GLORIOUS SUMMER

GLORIOUS SUMMER

The Story of the Battle of Britain

Air Vice-Marshal J. E. (Johnnie) Johnson
CB, CBE, DSO, DFC

Wing Commander P. B. (Laddie) Lucas
CBE, DSO, DFC

STANLEY PAUL
London Sydney Auckland Johannesburg

Stanley Paul and Co. Ltd

An imprint of Random Century

20 Vauxhall Bridge Road, London SW1V 2SA

Random Century Australia (Pty) Ltd
20 Alfred Street, Milsons Point, Sydney, NSW 2061

Random Century New Zealand Limited
191 Archers Road, PO Box 40–086, Glenfield, Auckland 10

Century Hutchinson South Africa (Pty) Ltd
PO Box 337, Bergvlei 2012, South Africa

First published 1990
Compilation Copyright © P. B. Lucas and J. E. Johnson, 1990

The right of P. B. Lucas and J. E. Johnson to be
identified as the authors of this work has been asserted
by them in accordance with the Copyright, Designs and
Patents Act, 1988

Set in 10½/12pt Linotron Sabon by
Deltatype Ltd, Ellesmere Port, Cheshire
Printed and bound in Great Britain by

British Cataloguing in Publication Data

Glorious Summer: the story of the Battle of Britain
1. World War 2. Battle of Britain
I. Johnson, J.E. (James Edgar)
II. Lucas, Laddie
940.5421

ISBN 0 09 174439 3

PHOTOGRAPH ACKNOWLEDGEMENTS

The author and publishers wish to thank the following
for permission to reproduce photographs:
Hulton-Deutsch Collection, pages 12 *below*, 14 *below*,
15 *above and below*, 16 *above and below right*; Imperial
War Museum, London, pages 2 *above left, above right
and below*, 3 *above left, above right and below*, 4 *above
left, above right, centre left, centre right, and below*, 5
below, 7 *above left, centre left, centre right, and below*, 8
above left, above right, and below, 9 *above*, 10 *above
and below*, 12 *above*, 13 *below*, 14 *above*, 16 *below left*;
RAF Museum, Hendon, pages 1, 6 *above left, above
right, below left, and below right*, 9 *centre and below*, 11
above, 13 *above*; Topham Picture Library, page 11
below.

The photgraph on page 5 *above* is from a private
collection
   Whilst every effort has been made to trace sources for
all extracts, in some cases this has not been possible. The
publishers would welcome notification of any error or
omission

Let us recollect what we contend for. It is for our property, it is for our liberty, it is for our independence, nay, for our existence as a nation; it is for our character, it is for our very name as Englishmen, it is for every thing dear and valuable to man on this side of the grave.

(William Pitt)

Contents

ACKNOWLEDGEMENTS

The editors thank collectively all those authors, many of them former comrades-at-arms and old Service friends, who have kindly and willingly allowed extracts from their work, published and unpublished, to be included in this collection. By so doing, they have contributed notably to the record of one of the far-reaching battles of history.

Thanks are particularly reserved for those who have so thoughtfully supplied family material which must still, even with the passage of time, arouse poignant memories of devoted relatives who made the ultimate sacrifice in support of a noble cause.

Lastly, the editors do not forget the help which was so readily offered by the staff of Stanley Paul, the publishers of this work, and their associates, in the preparation of this Battle anthology. Without it, a tight timescale could not have been met.

Explanation

For simplicity, the Battle of Britain has been divided in this collection into three separate and distinct phases covering five months or so in the summer and autumn of 1940.

The first phase, embracing the weeks in June and July, following the withdrawal from Dunkirk and the fall of France, comprises the time when the Luftwaffe was concentrating its gathering effort against shipping in the Straits and the Channel, and on fringe coastal targets and ports.

The second – in August through to 6 September – covers the German Air Force's critical onslaught against the whole paraphernalia of Fighter Command of the Royal Air Force – the airfields in southern and south-east England, the sector stations, the radars and the major ports.

The third daylight phase, from 7 September to 31 October, is starred by the German High Command's fatal switch of targets from the 'nerve' points of Fighter Command to the bombing of London and the adjoining docks. This diversion was to cost Hitler and the Nazis the first decisive battle of the war.

Split in this way, it is easy for the reader to see from the writings, speeches, memoranda and other material contained herein, how acute was the balance between British victory and defeat – and German reverse and triumph.

THE BATTLE

'He's a cheery old card,' grunted Harry to Jack
As they slogged up to Arras with rifle and pack.

But he did for them both by his plan of attack.
(Siegfried Sassoon)

In June of 1940 Hitler was master of Europe. German grand strategy relied on Operation 'Sea-lion' by which Hitler aimed to conquer Britain within the next few months: first of all the Royal Air Force (RAF) would be destroyed like the continental air forces; then invasion and the destruction of the British Army, not yet recovered from Dunkirk, on our own soil. Thus, with their western seaboard secured, a neutral America, the added industrial power of the conquered nations, and Europe held by the vicious Gestapo, the German legions could turn to the east and deal with their arch enemy, Russia.

The strategy of Operation Sea-lion was to be that of the recent campaign in the Low Countries and France, but on a far greater scale. There would be massive attacks against the RAF, the Channel would be a major river crossing and the German armies, well supported by the Luftwaffe, would, as before, carry all before them.

By the end of July the Luftwaffe forces poised to crush Britain comprised 2,600 aeroplanes of which 1,200 were bombers, 280 Stukas and 980 fighters. This was a formidable force, much bigger than its adversary and tactically well ahead of Fighter Command, whose training unfortunately was based on the theory that the air threat to Great Britain would be hordes of German bombers flying in close formation, and not escorted by fighters, since the Messerschmitt 109 could not reach our shores from airfields in Germany. Those who made this decision apparently did not take into account the possibility of closer airfields becoming available to the Luftwaffe or that Willi Messerschmitt might increase the range of his formidable fighter by fitting long-range drop tanks under the fuselage or wings. Dog-fighting, said Fighter Command, was a thing of the past, and introduced rigid air fighting tactics, which, by a series of time-wasting and complicated manoeuvres, aimed at bringing the greatest number of guns to bear against the bombers.

The tactical unit was the tight 'vic' of three fighters and our squadrons flew in four vics line-astern of each other. Although this looked fine at air shows and fly-pasts, in combat it was far too rigid.

1

From the unfortunate 'vic' of three fighters Fighter Command worked out six types of formation attacks against unescorted bombers on which squadron training was based. The stupid, time-consuming Fighter Attack No. 6 will be found in the diagram on page 205 (Appendix A).

Dowding's squadrons were based throughout the land from Caithness to Cornwall, and their day-to-day operations were controlled by four fighter groups which were subordinate to Fighter Command; the groups were divided further into sectors, each a geographical area containing a sector station and satellite airfields. 11 Group, bounded by Lowestoft, Dover, Bournemouth and Northampton, contained eighteen day fighter squadrons and four night fighter squadrons, while 12 Group's thirteen squadrons defended the Midlands and could, if need be, reinforce 11 Group. Farther north, twelve squadrons, including six obsolete Gladiators, guarded the industrial cities of the north-east and Scotland, while four squadrons were deployed in the west country. A further eight non-operational squadrons would take their places in the front line after more training.

Fighter Command was about the same size as that force which had been reckoned a sufficient defence against the Luftwaffe bomber arm operating unescorted from Germany: Dowding could put some 600 fighters into the sky, but he would keep some squadrons in reserve, and fighters based in Cornwall were too far away to be used against raids on London and the Midlands. If, as seemed probable, enemy formations crossed the coasts between the Thames Estuary and Bournemouth, about 220 fighter pilots of 11 Group would bear the brunt of the fighting with a little help from 10 and 12 Groups. It was estimated that about one-third of the Luftwaffe's strength would always be out of commission for repairs and inspections. This meant that they could mount raids involving some 1,800 aeroplanes of which about 550 would be Me 109s. Hence, Dowding's pilots would face heavy odds; but if radar, the magic eye, saw, and went on seeing, his fighter pilots would be fully briefed on the tactical situation from take-off until they opened fire. Radar gave them eyes which saw for about 120 miles, whereas German pilots, having no radars in France to back them, could only see four or five miles and would know little about the ebb and flow of the air battle.

Morale was high in the Luftwaffe. Their young fighter leaders had fought in the Spanish Civil War and had then blazed their way across half of Europe. Their fighter tactics were more advanced than ours and they were highly critical of our tight fighter formations.

In Spain the German fighter pilots soon realized that the speed of their 109s made close formations impracticable for combat. The large turning circle of the curving fighters dictated that a loose pattern was the only method by which individual pilots could hold their position in the turn and keep a sharp look-out at the same time. The high closing speeds, especially from head-on positions, made it essential to pick out and identify enemy aircraft as soon as possible, so that the leader could work his way into a good attacking position.

The simple requirement was for a loose, open type of combat formation with the various aeroplanes flying at separated heights which would permit individual pilots to cover each other and search a greater area of sky than before.

Credit must be given to the Germans for devising the perfect fighter formation. It was based on what they called the *rotte*, that is the element of two fighters. Some two hundred yards separated a pair of fighters and the main responsibility of the number two, or wingman, was to guard his leader from a quarter or an astern attack. Meanwhile the leader navigated his small force and covered his wingman. The *schwarme*, four fighters, simply consisted of two pairs, and when we eventually copied the Luftwaffe and adopted this pattern, we called it the 'finger-four' because the relative positions of the fighters are similar to a plain view of one's four fingertips.

The Luftwaffe possessed some excellent aeroplanes, and the Messerschmitt 109E had a higher ceiling and better guns than either the Spitfire or the Hurricane. The enemy fighter normally carried two machine guns and two cannon and compared very favourably with our eight Browning machine guns. During the fighting over France, our fighter pilots found that their Spitfires had slight margins of speed and climb over the 109E. But most of these flights took place below 20,000 feet, and later, when we had to fight well above this height, it was soon discovered that the enemy fighter was decidedly superior because its super-charger was designed to operate more efficiently at the higher altitudes. When the Messerschmitt took evasive action by 'bunting'* or half-rolling and diving vertically for the deck, we found that we couldn't stay with it in this manoeuvre. Certainly the Spitfire was more manoeuvrable, but manoeuvring does not itself win air battles, and tight turns are more of a defensive than an offensive tactic. The Spitfire's rate of turn would get you out of trouble if you saw your attacker in time, but only superior height would save you from the 'bounce'.

The Luftwaffe pinned great hopes on the stable companion of the 109, the twin-engined Messerschmitt 110C, 'destroyer' fighter. It had a greater range than the 109 and was accordingly often employed as a close escort to the bomber formations. It carried four machine guns and two cannon firing forward and one machine gun firing aft, but it could not hold its own particularly against the Spitfire. On more than one occasion the 109 had to help the twin-engined fighters out of a tight spot.

* An outside loop.

The Junkers 87 dive-bomber, the Stuka, had enjoyed great success as a close-support weapon in the recent campaigns. It was little more than a piece of flying artillery and it could dive very steeply at a low forward speed. This meant that the pilot could line up his diving aircraft against a ground target with great accuracy and release his bombs at low level and still pull out. But one of the basic principles of the employment of close support aircraft is that they must be capable of holding their own against contemporary fighters. The Stuka contradicted this simple truth and paid the price in full when it met our Spitfires.

Of the three other types of enemy bombers, the Heinkel III, the Dornier 17 and the Junkers 88, the last-named was superior to the other two and quite the most difficult to catch. It had a high top speed, and when it dived away with wide-open throttles our Spitfires had a difficult time trying to overhaul it.

In his subsequent Despatch, the Commander-in-Chief said that the Battle divided itself broadly into four phases. First, the attack on shipping convoys, ports, coastal airfields and radar stations; second, the onslaught against inland fighter airfields; third, the bombing of London; and fourth, the fighter-bomber stage.

Dowding clearly saw that during the July attacks against shipping the Luftwaffe was far less interested in sinking ships than in bringing our fighters to battle in conditions which favoured the attacker. Convoys were difficult to defend because our radar warning was so short that small standing patrols over the ships could only be reinforced by a few fighters from our forward airfields before the sky was full of German aeroplanes.

This probing and sparring continued for more than a month with little satisfaction to the Germans, whose Stuka pilots, not accustomed to the rough treatment handed out by our Hurricanes and Spitfires, called for larger fighter escorts. By 12 August the Luftwaffe had sunk eighteen small ships and four destroyers at a cost of 196 aeroplanes. We lost 148 fighters, replaced by one week's factory production, but this preliminary fighting gave Dowding, and especially Keith Park, a fine opportunity to perfect their defensive arrangements. At the beginning of August the Command was in good heart, with fifty-five squadrons on the order of battle, another six in reserve and a total of 1,434 fighter pilots.

On 12 August Göring launched the type of attack we had most reason to fear, the bombing of five radar stations on the south coast. All suffered damage but only one was wrecked, and on the following day the four damaged radars were repaired and helped identify German bombers at a range of 100 miles.

13 August was *Eagle Day* and saw heavy raids against southern ports and airfields. The enemy was trying to destroy our aeroplanes and vital communications on the ground but their intelligence was poor. Eleven

airfields were attacked but only one was used by our fighters. The Luftwaffe recorded that eight major airfields were destroyed. The attacks would have been much heavier had not Göring cancelled operations because of an unfavourable weather report. This caused much confusion because some squadrons were already in the air when the recall was received.

Between 13 and 18 August some thirty-four airfields and five radar stations were attacked. The size of the enemy bomber formations was increased and Göring ordered that each Stuka squadron be escorted by three fighter squadrons. Nevertheless the dreaded Stuka – that integral tool of *Blitzkrieg* – had met its match and on 18 August Göring withdrew them from the battle. Thus, one-fifth of the German bombers were no longer available.*

Four days of bad weather brought a lull in operations until 24 August when the Luftwaffe returned to the fight with further instruction from the *Reichsmarschall*. The bombers received larger fighter escorts and the fighter escorts were ordered to fly closer to the bombers, a stupid order which restricted the German fighter pilots' freedom of action and incensed able young fighter leaders like Adolf Galland and Werner Mölders.

During the following few days the bombers hammered at our fighter airfields, and the change in enemy tactics and their strong fighter escorts made life much more difficult for our fighters.

Park's squadrons usually fought singly because he did not have time to form his squadrons into wings. Leigh-Mallory, with bases in Cambridge-shire and Essex, did have the time and on 30 June Harry Braodhurst first led the Wittering Wing (229 and 226 Squadrons). Douglas Bader first led the Duxford Wing (19, 242 and 310 Squadrons) on 6 September.

This bombing of our sector airfields, with their operations rooms and essentials communications, was the most critical phase of the battle. Between 24 August and 7 September there were thirty-three major bombing attacks, and twenty-three were concentrated against our vital nerve centres – the fighter airfields and sector stations of 11 Group whose job was to defend London and the south-east. By 5 September, Park was reporting to Dowding that the damage by bombing was having a serious effect on the fighting efficiency of his group.

Thanks to their larger fighter escorts the enemy bombers were getting through to our airfields, and their casualties were reduced. During a four-day period of fighting we shot down 106 enemy aeroplanes, including a small proportion of bombers, and lost 101 fighter pilots.

During the first three days of September the bombing attacks, with

---

* The Stuka remained on the German Order of Battle until 1944 and was used in other theatres when there was little air opposition.

packs of escorting fighters, continued and we shot down ninety enemy aeroplanes and lost eighty-five pilots. The total wastage in our fighter pilots was about 120 pilots each week. Our operations training units produced sixty-five inexperienced pilots each week and it was quite apparent to Dowding and Park that they were fighting a battle of diminishing returns. They realized that if the Luftwaffe kept up the pressure, the control and reporting system would gradually disintegrate, and it would only be a question of time before the Germans dominated the air over southern England.

Fortunately, at this time the conduct of the battle changed. On the night of 24/25 August the first bombs fell on central London. Winston Churchill ordered a retaliation raid against Berlin, and during the next week there were four more. Hitler demanded immediate reprisals and shouted in a hysterical broadcast: 'If they attack our cities, we will rub out their cities from the map. The hour will come when one of us two will break, and it will not be Nazi Germany.'

Göring eagerly responded, and late in the afternoon of Saturday, 7 September, sent over 372 bombers and 642 fighters to make two concentrated attacks against London in rapid succession. Dowding, however, anticipating daylight attacks against our capital, made more use of the big wings from 10 and 12 Groups, and Park instructed that whenever time permitted his squadrons were to be used in pairs.

The attacks on London and its suburbs continued with little respite from 7 September until 5 October. This was the turning point of the battle, for it gave Park the opportunity to repair his battered airfields and restore his communications. On Sunday, 15 September, Göring provided the strongest escort so far, five fighters for every bomber, to try and saturate our defences. These big enemy formations took a long time to assemble. Our radars gave ample warning, and Park had the precious time to form some of his squadrons into wings and to ask for reinforcements from the flanking groups.

The defensive arrangements, so carefully tended throughout the long weeks of fighting by Keith Park, worked so well that the Biggin Hill Wing fought escorting 109s south of Canterbury, the Kenley Wing made a head-on attack near Maidstone, and two squadrons were in action over Gravesend. Nevertheless, the three German formations forced on and were met over south London by the North Weald Wing, who sorted out the bombers with surprisingly little interference from enemy fighters. The Duxford Wing, big even by Luftwaffe standards, was next in action, but Bader had to delay his attack until some friendly fighters had cleared away. Then, as carefully rehearsed, his three Hurricane squadrons went for the bombers while his two Spitfire squadrons held off the 109s. Some bombs were dropped but they did only a little damage to some property, an electricity station, and a bridge or two. An unexploded bomb lodged near Buckingham Palace. Thirty Germans were brought down at a cost of seven RAF pilots. The arithmetic was improving.

After a two-hour break, which gave the defending squadrons ample time to rearm and refuel, the Luftwaffe put in its second big attack, again consisting of three heavily escorted bomber formations which crossed the coast on a twenty-mile front between Dover and Dungeness, within five minutes of each other. This time the radar warning was shorter, but nine defending wings and several independent squadrons came into action over south London, where there was some stiff fighting. Once again, the defenders had the best of the exchange. There were fewer 109s than usual and these seemed less aggressive so that some of the bombers were very roughly handled. Two formations were broken up near London – one returning after a head-on attack by a lone Hurricane – and bombs were scattered over a wide area. The Germans were harried by more Spitfires and Hurricanes as they withdrew. During this action RAF pilots claimed to have destroyed fifty-nine bombers and twenty-one fighters at a cost of eleven of their own.

The fighting over London was at its height when about twenty Heinkels bombed Portland harbour. Only one squadron succeeded in intercepting, and that after the bombing. The final daylight operation was an attempt by twenty bombers to hit the Supermarine works near Southampton, but the anti-aircraft gunners put up a heavy barrage and the factory was not damaged. At dark the bombers returned to London and continued their work throughout the night.

The day's fighting cost the Luftwaffe fifty-six aeroplanes against our twenty-six pilots. More bombers struggled back to France, some on one engine or badly shot-up, and with many crew members dead or injured. At the debriefings the bomber captains complained bitterly of incessant Hurricane and Spitfire attacks from squadrons that had long ceased to exist – if they could believe their own intelligence and the Berlin radio.

The fighting on this day clinched the victory, for two days later, on Hitler's instructions, Operation Sea-lion was called off, never to be repeated, and the German invasion fleet left the Channel ports for safer harbours.

The daylight offensive against London continued for another six weeks (phase four), but from the beginning of October without the enemy bombers, which now only operated at night. The Blitz, in all its fury, was upon us. The daylight offensive passed to enemy fighters and fighter-bombers only. These raids, flown at great heights and taking every advantage of cloud cover, set Dowding new problems of high altitude interceptions, but they achieved little else, and Fighter Command continued along the path of recovery.

Thanks to Lord Beaverbrook, Minister of Aircraft Production,

Hurricanes and Spitfires came out of the factories at an astonishing rate and Dowding's squadrons were never short of fighters. With courage and resolution he cut through all red tape in his determination to give the 'fighter-boys', including his own son Max, all the aeroplanes they so badly needed.

During the Battle the Germans made two big mistakes. First, flushed no doubt by resounding victories in Poland and the Low Countries, Göring estimated that Fighter Command could, like the continental air force, be written off within two weeks or a month, failing altogether to realize that our sophisticated radar defence-control system gave Fighter Command that high degree of flexibility not available to the continental air forces. Second, Hitler ordered Göring to switch the bombing from our airfields and aircraft factories to London, thus abusing the first principle of war, 'maintenance of the aim', at a time when victory was within his grasp.

These two failures were the beginning of their undoing. The remainder was provided by Fighter Command's radar shield, resolute leadership by the Commander-in-Chief, sound tactical handling by the 11 Group commander, Keith Park, and the courage and determination of the young fighter leaders such as Malan and Hugo of South Africa; Deere, Wells, Jameson and Gray of New Zealand; Gordie McGregor and Stan Turner of Canada; Witold Urbanowicz of Poland; Karel Myazek of Czechoslovakia; Bader, Broadhurst, Beamish, Carey, the brothers Dundas, Holden, Crowley-Milling, Kingaby, Lacey and Cunningham of Great Britain.

And so the great battle was fought and won over the Channel, over the fields of Kent and Sussex, and over the woods of Hampshire and Dorset, over the flat marshes of Essex and the sprawling mass of London. Unlike the previous battles of destiny – Waterloo, Trafalgar, the terrible roar and devastation of the Somme bombardments – there was little sound or fury. People on the ground went about their business with little idea of what was taking place high in the sky. They saw a pattern of white vapour trails slowly changing form and shape. Sometimes they saw the contestants as a number of tiny specks, scintillating like diamonds in the splendid sunlight of those cloudless days. The skilful parries of the defence continued throughout those long days of the late summer and had they not done so London would have suffered the fate of Warsaw and Rotterdam.

Although 'the gayest company who ever fired their guns in anger'* are called 'The Few', nearly 3,000 aircrew (Blenheim and Defiant fighters carried aircrew as well as the pilot) fought in the battle, but less than half were in the front line at any one time. Of these 3,000, one in three was killed or wounded.

The aircrew formed only a small minority of those who helped to win. There were the ground crews, the controllers and their operations room

* Denis Richards, *Royal Air Force 1939–1945*, vol. 1, HMSO.

staff, the radar operators, the intelligence, training and operations staff and the commanders; and backing up were the drivers, the suppliers, cooks and clerks. Nor was it won by Fighter Command alone for, to some extent, all other Commands played their part as well as the guns and searchlights of Anti-Aircraft Command.

'How dare those bloody Krauts', said Douglas Bader on more than one occasion, 'fly over our country with those dirty black crosses on their aeroplanes!' And he often said that the victory was the people's victory; other governments and peoples had cracked under *Blitzkrieg* but the British people never failed in their determination to see it through.

Towards the end of 1940 the ambitious Sholto Douglas replaced Dowding, the victor, and the agreeable Leigh-Mallory took over from the loyal Park who had fought the day-to-day battles so well. It was not Dowding's departure – for he was fifty-eight and had been Commander-in-Chief for four years – but the manner of his going which cast a dark shadow. He, like dozens of other senior officers, was made a Knight Grand Cross of the Order of the Bath, and later received a Barony, but his pilots thought, and still do, that their commander, who takes his place with Wellington and Nelson, should have been made a Marshal of the Royal Air Force.

(J. E. [Johnnie] Johnson, personal collection)

Flight

How can they know that joy to be alive
    Who have not flown?
To loop and spin and roll and climb and dive,
    The very sky one's own,
The urge of power while engines race,
    The sting of speed,
The rude winds' buffet on one's face,
    To live indeed.

How can they know the grandeur of the sky,
    The earth below,
The restless sea, and waves that break and die
    With ceaseless ebb and flow;
The morning sun on drifting clouds
    And rolling downs –
And valley mist that shrouds
    The chimneyed towns?

So long has puny man to earth been chained
    Who now is free,

And with the conquest of the air has gained
   A glorious liberty.
How splendid is this gift He gave
   On high to roam,
The sun a friend, the earth a slave,
   The heavens home.

(Flight Cadet Brian Young*)

---

* Born and educated in South Africa, Brian Young wrote this poem in 1938 while a twenty-year-old flight cadet at Cranwell where he won the Sword of Honour. He was shot down in 1940 in a Hurricane of 615 Squadron. After months in hospital, he returned to operations two years later as a flight commander in 422 (RCAF) Squadron of Coastal Command. He retired as an Air Vice-Marshal in 1973.

Part One

JUNE AND JULY 1940
The Shooting Starts

Thank God we are now alone.

(Air Chief Marshall Sir Hugh Dowding, Air Officer
Commanding-in-Chief, Fighter Command)

Between the acting of a dreadful thing
And the first motion, all the interim is
Like a phantasma, or a hideous dream
William Shakespeare,
(Julius Caesar, act 1, scene II)

THE LEAD CHURCHILL GAVE

To form an Administration of this scale and complexity is a serious undertaking in itself, but it must be remembered that we are in the preliminary stage of one of the greatest battles in history . . . In this crisis I hope I may be pardoned if I do not address the House at any length today. I hope that any of my friends and colleagues, or former colleagues, who are affected by the political reconstruction, will make all allowance for any lack of ceremony with which it has been necessary to act. I would say to the House, as I said to those who have joined this Government: 'I have nothing to offer but blood, toil, tears and sweat.'

We have before us an ordeal of the most grievous kind. We have before us many, many long months of struggle and of suffering. You ask, what is our policy? I will say: It is to wage war, by sea, land and air, with all our might and with all the strength that God can give us: to wage war against a monstrous tyranny, never surpassed in the dark, lamentable catalogue of human crime. That is our policy. You ask, What is our aim? I can answer in one word: Victory – victory at all costs, victory in spite of all terror, victory, however long and hard the road may be; for without victory, there is no survival. Let that be realized; no survival for the British Empire; no survival for all that the British Empire has stood for, no survival for the urge and impulse of the ages, that mankind will move forward towards its goal. But I take up my task with buoyancy and hope. I feel sure that our cause will not be suffered to fail among men. At this time I feel entitled to claim the aid of all, and I say. 'Come, then, let us go forward together with our united strength.'

(Winston S. Churchill, House of Commons, 13 May 1940)

Turning once again, and this time more generally, to the question of invasion, I would observe that there has never been a period in all these long centuries of which we boast when an absolute guarantee against invasion, still less against serious raids, could have been given to our

13

people. In the days of Napoleon the same wind which would have carried his transports across the Channel might have driven away the blockading fleet. There was always the chance, and it is that chance which has excited and befooled the imaginations of many Continental tyrants. Many are the tales that are told. We are assured that novel methods will be adopted, and when we see the originality of malice, the ingenuity of aggression, which our enemy displays, we may certainly prepare ourselves for every kind of novel stratagem and every kind of brutal and treacherous manoeuvre. I think that no idea is so outlandish that it should not be considered and viewed with a searching, but at the same time, I hope, with a steady eye. We must never forget the solid assurances of sea-power and those which belong to air power if it can be locally exercised.

I have, myself, full confidence that if all do their duty, if nothing is neglected, and if the best arrangements are made, as they are being made, we shall prove ourselves once again able to defend our island home, to ride out the storm of war, and to outlive the menace of tyranny, if necessary for years, if necessary alone. At any rate, that is what we are going to try to do. That is the resolve of His Majesty's Government – every man of them. That is the will of Parliament and the nation. The British Empire and the French Republic, linked together in their cause and in their need, will defend to the death their native soil, aiding each other like good comrades to the utmost of their strength. Even though large tracts of Europe and many old and famous States have fallen or may fall into the grip of the Gestapo and all the odious apparatus of Nazi rule, we shall not flag or fail. We shall go on to the end, we shall fight in France, we shall fight on the seas and oceans, we shall fight with growing confidence and growing strength in the air, we shall defend our island, whatever the cost may be, we shall fight on the beaches, we shall fight on the landing grounds, we shall fight in the fields and in the streets, we shall fight in the hills; we shall never surrender, and even if, which I do not for a moment believe, this island or a large part of it were subjugated and starving, then our Empire beyond the seas, armed and guarded by the British Fleet, would carry on the struggle, until, in God's good time, the new world, with all its power and might, steps forth to the rescue and the liberation of the old.

(Winston S. Churchill, House of Commons, 4 June 1940)

I stayed with Halifax [Foreign Secretary] in the subordinate role of Under-Secretary, until the turn of this historic year when he was dispatched to Washington. He did not want to go a bit, and I was very sorry to lose him, but he fulfilled his time at the Foreign Office by becoming an exceptional Ambassador. One of the last memories I have of working with Halifax and Churchill was when we were invited to march up and down in the garden of No. 10 while Winston was rehearsing his speech 'We shall fight on the beaches'. There we were, the lanky Edward, the stocky Winston and myself. As Winston declaimed, he turned to us and said, 'Would you fight in the streets and on the hills?' Pacific as we were we warmly agreed, saying 'Yes, certainly, Winston', and then continued to march up and down with him.

(R. A. Butler, *The Art of the Possible: The Memoirs of Lord Butler*,
Hamish Hamilton, 1971)

ENTER LORD BEAVERBROOK

Lord Beaverbrook, the mercurial and dynamic Canadian, who, between the wars, had masterminded his brilliantly successful Express Newspapers Group, joined Churchill's National Coalition as Minister of Aircraft Production on 14 May 1940 at a moment of gathering crisis. His single remit from the Prime Minister? 'Get us the aeroplanes.'

Hurry, hurry!

[With Beaverbrook's appointment], a new spirit flowed through the world of aircraft manufacture and repair. Hurry, Hurry, Hurry, for we have so little time. Then the Battle of Britain was on us. The pirate of Whitehall really hoisted the Jolly Roger so far as service practice and methods [were concerned] . . . The old Air Ministry supply system said that if one Hurricane was at Cramlington, Northumberland, unserviceable with a broken airscrew, the damaged component had to be replaced by indent through its own group. If another Hurricane was unserviceable at Northolt with a broken undercarriage, the same local indenting procedure for replacement parts had to be gone through. Beaverbrook would have none of this. To the confusion of accounting and issuing departments now the two unserviceable Hurricanes would be thrown together to make one airworthy fighter. Technical experts laid down that each set of piston rings had to be fitted carefully to individual Rolls-Royce Merlin engines. Now any set of rings was to go into any Merlin and they all worked just as well as before.

Any hen roost was robbed to produce just one more fighter. Risks were taken. Experimental units were robbed of test aircraft. Training stations had to give up Service types. Factory management was bullied, praised, cajoled. Each week's effort was taken as the starting point of exhortation for a bigger and better next week. Bosses of great aircraft concerns learnt not to play golf on Sunday mornings but to stand by the telephone for this was Beaverbrook's favourite hour for telephone talk with these men. His minions went round the country with delegated powers to requisition any and every building wanted for dispersed component manufacture or for storage. The Archbishop of Canterbury complained to Churchill. One of

Beaverbrook's travelling staff served a requisition on a garage in Salisbury where the Bishop and other clerics of the Cathedral housed their cars. The Bishop protested whereupon the MAP* official took out a blank requisition form and threatened the Bishop that any more resistance and he would requisition the Cathedral.

One night London had a bad thunderstorm. A whole lot of barrage balloons were struck by lightning. This form of barrage defence had been extended to provincial cities and this had depleted reserves. Now, on the morning after the storm, we woke up to the fact that we just could not replace the previous night's casualties. MAP officials advised us there was little hope of increased supplies due to cotton shortage and other manufacturing difficulties. At the Air Ministry we could not accept this. I rang Beaverbrook and told him the position. His reply: 'Leave it to me.' This was Saturday. He asked me to come to a meeting on Sunday, next day, armed with figures of our monthly needs. Next morning I found seated round his office table a dozen chiefs of the Lancashire cotton industry called up by train, car or aeroplane. I stated our needs. Within an hour the meeting closed with a complete production programme fitting our needs, immediate and future. No more balloon trouble.

I do declare that from my first-hand knowledge, even though on the Air Ministry side of the fence, the margin for victory in terms of aircraft and pilots was knife-edged.

I do declare that if there had been no Beaverbrook and no MAP I do not believe the balance would have been tipped in our favour.

[But] a policy of 'everything for the hour' had to be paid for later.

(Harold Balfour Lord Balfour of Inchrye, Under-Secretary of State for Air,
Wings over Westminster, Hutchinson, 1973)

There was a third decisive figure in the Battle of Britain. . . . Lord Beaverbrook's task was to produce aircraft as quickly as possible without regard to established procedure. He discharged this task successfully and to the great annoyance of the Air Marshals. Beaverbrook was an isolationist who had little interest in the continental war. He came alive only when the defence of Great Britain was in question. He formed a close alliance with Dowding, who shared his outlook. Beaverbrook turned out fighters where the Air Marshals called for bombers. He sent new fighters direct to the squadrons. He trampled over all bureaucratic obstacles. Dowding paid him this tribute: 'The country owes as much to Lord Beaverbrook for the Battle of Britain as it does to me. Without his drive behind me I could not have carried on during the battle.' Thanks to Beaverbrook, Fighter Command possessed more aircraft at the end of the

* Ministry of Aircraft Production.

16

Battle than it had possessed at the beginning. But ... not even Beaverbrook could remedy the wastage of pilots.

(A. J. P. Taylor, Introduction, in Len Deighton, *Fighter: The True Story of the Battle of Britain*, Jonathan Cape, 1977)

'*Magic with a nasal twang!*'

Beaverbrook's critics have always maintained that he was little more than a play-actor and that his main object was self-glorification. The same criticism might also be levelled at the magnificent and flamboyant rhetoric to which, at the same time, Churchill was treating the House of Commons. Certainly the personal touch which the Minister of Aircraft Production used with high and low made him for a time the second most popular man in the country. It was rough magic worked with a nasal twang. It was effective as never quite again. In any case his critics were wrong. In all the six and a half years I worked for him I never knew him so selfless as in the months of his adopted country's greatest danger.

Nor could play-acting have got the results which were achieved. They came in the last resort from a rapid mastery, by the quickest and sharpest brain I have ever known, of all the problems and intricacies of the aircraft industry, allied to an incomparable drive. The final ingredient was a ruthlessness bordering sometimes on sharp practice which was perhaps natural in a man who had made a million before he was thirty, but which now was applied in the national interest. The 'personal touch' was the ingredient which fused these qualities into success. . . .

For me, who in this doom-laden time of late spring and early summer, saw him day in day out (including Sundays), and sometimes part of the night as well, the days had often the quality of a nightmare. The hasty scurryings between Stornoway House and Millbank, the increasing number of letters and documents for which I had to provide first drafts, the often brusque and always telegraphese instructions which had to be interpreted for onward transmission in the shortest form possible to the relevant individual or department, the absolute uncertainty as to what I was going to do next – all this put a strain on Beaverbrook's junior personal secretary that left its mark. Whenever I was not with him and my telephone rang I would jump in near panic out of my chair before I could bring myself to answer it. I had, after all, been catapulted into a strange alarming world for which nothing in my previous career had prepared me. . .

It was a nightmare, but one in which, like other junior members of 'Operation Beaverbrook', I grew increasingly proud to share. For Beaverbrook it was a nightmare of a different kind, for if his nightmare turned into truth there would be a German occupation of Britain.

This nightmare can be simply described. On the day he took office there were more trained pilots than there were aircraft in the front line of the RAF, and in Fighter Command there were only five fighter aircraft immediately available in reserve. The tensest, most nervous moment of the week was Saturday afternoon when Beaverbrook received the weekly production charts. From the start they rose steeply, and before the Battle of Britain was finally joined they showed a total reserve of 65 per cent of the Fighter Command's operational strength, which at the same time exceeded the number of trained pilots available to man them. Such was the achievement which by every manner of means, adding up to an inspired unorthodoxy, Beaverbrook had made possible. It came just and only just in time. In my view the Minister of Aircraft Production had his 'finest hour' even before Churchill had called upon the people of Britain to rise to theirs. . . .

So, as far as MAP was concerned, by early August the stage had been set, the chief actors assembled, for the high drama of the Battle of Britain and the Blitz. There had been minor dramas already, with happy endings and Beaverbrook taking all the bows while distributing bouquets to all around him. And there had been comedies too, in one of which *in absentia* I took part.

Beaverbrook had instituted a rule whereby letters written for his signature by Thomson [George Malcolm Thomson, senior personal secretary to Lord Beaverbrook] had to have a small 't' in the top right hand corner, those written by me a small 'f'. One evening about half past eight, with his full council surrounding him, Beaverbrook pressed the bell which summoned me to his presence. I had gone home, so Thomson, with an air of conscious virtue answered the summons. Beaverbrook looked up as he entered the room. 'Where's little f?' 'Little f,' replied Thomson, 'has effed off.'

In the ensuing gale of laughter at this unexpected sally, my truancy was forgotten. It was a very human ministry to work in, led by a very human man.

(David Farrer, G – for God Almighty: A Personal Memoir of Lord
Beaverbrook, Weidenfeld & Nicolson, 1969)

Orders of the day

This is an appeal to all workers in the aircraft industry. Urgently we ask for the fullest output this week and next. . . . I want to reach all of you with my words: the work you do this week fortifies and strengthens the font of battle next week. The production which you pour out of your factories this week will be hurled into the desperate struggle next week.

And make no mistake, in meeting this crisis we have none to rely on but our own energy and driving force. Britain stands or falls on her own resources. You have the power to multiply and to magnify them. The young men of the air force, the pilots and gunners are waiting to fly the machines. We must not fail them. We must provide the aircraft, engined, armed, equipped, and ready for battle.

(A few days later, Beaverbrook announced that aircraft production had increased 62 per cent.)

Women of Britain, give us your aluminium. We want it and we want it now. We will turn your pots and pans into Spitfires and Hurricanes, Blenheims and Wellingtons. I ask therefore that everyone who has pots and pans, kettles, vacuum cleaners, hat pegs, coat hangers, shoe trees, bathroom fittings and household ornaments, cigarette boxes or any other articles made wholly or in part of aluminium, should hand them in at once to the local headquarters of the Women's Voluntary Services.

(Lord Beaverbrook, 1940)

DOWDING'S DREADFUL DILEMMA

I was responsible for the Air Defence of Great Britain, and I saw my resources slipping away like sand in an hour-glass. The pressure for more and more assistance to France was relentless and inexorable.

(Air Chief Marshal Sir Hugh Dowding, Air Officer Commanding-in-Chief, Fighter Command, Battle of Britain Dispatch, 20 August 1941)

DUCAL MISSION

At this bleak juncture, as the French armies were falling back in the face of the German onslaught, Hugh Dowding (Air Chief Marshal Lord Dowding), Air Officer Commanding-in-Chief, Fighter Command, sent a personal emissary to France to report directly on the worsening situation.

It was an unusual arrangement. The officer assigned to the task was Wing Commander The Duke of Hamilton, the first man to fly over Everest and one of four remarkable air force brothers, each of whom, at one time, became a squadron commander. Hamilton flew this three-day mission . . . to the battle area in a tiny Miles Magister, a light, single-engined aircraft with a top speed which would have compared unfavourably with a modern small motor car. He was then serving as a controller under Keith Park (Air Chief Marshal Sir Keith Park) at Headquarters, 11 Group.

For the historical record, it is worth reproducing the relevant entries in the pilot's flying log book.

The report which Hamilton brought back convinced the C-in-C that, with the French crumbling, no further fighter squadrons should in any circumstances be sent to France. From this stance, Dowding fought his corner with great courage. Meanwhile 'Douglo' Hamilton received a mention in despatches for his exploit.

(Laddie Lucas, *Wings of War: Airmen of all Nations tell Their Stories, 1939–1945*, Hutchinson, 1983)

19

BROADHURST GIVES THE C-IN-C HIS ANSWER

Harry Broadhurst's character was aptly described by 'Laddie' Lucas who wrote* 'He was a rugged, competent buccaneer who knew exactly what he was about and where, the Lord willing, he intended to go. He and Douglas (Bader) had several similarities. Neither was an easy man and each was strongly assertive. Both were controversial figures and always prepared to swim against the current to sustain a personal conviction. As a pair of officers they were outstanding by any test. With 'Sailor' Malan, the South African commander of 74 Squadron, and later the highly distinguished leader of the Biggin Hill Wing, they possessed the three most resourceful brains among the senior pilots in Fighter Command . . .' All of which was just as well because 'L-M',† and most of his contemporaries, seldom took to the air and therefore had to rely for tactical advice on their active wing commanders.

In the late spring, 'Broady', as he was universally known, 'volunteered' to command a wing of Hurricanes in France just as the German legions were blasting their way south. After five hectic days he was ordered to withdraw to the UK and to destroy all his remaining ground stores. When he returned Dowding appointed him to command the fighter station at Wittering and he had only been there a few days when he received a telephone call from Fighter Command to say that the Commander-in-Chief would like to come to lunch. He was a bit suprised especially when he rang 'L-M' and found he knew nothing about it, but 'L-M' decided to come too. On the following day Broady found himself sitting between his C-in-C and his AOC and trying to stimulate conversation over lunch. After lunch, 'L-M' muttered something about having to return to Watnall to get on with the war, and Broady saw him to his car to take him to the airfield. Immediately Broadhurst returned to the lunch table, Dowding said to him: 'If I were to offer you a wing of fighters to take to France, what would you say?' This remark startled Broady who had only recently returned from the disaster in France; but he collected his wits and replied:

'Well, I'd go, sir . . .'

'Of course you'd go,' interrupted Dowding, 'but what would you think? What success would you have?'

'Judging by my recent experience, I doubt if we would last a week.'

Dowding said: 'Thank you very much. That is all I wanted to know'; and soon after he flew back to Fighter Command.

(J. E. [Johnnie] Johnson, personal collection)

---

* Laddie Lucas, *Flying Colours: The Epic Story of Douglas Bader,*Hutchinson 1981.
† Air Vice-Marshall Trafford Leigh-Mallory.

CAS* STANDS UP TO CHURCHILL

'I was very fond of Cyril Newall* and we were close friends . . . As his Director of Plans, he took me into his confidence on most things, but I do not recall him ever talking to me about Fighter Command matters during the Battle. Earlier, I did express to him strong views about the folly of sending more and more fighter squadrons to jack up a lost cause in France; and I don't think [Cyril] . . . ever received the credit that was his due for Winston's final decision [not to send more Hurricane squadrons to France] . . . Stuffy's was not the 'lone stand' against Churchill in the Cabinet on 15 May [that has been] made out.

(Marshal of the Royal Air Force Sir John Slessor [see under 'Dowding' on page 23]: correspondence with Lord Balfour of Inchrye, 28 October 1969)

THE COMMANDERS

Air Chief Marshal Sir Hugh Dowding†

A difficult man, a self-opinionated man, a most determined man, and a man who knew, more than anybody, about all aspects of aerial warfare.

(General Sir Frederick Pile, GOC, Anti-Aircraft Command, 1939–45)

Personally, I think [Dowding] is one of the very best men you have got, and I say this having been in contact with him for about two years. I have greatly admired the whole of his work in the Fighter Command, and especially in resisting the clamour for numerous air raid warnings, and the immense pressure to dissipate the Fighter strength during the great French battle . . . He has my full confidence.

(Winston S. Churchill to the Secretary of State for Air, 10 July 1940)

The C-in-C of Fighter Command was 'an unpopular little boy' at Winchester College because, in his own words, 'he was too cheeky'. Stuffy Dowding said of himself, 'Since I was a child I have never accepted ideas purely because they were orthodox, and consequently I frequently found myself in opposition to generally accepted views.'

This was the philosophy behind his energetic and far-sighted efforts to build an efficient air defence. His requirements were enormous – in men, aircraft, ground equipment, buildings and telecommunications – which included radar, then still in its infancy. Everything had to be done and

---

* Air Chief Marshal Sir Cyril Newall, Chief of the Air Staff throughout the Battle of Britain.

† Air Officer Commanding-in-Chief, Fighter Command.

time was against him. Dowding was not a man for half measures. He was resolved to get what he needed to make the 'base' – Britain – safe and secure. On one occasion a senior officer propounded to him at length, as if they were sacred words of truth, the Trenchard doctrine, 'attack is better than defence'. Stuffy disagreed vigorously: 'It's a shibboleth, a play on words with just enough truth, but not enough to make it a clear case. Why must it be accepted without question? Only because you think that you are going to do so much damage that the enemy will be smashed right at the outset. And how are you going to do that?' Fiercely he insisted that, 'the one thing vital before going over to the offensive is security of the base. That overrides all considerations.' His unshakeable belief in the principle and his obstinate insistence that all his demands should be met, did not endear him to all his brother officers. 'Always remember,' he would say later, 'that my name stank on the Air Staff.'

(Peter Townsend, Duel of Eagles, Weidenfeld & Nicolson, 1970)

Sir Hugh Dowding was the senior member of the Air Council. He had every claim to become Chief of Air Staff in 1937. But he was a quiet, reserved man, obstinate in pressing his views and not a good mixer. He was pushed off to become head of Fighter Command, then regarded by the other Air Marshals as a second-rate post. Dowding considered the problem of fighter strategy in his cool, rational way. Far from him was any romantic idea of vast armadas contending in the skies or of dog-fights such as there had been in the First World War. The sole task of Fighter Command, as Dowding saw it, was the defence of Great Britain and this could be accomplished by defeating the German bombers. Without them the German fighters would be harmless. Dowding planned an economical campaign to husband his fighter force at all costs.

Dowding's single-minded concentration on the defence of Great Britain often brought trouble for him after the war started. When the Germans broke through in Flanders the French pleaded for more British fighter squadrons. Churchill acquiesced. Dowding resisted this emotional decision and got his way after the Chief of Air Staff appealed to the Cabinet on his behalf. In July, when the Germans began to attack British shipping in the Channel, Dowding again refused to involve his fighters in this to him irrelevant conflict. Dowding also had trouble within his own force. Some of the area commanders resented Dowding's cautious policy and clamoured for the tactic of the 'big wing'. All along Dowding suffered from disloyalty as well as from lack of understanding.

(A. J. P. Taylor, Introduction, in Len Deighton, Fighter: The True Story of
the Battle of Britain, Jonathan Cape, 1977)

Dowding was an enigmatic man. His inability to make intimate friends . . . probably [kept] him so. It is difficult to reconcile a man who put on his

22

hat before stepping into the next office, with a ski champion who seldom missed a season on the slopes, and eventually became president of the Ski Club of Great Britain. There was Dowding the diligent administrator, and Dowding the impatient technician; Dowding the devout and courteous, and Dowding of whom the Air Ministry was afraid. If Dowding remains an enigma there can be little doubt that that is exactly what he wished . . .

He was indifferent to the boardroom politics of higher office, impatient and abrasive to men who failed to understand his reasoning. When he told an Air Ministry conference that he wanted bullet-proof glass for the Hurricanes and Spitfires, everyone laughed. 'If Chicago gangsters can have bullet-proof glass in their cars I can't see any reason why my pilots cannot have the same,' he said, and was irritated by their laughter. He delegated authority readily and seldom interfered with subordinates he trusted. Not unreasonably – but unrealistically – he expected the same treatment by the men in the Ministry.

Although Dowding's concern for the fighter pilots was central to every decision he made, he seldom met them or talked with them, believing that the presence of the Commander-in-Chief would merely provide an extra burden for them. But it is an attractive aspect of this reserved man's character that his staunchest supporters should be low-ranking subordinates who worked at his HQ, including his personal assistants and his office staff.

(Len Deighton, *Fighter*)

For all his undoubted qualities, I do not think Stuffy [Dowding] was a very good Commander-in-Chief – actually in the heat of battle. His technical qualities were good and his strategy was good; but he did not control his subordinate commanders as he, or any C-in-C should have done. All this controversy about Big Wings . . . should never have reached Air Ministry level. It should have been decided by Stuffy himself; and if Leigh-Mallory was disloyal and not implementing Stuffy's strategic plans, should have sacked him . . . That sort of thing is what Cs-in-C are paid for.

(Marshal of the Royal Air Force Sir John Slessor, former Chief of the Air Staff: correspondence with Lord Balfour of Inchrye [Captain Harold Balfour], Under-Secretary of State for Air 1938–44, 28 October, 1969)

Air Vice-Marshal Keith Park*

His active fighting background [as the CO of a fighter squadron in World War I] was to be of inestimable value when, as AOC, 11 Group of Fighter Command in 1940, Keith Park was to assume operational control of all the Hurricane and Spitfire squadrons defending this country against the

---

* Air Officer Commanding, 11 Group, Fighter Command.

massive German air attacks from occupied France over our south-east coast. I suppose every squadron in Fighter Command was involved in the Battle of Britain. Some came down from the north to replace badly mauled squadrons in the south; others operated from airfields like Warmwell in neighbouring 10 Group and Duxford in 12 Group. Every single one of these squadrons was under the operational control of 11 Group headquarters at Uxbridge and its outlying-sector Operations rooms . . .

Air Chief Marshal Lord Dowding . . . has often been acclaimed as the saviour of this country. Rightly so, because in the pre-war years he laid down an air defence system which, in the event, proved to be impregnable. Nevertheless, the Battle of Britain had to be fought in that high summer [of 1940]. It is right and proper for me to say on this occasion . . . something which I do not recall has been said before. It is this. That great and vital air battle was controlled, directed and brought to a successful conclusion by [Keith Park]. The awesome responsibility for this country's survival rested squarely on his shoulders. Had he failed, Stuffy Dowding's foresight, determination and achievement would have counted for nought.

During the battle this splendid officer flew himself around in his Hurricane to see what was going on. He had done the same during the Dunkirk episode . . . This was leadership indeed of the sort that was to become traditional in the Royal Air Force.

I saw Keith Park in December 1940. He was lean, upright, immaculate as usual, but haggard with fatigue from the colossal strain of the events of the preceding months.

This tired officer was rested in Training Command during 1941. His subsequent career continued with distinction and resolution, but always overshadowed by his tremendous Battle of Britain achievement.

> (Douglas Bader, address at a Service of Thanksgiving held at St Clement Danes in the Strand, 12 September 1975, for the life and work of Air Chief Marshal Sir Keith Park)

I was not very fond of [Park] and he was an awkward customer – but, I think, a superb Fighter commander as he [was to] prove again [later] in Malta.

> (Marshal of the Royal Air Force Sir John Slessor [see under Dowding, page 23]: correspondence with Lord Balfour of Inchrye, 28 October 1969)

Air Vice-Marshal Trafford Leigh-Mallory*

Here was a squadron commander's AOC. A solid, upstanding man of forty-eight, a product of Haileybury and Magdalene, Cambridge, he seemed to work at the business of conveying authority. Always trim and

---

* Leigh-Mallory was the Air Officer Commanding, 12 Group, Fighter Command.

spruce, he guarded his dignity with care. It was important to him. At first he could give the impression of stiffness, even pomposity; but this was an outer crust. It could just have been a cover for some inner uncertainty or doubt.

L-M was a First World War aviator, but, unlike his opposite number in 11 Group, he hadn't been a fighter pilot; reconnaissance and Army co-operation was his business. Although, by 1940, he had already had some three years in command of 12 Group, this deficiency in fighter experience may well have weighed in his mind and caused him to adopt a somewhat elevated stance to disguise it. All the same, this pride would never blind him from seeking and, if convinced, adopting a squadron or wing leader's advice. Behind a determined and rather haughty exterior, there was warmth, kindness and loyalty. When L-M was satisfied and confident with a commander, he would stand at his shoulder and never leave him exposed. Difficult he might be, but for those who served him he possessed the virtue of dependability . . . He could make a squadron commander feel that he was walking tall.

(Laddie Lucas, *Flying Colours: The Epic Story of Douglas Bader*,
Hutchinson, 1981)

Leigh-Mallory was an old friend of mine from Haileybury days; I liked him and worked closely with him for some years when we were both active members of the Army Cooperation trade union. But he really knew nothing about the use of fighters, and was not still an active pilot in 1940 – as Keith Park was.

(Marshal of the Royal Air Force Sir John Slessor [see under 'Dowding', page 23]: correspondence with Lord Balfour of Inchrye, 3 November 1969)

THE NERVE CENTRE OF FIGHTER COMMAND

'The hole'

The 11 Group controller walked down a long flight of concrete steps to Park's battle headquarters, known to all who laboured there as 'the hole'. A short time ago he had commanded a fighter squadron, but he was wounded in a dog-fight, and it would be some months before he could return to flying. So he had become a controller and admitted that controlling was the next best thing to flying. He and his fellow controllers, most of whom had flown operationally, knew the problems of fighting and flying; they spoke the same language as the fighter boys, and there was a good understanding between fighter leader and controller. They found that directing the fighter squadrons was a wonderful outlet for their energies, and their heavy responsibilities gave them a sense of power and achievement.

The controller entered a room which overlooked a lower and larger room where several WAAFs, wearing headsets, sat round a large map, known as 'the table', on which they plotted the movements of friendly and enemy aeroplanes. This underground building sometimes reminded him of a small, intimate theatre, for the controller and his assistants sat, as it were, in the sound-proofed, glass-partitioned dress circle, flanked by teams from the gunners and the Observer Corps, so that all could watch the drama below: sometimes when Park came down to follow the battle and sat in his special place it reminded him of the bridge of a great ship.

This building was the hub of a nerve system which had two distinct functions, reporting and controlling. The reporting of enemy raids came from the radars, and from thousands of field observers, who with glasses and telephone took over from radar once the Germans had crossed the coast. All this information was filtered before being plotted on the table, and this process took some time, but a controller could usually reckon on about fifteen minutes' warning from the radars before a high-altitude formation crossed the coast. The other half of the system was used by the controller to get the fighter squadrons into the air to intercept.

The WAAFs placed small counters (red for attackers and black for defenders) on the table, and these gave the estimated height and number of an enemy raid. Each raid was given a number, and as the counters were moved to and fro across the table the group controller and the six sector controllers, who had similar presentations, could watch the build-up of big raids and follow their own defensive moves.

Opposite the control bridge was a huge board displaying, by a system of coloured lights, the squadrons' ever changing order of battle – released, available (thirty or fifteen minutes), readiness (five minutes) and cockpit readiness (two minutes). Once they were scrambled more coloured lights indicated their progress, so that the controller could see at a glance the number of squadrons in the air, how many had sighted the enemy, what proportion were in action, those returning home, and what he had in reserve. This display was called 'the Tote'.

The nerve system stretched out across the land, over the Channel, over the North Sea, and into the air. It gave the group controller a minute-to-minute picture of an air battle fought a hundred miles away. But it was a complicated instrument of war, and because of this complexity some of its components – especially radar stations, surface operations rooms and land-lines – were vulnerable to bombing.

(J. E. [Johnnie] Johnson, *The Story of Air Fighting*, Hutchinson, 1985)

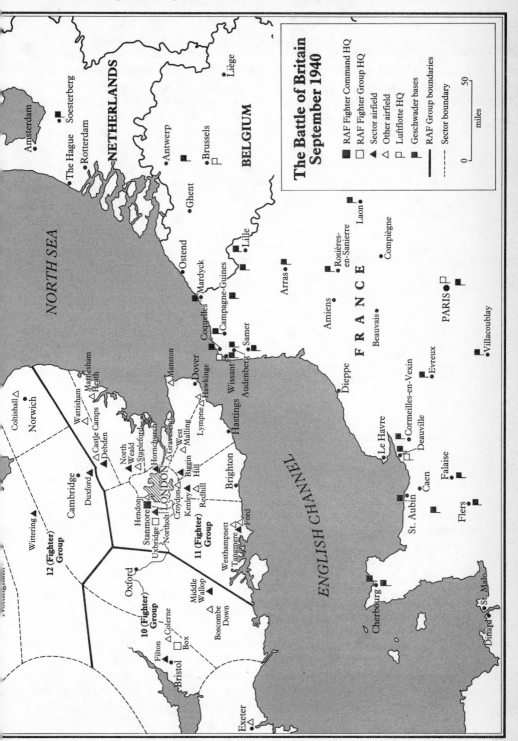

The Battle of Britain September 1940

- ■ RAF Fighter Command HQ
- □ RAF Fighter Group HQ
- ▲ Sector airfield
- △ Other airfield
- ⌷ Luftflotte HQ
- ■ Geschwader bases
- ▬ RAF Group boundaries
- ┈ Sector boundary

0   50
miles

NETHERLANDS

Amsterdam
The Hague
Soesterberg
Rotterdam

Liège

Antwerp
Brussels
Ghent

BELGIUM

NORTH SEA

Ostend
Mardyck
Campagne-Guines
Coquelles
Samer
Audenberg
Wissant

Lille
Laon
Rosières-en-Sanierre
Compiègne

Arras

FRANCE

Amiens
Beauvais

PARIS
Villacoublay

Coltishall
Norwich
Wattisham
Martlesham Heath
Castle Camps
Debden
Duxford
Cambridge

Manston
North Weald
Stapleford
Hornchurch
Gravesend
Biggin Hill
Kenley
Croydon
Redhill
West Malling
Lympne
Hawkinge

Dover

Dieppe

Manston

Hendon
Stanmore
Uxbridge
Northolt
LONDON

12 (Fighter) Group

Wittering

Hastings
Brighton
Ford

Westhampnett
Tangmere
Thorney

11 (Fighter) Group

ENGLISH CHANNEL

Le Havre
Cormeilles-en-Vexin
Deauville
Evreux
Falaise
Caen
St. Aubin
Flers

Oxford
Middle Wallop
Boscombe Down
Coleme
Filton
Box
Bristol

10 (Fighter) Group

Exeter

Cherbourg

Dinard
St. Malo

27

Listening to the enemy

'Everything', says Ronald Lewin, 'began with the intercept.' The monitoring of all German signals 'whether in low-grade or high-grade cipher, radio-telephony, or non-Morse transmissions, was the responsibility of the Y Service'. And utterly dependent upon 'Y' was 'Station X', Bletchley Park, the war station of the Government Code and Cypher School, with its astounding assembly of dedicated genius which broke the German Enigma codes and thus endowed the Western Allies with the priceless gift of Ultra. Throughout the whole critical – and at times nerve-racking –period of the invasion threat, Ultra played a significant part in permitting the British leadership to build up a 'meaningful mosaic' (in Lewin's words) of German intentions. In the Battle of Britain, 'The early and authentic information that came from Bletchley about forthcoming raids was a strong buttress for Dowding in his conduct of the battle.'

'Buttress' would seem to be a well-chosen word: a useful support to a building, but not part of the main structure. It is possible to picture a strong building without a buttress, but a buttress without a building is nothing – and so it was with Air Intelligence in 1940.

(John Terraine, *The Right of the Line: The RAF in the European War: 1939–1945*, Hodder & Stoughton, 1985)

THE CONTROLLERS

Squadron Leader Ronald Adam

Controllers had to cope with poor radar reports, poor communications and mistakes by the Observer Corps. They had to do an awful lot of coordinating of information. It was true they sometimes put lame ducks – who weren't much good at flying and fighting – in the Ops Room. But that didn't necessarily mean they were poor controllers. The good controllers were very good indeed. The controllers we trusted, we trusted implicitly. Ronnie Adam was one of those. There were times when we'd say among ourselves 'Oh hell, Ronnie isn't on today . . .'

(Squadron Leader James Leathart)

In the Hornchurch operations room

We all knew how limited our resources were, how few aircraft and trained pilots we had got ready for action, and we did not – we could not –understand why the enemy did not come for us at once . . . We held our breath . . . and then . . . the radar plots began to show the enemy assembling in the air behind Cape Gris-Nez in France. There he was milling around as one formation after another joined up, and we went to our loudspeakers when our Group Headquarters gave the order telling the squadron to take off . . . 'Scramble' we would say and Spitfires would tear into the sky . . . We would sit there on the ground and watch the plots . . . We would pass information to the pilots, telling them all changes in the enemy's direction, how he was splitting up into different formations, what height he was flying at and guiding our fighters to the most advantageous position up in the eye of the sun, ready to attack. The Battle of Britain is summarized for me in one snatch on the radio-telephone from a famous New Zealand fighter . . . I heard his voice in my ear as he sighted the enemy: 'Christ Almighty, tally ho! Whole bloody hordes of them.'

(Squadron Leader Ronald Adam, in Norman Gelb,
Scramble, Michael Joseph, 1986)

A great test pilot remembers

In the air everyone, quite naturally, became tense and excited. Often it was difficult enough to know what was going on anyway and this was when a really good controller was a fighter pilot's best friend – he could calm everything down and make everyone feel relaxed and well informed. At Hornchurch we had some splendid controllers but one in particular stands out in my memory: his name was Ronald Adam and in civilian life he was an actor of some distinction. Apart from being highly competent at the actual job, his voice had a quality of calm and unhesitating certainty which would have done credit to an archbishop in his pulpit. Often after an engagement one found oneself alone and disoriented in a hazy sky and calling for a homing course to steer. Adam's voice then almost shamed one into feeling 'What the hell am I getting all steamed up about?' The contribution of such men to the outcome of the Battle of Britain was incalculable.

(Jeffrey Quill, *Spitfire: A Test Pilot's Story*, John Murray, 1983)

Group Captain A. B. Woodhall

Woodhall . . . the controller with a cool, unruffled ability to size up the situation presented to him on the big board in his operations room and then give directions to his pilots in a voice which invariably remained calm and sonorous, even at times of greatest stress.

(Hugh Dundas, *Flying Start: A Fighter Pilot's War Years*,
Stanley Paul, 1988)

Woodhall, affectionately known as Woody, was a veteran of the Kaiser's War, and was one of the best and most trusted controllers in Fighter Command. His calm and measured tones seemed full of confidence and assurance, and he was fully aware of the limitations of radar which, at this time, was often distorted . . . Woodhall knew that his wing leader was in the best position to judge how and when to attack, and therefore his controlling technique was to advise rather than to instruct.

(J. E. [Johnnie] Johnson, *The Story of Air Fighting*, Hutchinson, 1985)

242 Squadron had moved down to Duxford from Coltishall . . . to be nearer the battle. Now it was being controlled from the local operations room and, in particular, by Wing Commander A. B. Woodhall, the station commander. A well-tried First World War pilot, with a resourceful and tactical mind, Woodhall was to become the star among the Royal Air Force's wartime fighter controllers. Within two years, he had transferred to the great air battle for Malta the lessons he was learning in the struggle for command of British . . . skies. Profiting from his association with Bader, he was developing a genius for this exacting and responsible role.

(Laddie Lucas, *Flying Colours: The Epic Story of Douglas Bader*, Hutchinson, 1981)

Squadron Leaders the Hon. Roger Frankland and W. A. K. (Bill) Igoe

A normal day during 1940 usually began with us lying around in our Mae Wests at the dispersal point waiting for some sort of show to start. When the alarm sounded we scrambled and, once airborne, heard through our earphones the clarion calls of such great controllers as Bill Igoe or Roger Frankland, instructing us to patrol Mayfield or Tenterden [Sussex and Kent] at angels two five (twenty-five thousand feet).

These were remote little villages that could not be seen from five thousand feet let alone twenty-five thousand. Dover or Hastings would have surely been simpler. If you survived the action in the evening you went off to the local pub (in our case the *Unicorn* in Chichester) and got pissed and hopefully hurried home with one of the WAAFS.

(Paddy Barthropp, *Paddy: The Life and Times of Wing Commander Patrick Barthropp*, DFC, AFC, Howard Baker, 1986)

THE GIRLS IN BLUE

Now and then a pay-off

Radar and the Observer Corps gave no rest all day to the controllers and the apparently untirable WAAF plotters both at Fighter Command and Group Headquarters. I managed occasionally . . . to watch the incredible speed and accuracy with which the WAAFs plotted the raids in the operations room. On one occasion I noticed a lovely girl who was working harder than most. She looked up and I saw a pair of laughing brown eyes. She became my wife.

(F. W. Winterbotham, *The Ultra Secret*, Weidenfeld & Nicolson, 1974)

In charge at Biggin Hill

My first husband – he was a fighter pilot – was killed before the Battle of Britain began . . . So when I became an officer – I was twenty-four years old then – I had already been made a widow by the war. It was quite a shock, coming at the beginning . . . I had experienced what might happen to other people, which, I suppose, wasn't really a bad thing when I was put in charge of the airwomen, about 250 of them, employed at Biggin Hill – plotters, drivers, cooks, people in the armory, equipment assistants, everything. One of my code and cipher officers married a pilot on the base. He was shot down and she didn't know whether he'd reappear. But he did, thank goodness.

The girls came from all walks of life. Some were well educated, others were not. There were so many wanting to join that you could sort them out as suitable for this or suitable for that. We had no difficulty recruiting. We had some difficulty absorbing them all at short notice.

(Assistant Section Officer Felicity Hanbury)

Plotting

I was in a repertory company on Hastings Pier before the war began. I was twenty-one years old and supposed to be the costume designer, but in a repertory company you did all sorts of things. I played all the maids on stage, all the nannies, all those things.

I had shared a dressing room with Dulcie Langham. She disappeared just before the war started. She said she was going to join the WAAF and that if I ever wanted any help or anything, I was to contact her. So when the war started, I did just that and Dulcie told me what to do. She told me I ought to become a plotter in the WAAF. I hadn't the slightest idea what a plotter was. But that's what I became. I went to a school and was taught how to use these great long rods with arrows on the end for plotting. We were given a rough idea of what it was all about. We were – myself and seven other girls – the first ones to arrive at Tangmere (an 11 Group Sector Station). It was February. We had practically no uniforms. We were given bloomers – they were called passion-killers in those days. We were given a shirt and a tie and a mackintosh and a beret. But we wore our own shirts. All we had really been taught was to manipulate those enormous rods. They had a battery at one end and a magnet at the other. We were supposed to pick up small metal arrows with them and place them where they had to be put on the plotting table. That was the basic business of plotting aircraft. You'd get a grid reference and you'd plot one arrow after the other across the board.

But of course, when we got to Tangmere, they hadn't got any of those sophisticated rods. All they had was a bit of wood with a thumb stall in the end – that rubber thing bank clerks put on their fingers to count paper money. So you were throwing the arrows on the table and sort of pushing them into place. And we had a croupier thing for pulling the arrows off. It was very primitive. The table was arranged in such a way that you could really reach to put most of the arrows in the proper grid references by hand.

We were connected by headphones to two sources, to various Observer Corps posts and to what was known in those days as RDF – radio direction finding. We know it as radar today. The plots were passed to us in a four-figure grid reference . . .

In front of the plotting table was a raised dais where sat the controller, who was the boss man, an Ops A, often an airwoman, who would take down instructions from Group when they came in, an Ops B, who was the controller's assistant, and an Ops B1. Also there on the dais was the Army, who passed on the information on the table to warn the anti-aircraft batteries of what was happening. The order for any forms of readiness, scramble, do anything, was not the responsibility of the controller at Tangmere before anything happened. He was only responsible once the battle was joined in his Sector. Up to that point, it was the controller at Group Headquarters who was responsible. He had a similar, but much more comprehensive, picture of the entire Group area. We just had a picture on our table of our Sector and a little bit outside it. So up at Group the controller there would decide when something was happening and it was time to bring a squadron to readiness.

When you think of it, it was so laborious it wasn't funny. Ops A had a pink form in front of her. Until that moment, she'd probably just been sitting around. But as soon as she put her hand to her headphone and braced herself to take a message from Group, everybody was alerted. We knew something was coming down. The message would come through and if it said 'Tangmere' she would write down 'Tangmere'. Then it would say, 'Such-and-such Squadron.' She'd write down the squadron. Then it would say, ' "A" Flight to readiness' or ' "A" Flight ten minutes.' She'd write all that down and hand it to the controller and he would see what was happening. He would hand it to Ops B. Ops B would action it. He would lift his telephone and say, 'Squadron "A" Flight five minutes' or 'Come to readiness' or 'Stand by' or whatever it was. The pink form would then be passed to Ops B1, who would tick it off as actioned. The pink form would then be passed to a teleprinter operator in a little cubbyhole who would make a record that it had happened. . . .

. . . Our controller would be getting instructions from Group while using what we were plotting on the table as a reference to see what it was all about. The raid would come up toward the coast, and as it arrived within, say, ten miles of the coast, at a distance where it could be seen from the ground, the plotting of that particular plane would be stopped by the radar and taken over by Observer Corps, who would then plot it until it went out of their area into the next Observer Corps area . . . As the enemy moved from one Observer area to the next, the girl connected by phone to that area would take over plotting its movements on the table . . . A supervisor went around in the Ops Room, seeing what was happening and tidying up . . .

We did the twenty-four hours between us. We had a weekend every three, and a day off every week. Three days a week we had a three-watch shift, but the other four days two watches were operating and that was pretty rough. Then it was usual for us to do one four-hour and one eight-hour shift in every twenty-four hours.

Fairly soon after the start of the Battle of Britain, I stopped plotting. I was made a corporal and my job was to do a liaison between RDF and the Observer Corps. As a raid came up, I assessed which Observer Corps area it was going into, got onto the appropriate Observer Corps, gave the warning, and arranged the hand-over of the plotting as best I could. I was on duty at Tangmere the day North Weald was bombed. The girl on the table who was on to North Weald got word over her headphones and said, 'Oh my God, they've been bombed.' The supervisor snapped, 'Shut up and get on with your job.'

But up until the day France fell, everything was free and easy. We didn't wear uniforms, for instance, on the evening shift because if you were going out, you'd just put on your high-heeled shoes. I remember a remarkable girl called Sunneva. She appeared on duty in a black dress, wearing earrings. That was the order of the day. Nothing was happening. We used to take our knitting and our sewing around the table. . . . We had a super controller, Squadron Leader Vick. He went along with all of this.

The day France fell, we went on duty as usual with all our bits and pieces and the sewing and what have you. And Vick came on duty and stood there and looked sternly at us and cried out, 'Flight Sergeant!' The flight sergeant said, 'Yes, sir.' Vick shouted, 'Get these bloody women out of here!' One by one we were all sent out, relieved one by one by men, and we were herded off into a rest room. We sat there a half hour, three-quarters of an hour, and eventually the flight sergeant appeared and said, 'Now, you lot, you listen to me.' We were told in no mean fashion that all this was to stop.

(Corporal Claire Legge)

Anxious waiting

Richard (Pilot Officer Richard Jones) and I were engaged during the Battle. When I had a long weekend off, I'd go . . . and find . . . a room near where he was stationed . . . I knew the day-to-day danger he faced. There was always the possibility that . . . he'd be killed . . . The husband of one of my friends, also a pilot, was killed. It could have been Richard. We just lived for the day. I lived for the time we could be together.

(Elizabeth Cook)

I had got to know the men of 54 Squadron very well. I felt deeply when people like Johnny Allen were killed. I remember saying to James's [Squadron Leader James Leathart] father 'I don't think there will be any of them left.' The men were right in it, doing something. But we were just sitting there waiting.

(Elaine Leathart [Mrs James Leathart], in Norman Gelb, *Scramble: A Narrative History of the Battle of Britain*, Michael Joseph, 1986)

Dusk take-off, 1940

At the end of the runway
   The WAAF corporal lingers,
Nervously threading
   A scarf through her fingers.

Husband? Or lover?
   Or friend for a night?
Her face doesn't tell
   In the dim evening light.

The Squadron is airborne,
   But still the WAAF lingers,
Nervously threading
   A scarf through her fingers.

(Ronald A. M. Ransom)

IN R/T* TOUCH?

In January 1937 a requirement was issued for a very high frequency (VHF) radio-telephony set with 100 miles range. The Royal Aircraft Establishment were entrusted with development following its research work over the two previous years. The demand presented problems and by mid-1938 it was reported that it might still take four years to perfect fighter VHF. . . .

  * Radio telephone.

The Chief of Air Staff approved revised plans and orders were given for the re-equipping of four sectors each in Nos. 11 and 12 Groups. Hornchurch, North Weald and Debden were to operate both HF and VHF simultaneously.

The whole VHF programme became a race against time, which was lost. By August 1939 the first sets, designated TR 1133, were ready for delivery and in October trials began with six Spitfires of No. 66 squadron based at Duxford. The results were excellent. For the second stage of the programme it was anticipated that by May 1940 all Fighter Command aircraft would be equipped with an improved VHF radio, TR 1143.

Serious delays occurred in deliveries of both sets and at the time of Dunkirk VHF was held in reserve. Aircraft continued with the TR9 HF set. In the main the Battle of Britain was fought using the old and well-tried HF network. It was not until the end of September 1940 that sixteen day-fighter squadrons had been re-equipped with VHF. It was a case of too little too late.

(Derek Wood with Derek Dempster, *The Narrow Margin: The Battle of Britain and The Rise of Air Power, 1930–1940*, Hutchinson, 1961)

A serious handicap ... was the fact that the change over from 'High Frequency' to 'Very High Frequency' radio telephony was still in progress. The VHF was an immense improvement on the HF, both in range and clarity of speech; but the change over, which had started nearly a year before, was held up by the slow output of equipment. This meant that much work had to be done on aircraft radio equipment during the Battle, and squadrons equipped with VHF could not communicate with HF ground stations, and *vice versa*.

(Air Chief Marshal Sir Hugh Dowding, Air Officer Commanding-in-Chief, Fighter Command, Battle of Britain Despatch, 20 August 1941)

AFTER FRANCE – JUNE 1940

Since my wound I had had an incredible capacity for sleep, and I slept now. I awoke over the Channel Islands; they were bathed in sunlight and stood out very clearly in a smooth sea. Soon we were crossing the Dorset coast; and as I looked down on the calm and peaceful English countryside, the smoke curling, not from bombed villages, but from lazy little cottage chimneys, I saw a game of cricket in progress on a village pitch. After the poor war-torn France I had just seen in its death agony, I was seized with a sudden disgust and revulsion at this smug insular contentedness and frivolity that England seemed to be enjoying behind her sea barrier. I thought a few bombs would wake those cricketers up, and that they wouldn't be long in coming, either.

As we glided down on to Hendon aerodrome, my feelings were so mixed that I had difficulty in controlling them. I cannot describe them very well, and they don't really matter much anyway. I suppose it was a culmination of emotion that brought the tears to my eyes – something to do with the things I had done and seen, perhaps, with the friends I had left, and the almost unbelievable fact that I was home.

Well, as everyone knows, the Luftwaffe came to England. Many of us who fought in France were unable, through wounds or because we were doing other jobs, to take part in the Battle of Britain. But even so, and even though the Battle of France was lost, we like to think we had something to do with the saving of this Island. We like to think that we gave the Luftwaffe a little bit of a shaking up when we took the first shock in May 1940. We like to think, too, that our experience helped the British Fighter Squadrons to inflict their first defeat on the Luftwaffe in August and September, 1940.

But that is another story.

> (Paul Richey, *Fighter Pilot: A Personal Record of the Campaign in France*, Batsford, 1941)

FROM NO. 10

On 29 May, I, like every other member of the administration of whatever rank, received a printed circular from the Prime Minister which I have long preserved among my cherished possessions. It ran as follows:

STRICTLY CONFIDENTIAL

In these dark days the Prime Minister would be grateful if all his colleagues in the Government, as well as high officials, would maintain a high morale in their circles; not minimizing the gravity of events, but showing confidence in our ability and inflexible resolve to continue the war till we have broken the will of the enemy to bring all Europe under his domination.

No tolerance should be given to the idea that France will make a separate peace; but whatever may happen on the Continent, we cannot doubt our duty and we shall certainly use all our power to defend the Island, the Empire and our Cause.

W.S.C.

> (Harold Macmillan, *The Blast of War, 1939–45*, Macmillan, 1967)

One June morning in 1940 I was at my desk at 10 Downing Street, immersed in the frantic activities of those anxious days, when a messenger informed me that Lord Mottistone was at the front door, demanding to see me. 'Bring him in, of course,' I said. The messenger said he had indeed invited him in, but His Lordship had declined. So I went to the front door and there, resplendent in the full dress uniform of a Lord Lieutenant, stood the seventy-year-old general.

'Winston,' he said to me, 'is one of my oldest friends. But I don't wish to disturb him at this moment when the future of the world rests on his shoulders.' He fumbled in his pocket and I thought for one moment that he might be going to give me half-a-crown. Instead he brought out a piece of paper on which were written the words: 'Hampshire is behind you.' 'Give that to Winston from me,' he said, and with a gallant smile turned to walk back to Waterloo Station. I gave the Prime Minister the message. He shook with laughter as he read it and then, quite suddenly, he wept.

(John Colville, *Footprints in Time*, Collins, 1976)

What General Weygand called the Battle of France is over. I expect that the Battle of Britain is about to begin. Upon this battle depends the survival of Christian civilization. Upon it depends our own British life, and the long continuity of our institutions and our Empire. The whole fury and might of the enemy must very soon be turned on us. Hitler knows that he will have to break us in this island or lose the war. If we can stand up to him, all France may be free and the life of the world may move forward into broad, sunlit uplands. But if we fail, then the whole world, including the United States, including all that we have known and cared for, will sink into the abyss of a new Dark Age made more sinister, and perhaps more protracted, by the lights of perverted science. Let us therefore brace ourselves to our duties, and so bear ourselves that, if the British Empire and its Commonwealth last for a thousand years, men will still say, 'This was their finest hour.'

(Winston S. Churchill, House of Commons, 18 June, 1940)

TO DO OR DIE

We were likely to be left alone, as we had not been for centuries, with a powerful enemy at Calais and Cherbourg. But then, at the Table, [of the House of Commons] stood this one man, with the pale, round, bulldog face, grim but undaunted, precise and strong in speech and intention, ready to lead us 'if necessary, alone'. 'You ask me my policy. My policy is Victory.' Short words, but shattering, explosive, electric. I have been moved in theatres and churches, but never so deeply as those early speeches stirred me up there in the Gallery, the famous phrases which passed into history as soon as they were spoken. All knew at once that they were history. Some have said – Mr Churchill has modestly said – that he did no more than express what was already in the hearts of the people. I think there was rather more to it than that. The trumpet does not blow for nothing. It was one great difference between Mr Churchill and Mr Chamberlain. He, after all, was tough enough and, since the war began, had been heart and soul with Mr Churchill. But when he said the fine true thing it was like a faint air played on a pipe and lost on the wind at once. When Mr Churchill said it, it was like an organ filling the church, and we all went out refreshed and resolute to do or die.

(A. P. Herbert, *Independent Member*, Methuen, 1950)

To fight England is like fighting fate.

(Lord Dunsany)

THE CURTAIN LIFTS

Douglas Bader joins 242 (Canadian) Squadron

In June 1940 I was sent for by the Air Officer Commanding 12 Group who told me that he wanted me to take over 242 (Canadian) Squadron. They had had a very rough time in France. They were a pretty brassed-off bunch and lacked discipline. Leigh-Mallory thought I might be of some use in getting the thing straight.

The next morning I found myself at Coltishall with my Adjutant, a fine old gentleman who had been MP for the Isle of Wight for many years and who had fought in World War One. He took me into a dispersal hut where pilots were lounging in chairs and on beds, wearing Mae-Wests and flying clothes and all reading comic strips.

He said: 'Gentlemen this is your new Squadron Commander.

For some extraordinary reason, because I had been trained at the Royal Air Force College at Cranwell, I thought they might stand up. In fact most of them, still lying flat on their backs, lowered their comics, looked over the tops and did not care for what they saw. They raised their comics again and went on reading. There was one chap who was lying with his back to me who actually turned over and had a look; he then turned his back to me and went on reading.

I told the Adjutant that I wanted to see all the pilots in my office in half an hour's time and I gave them what I thought was a reasonable three-minute talk on what I expected of them. As I finished I asked whether anyone had got anything to say.

There was a long silence but eventually from the back came a voice which said 'Horseshit'.

Again, they hadn't taught me at Cranwell what to do in such a situation and I got very red in the face and was about to make a bloody fool of myself when the same voice quickly added. 'Sir!'

After that, it was all right.

(Douglas Bader at the Wartime Pilots' and Observers' Association
Commonwealth Wartime Aircrew Reunion, Winnipeg,
Manitoba, September 1970)

A New Zealander's analysis

When did the Battle of Britain begin? The history of the Royal Air Force says mid-August;* other publications say July; some even as late as September when the assault on London was at its peak. The German General Kreipe,† says, and I quote, 'The date that I should ascribe to the opening of The Battle of Britain is May 1940.' . . . From a fighter pilot's point of view, I put it at July when enemy bombers, operating singly and taking advantage of extensive cloud cover, made repeated attacks on Channel shipping. Throughout this day the fighter squadrons in No. 11 Group were constantly alerted, ordered off and engaged in combat, and from then onwards there was to be little respite for the pilots defending our Channel shipping. Indeed, one or two slack periods apart, July 1940 was to be a particularly intensive phase of what we now know as the Battle of Britain.

German documents captured since the war confirm 3 July as the date intended for the re-opening of the air offensive. On 2 July the German Armed Forces Supreme Command issued its first operational instructions to the Luftwaffe for the campaign against the United Kingdom which was intended to culminate in the invasion of the British Isles. There were two basic tasks assigned to the Luftwaffe:

(1) The interdiction of the Channel to merchant shipping, by means of attacks on convoys, and the destruction of harbour facilities.
(2) The destruction of the Royal Air Force.

Between the date that this order was issued and 10 July bad weather conditions over the Channel precluded the mounting of large-scale bomber operations. It was not therefore until this latter date that operations in force were undertaken by the Luftwaffe when bomber formations, with heavy fighter escort, attacked two convoys in the Dover–Dungeness area. This operation was to be repeated many times in the weeks that followed, and with increasing effort, particularly in fighter support. Phase one of the Battle of Britain had begun.

No story of the Battle of Britain is complete, at whatever level it is written, without a brief survey of the opposing air forces. Only by doing this is it possible to bring home to the reader the immensity of the task faced by the fighter pilots of the Royal Air Force. Furthermore, the extreme fatigue reached by the squadron, flight and section leaders can be more readily appreciated when the odds against Fighter Command are related to the acute shortage of pilots, and in particular leaders, at the time.

At the end of the Dunkirk operations, Fighter Command could muster

---

* *The Fight at Odds*, HMSO.
† Werner Kreipe, Chief of Operations, Third Air Fleet, *The Fatal Decisions*.

only three hundred serviceable Spitfires and Hurricanes. This figure improved to about five hundred by July and was further increased until there were about six hundred Spitfires and Hurricanes in the battle by mid-August. It is interesting to note that this latter figure represented just half that considered by the Air Staff to be necessary for the defence of the United Kingdom, when they reviewed the strategical consequences of the fall of France. The pilot situation was more unfavourable. Despite the invaluable intake into the Command of fifty-two pilots on loan from the Fleet Air Arm – and what good pilots they were too – the squadrons were still under strength and embarrassingly short of experienced leaders [see Appendix B].

What of the opposition? The lull between the end of the French campaign and July had enabled the Luftwaffe to regroup its forces which were now disposed on captured and rebuilt airfields throughout the occupied territories. On 3 July, when the Armed Forces Supreme Command directive was issued, their forces amounted to some three thousand aircraft of which no less than fourteen hundred and eighty were fighters. As for their pilots, I again quote the erstwhile General Kreipe, who, referring to this period, said of the Luftwaffe: 'The power of the Air Force was now at a zenith which it was never again to achieve during the long years of war. . . . The pilots were highly skilled. . . . Their morale was very high and they were confident of victory.'

The outcome of the battle was to the Germans a foregone conclusion. 'It will take', reported General Stapf of German Intelligence to General Halder (German General Staff) on 11 July, 'between a fortnight and a month to smash the enemy air force.'

(Alan C. Deere, *Nine Lives*, Hodder & Stoughton, 1959)

THE FIGHTER PILOTS

We few, we happy few, we band of brothers;
For he today that sheds his blood with me
Shall be my brother; be he ne'er so vile
This day shall gentle his condition:
And gentlemen in England, now a-bed
Shall think themselves accurs'd they were not here,
And hold their manhoods cheap whiles any speaks
That fought with us upon Saint Crispin's day

(William Shakespeare, *King Henry V*, act iv, scene iii)

The right stuff

Before the war the Service undoubtedly had an indifferent reputation, not only among magistrates and insurance companies, but with a large body of well-meaning people. Its officers were often not considered to be

gentlemen and pilots as a whole were thought tough, wild and unman-
nerly. The horse was still the hallmark by which the officer-class was
judged, and manners and a correct address were still more important than
imagination or ability. By these standards the RAF was tried and failed.

What was it then which enabled the Service to command the loyalty of
squadrons recruited from Britain, the Dominions ... European
countries, and the United States? What was it that enabled all these
elements to mix together without favour or friction? ... It was a Polish
squadron which emerged from the Battle of Britain with the best record of
any unit of any nationality, yet I had never heard a hint of envy or
detractive explanation from British pilots on this score. The CO of this
squadron was an Englishman and one of his Flight Commanders a
Canadian ... In my first squadron, two Czech sergeant pilots had begged
to remain with us even when they were offered places in a Czech squadron
which was then being formed ... Cliques and national antipathies were
unknown ...

I wondered whether hatred of the enemy could account for this
fellowship, but rejected the explanation at once ... I wondered whether a
sense of common purpose would explain it, but this theory was no more
satisfactory than the others. The average pilot is too deeply involved in
the war to be able to think in terms of common enemies or common aims.
I wondered whether it could be explained as a fellowship of the air and
felt that this was nearer the mark.

The air is an element more brutal than the sea and more searching. It is
impossible to live by it and have many illusions either about yourself or
about those around you; if you do, it will expose you or them before long.
If there is one quality which pilots possess it is genuineness. I do not know
whether this is an element attracted by the air or an attribute imposed by
it, but I felt it was the virtue which underlay and explained what had
seemed so puzzling.

This theory seemed to fit the facts. What the layman had once regarded
as lack of manners was partly uncouthness or lack of consideration, but
partly also a refusal to show an interest which was not felt or say a thing
which was not believed. In this light the uncouthness of the airman
seemed pardonable and the manners of, say, Brett Young's Essendines
hollow and meaningless.

I began to understand why cowardice was merely pitied or disregarded,
but line-shooting was actively and cordially disliked. The coward was just
a poor devil who had not the nerve, as another might not have the
eyesight, to do a job; but a line-shooter was un-genuine and beyond the
pale. This was the criterion by which the RAF judged, and beside it other
things had small importance. Birth and upbringing counted for nothing;
nationality and creed did not matter; learning or ignorance, wealth or
poverty, skill or ham-handedness in flying, dullness or eccentricity in

everyday life, it was the same; if a man was genuine he was a good type, if un-genuine he was not.

It was this criterion of straightforwardness, I thought, which made it possible for all manner of men of all nations to work together as they did. A man was not judged by any of the old standards, race, birth, religion, wealth or membership of the best clubs, but according to his personal integrity; if he passed the test the other things did not matter, if he failed they would not help him. It followed naturally that a Service which applied a universal standard should command a universal loyalty.

(H. A. S. [Tim] Johnston,* *Tattered Battlements: A Fighter Pilot's Diary*,
Peter Davies, 1943; William Kimber, 1985)

A United States view

From Munich onwards the regular officers [of the Royal Air Force] were augmented by Volunteer Reserve pilots who had completed their flying training. These were the 'weekend pilots', the 'long-haired amateurs' who came from university squadrons or who had flown with their local flying clubs on weekends. In time of course these amateurs were to outnumber the professionals. But in 1939 and 1940 they were new. The professionals looked at them askance. Senior officers wondered, unnecessarily, what they would be like when the time came.

The fighter pilots, professional and amateur were as blithe and valorous a group as any in the war. Many actively disliked the military part of their training. They said with wonderful gusts of profanity that they could not understand why they had to learn to form threes on barrack square or study military etiquette. Others were willing enough, but hated the technical side of flying; they couldn't be bothered to learn about engines or map-reading. But one and all loved flying itself.

The Volunteer Reserve added a certain worldliness to the small, closed world of the professionals. Here were gay young men from Oxford and Cambridge ready to spend a month's pay on one wild 'night out' in London. Here were intellectuals, equally gay, who would sit up half the night discussing the war and its origins; subjects which the professionals left to the politicians and the high command. Here were solemn Scots and fervent Welshmen from towns and villages with queer Celtic names and some scores of brawny young men from Canada and Australia and South Africa and New Zealand who had joined the air force in Britain.

---

* Wing Commander Tim Johnston (he was – inevitably – 'Johnny' to the Royal Air Force) was an exceptional, and yet unsung, figure in the Service. A Domus Exhibitioner of Brasenose, Oxford, his intellectual qualities and perennial good humour and friendliness set him apart. He learnt about air fighting under Bob Stanford-Tuck in 257 Squadron. This, allied with his purpose and resolution, won him two Distinguished Flying Crosses in wartime to which, as a widely respected member of the Colonial Civil Service, he added a CMG and a CBE in peace. Tim Johnstone died prematurely in 1967, aged 54. Ed.

They drank and they wenched. Their behaviour on leave was a scandal to senior regular officers of all three services and their own immediate commanders found them a handful. As the battle wore on they developed an *esprit de corps* which few services have ever approached. Like all services with a high morale they had a tendency to look down on men less happily situated. Their name for the British Expeditionary Force, after Norway and Dunkirk, was 'Back Every Fortnight' and they held naval officers to be humourless fellows to be teased with questions about 'the sharp end' and 'the blunt end' of the 'boats'. The fame they won impressed them very little. I recall that shortly after the Battle of Britain some solemn fellow inquired in *The New Statesman and Nation* whether those pilots might in the future form the cadre for a British Fascist party. When I read this to a group of pilots it was greeted with roars of incredulous laughter.

The grass is long on their graves now; those whose graves are known. I wonder sometimes what they would think of the great memorial that rises on the hill by Runneymede that bears the names of those whose bodies were not recovered. Probably, 'Memorials are mouldy, old boy, much better have a noggin before closing time.' If heavenly justice has done its job, I hope there is some celestial pub where they can stand, with the top button of the tunics unbuttoned, pewter mug in hand and talk about the 'popsie' they met at the Savoy and 'that ass of an adjutant who thinks this is a bloody Guards regiment'.

> (Drew Middleton,* *The Sky Suspended! The Battle of Britain May 1940–*
> *April 1941,* Secker & Warburg, 1960)

By one of them

High summer, 1940 – that is a time to look back upon with wonder, a time to have been alive and British. Above all, perhaps, it was a time to have been a fighter pilot in the Royal Air Force.

> (Hugh Dundas, *Flying Start: A Fighter Pilot's War Years,*
> Stanley Paul, 1988)

Independent judgement

But what gave him [Richard Hillary] his determination? – His nature was complex, so the answer cannot be simple, but this should be remembered: he was a pilot who had lived, for a little season of intensified perception, in the thin bright air that is twenty thousand feet above the earth. In a man whose mind is deeply imaginative and equally capable of delight, flying

---

* Middleton, an exceptional US newspaperman, who died in 1990, was the London correspondent of the Associated Press during the Battle, joining the *New York Times* two years later to cover for it the remainder of the European war. He was made an honorary CBE by the British in 1986 – Ed.

must leave a hunger that nothing else can feed. Few of us know the sensation of handling a Spitfire to the altitude of the sky, but we have all seen pilots, in the enormous air of a summer day, drawing their patterns of exuberant delight: whatever the sensation may be, it must include a very joyous enlargement of the spirit. So there is that to think of when looking for an answer: in Dick's mind there was the flavour of an old delight. There was also a romantic image.

He liked the idea – as who would not? – of being a fighter pilot. He cultivated the appearance of one: a sedulous avoidance of that kind of smartness which suggests the formality of a parade-ground, top button of his tunic unfastened, a little air of brave dishevelment. He wanted to go on being a fighter pilot, and it would be odd indeed if he did not sometimes think of winning distinction as one.

(Eric Linklater, Foreword, in Richard Hillary, The Last Enemy,
Macmillan, 1942)

By a Commander-in-Chief

In the years that have passed since then – years which have brought with them an ever-increasing understanding of the importance of that one particular year [1940] – I have found myself becoming more and more deeply touched by the part played by the young air crews who fought the battles . . . For that reason alone, my becoming Commander-in-Chief of Fighter Command . . . was an experience about which I feel very strongly. I was keenly aware that I was to become responsible for the operation of a magnificent and battle-seasoned command.

While I was alive to, and a little overawed by, the weight of that responsibility, in my heart and mind I was able to accept it with a reasonable eagerness. I knew the breed of the men whom I was going to command through having been one of the first of them. I understood them, even if, in the arrogance of their youth, they might at times look with disdain on the 'scrambled eggs' on the peak of my cap, for I knew that it was particularly in the tradition of fighter pilots to look upon all authority with a pronounced irreverence.

I have never doubted that many of those young bloods who served under my command . . . thought that I did not understand the inclination which they showed towards a certain flamboyance of manner, and that the style of the cynicism which they appeared so casually to adopt was a mystery to me. The truth of it was that their outlook and spirit were expressed in just the same way as that known to those of us who had started it all not so many years before.

(W. Sholto Douglas, later Lord Douglas of Kirtleside, who followed Lord
Dowding as AOC-in-C of Fighter Command, Years of Command)

Pilot reflection

One Sunday morning . . . it was time to say goodbye to Cocky Dundas . . .
He was the last of the original Auxiliaries [of 616 Squadron] . . . and loath
to leave its splendid Yorkshire ground crews . . . Tired from [weeks] of
operational flying, [and after] two shattering experiences . . . he was
posted to a training unit which had a reputation for smart, unmodified
uniforms, collars and ties, and that sort of thing, and he was clearly not
dressed for this occasion . . . Fighting in that tiny cockpit had not
improved the appearance of his scarlet silk-lined tunic. One of the two
'As' on his lapels was missing, as was his tie, and a vivid yellow scarf
added a colourful touch to this ensemble.

We poured him into the open cockpit of the Maggie, which was not
intended for such a long, sparse frame. I stood on the wing, fastened the
safety straps, wished him well and shouted that a few whiffs of oxygen
might improve his state of health. He turned a pair of bloodshot eyes
upon me and shouted something about getting back on ops before
Christmas. . . .

. . . I did not see Cocky again until early 1945, when as Group Captain
Hugh Spencer Lisle Dundas, DSO and Bar, DFC, aged twenty-four, he
flew from Italy to Brussels Evêre, where I had a Canadian Spitfire Wing.
He had already been offered a permanent commission, but after the war
preferred to enter the harsher commercial world, where, because of his
outstanding qualities of leadership, he reached the top.

(J. E. [Johnnie] Johnson, in Laddie Lucas, Thanks for the Memory,
Stanley Paul, 1989)

Inner thoughts

85 [Squadron] was not ordered off that day. We sat around at dispersal
talking of trivial things, waiting . . . Ceaselessly the gramophone churned
out some well-known tune: *Tuxedo Junction, I'm in the mood for love,
Don't you ever cry.* They were the favourites.

> 'Don't you ever cry, don't ever shed a tear
> Don't you ever cry after I'm gone . . .'

There seemed nothing melancholy in those lilting words and the catchy
little tune seemed suited to our mood. Some of us would die within the
next few days. That was inevitable. But you did not believe it would be
you. Death was always present, and we knew it for what it was. If we had
to die we would be alone, smashed to pieces, burnt alive, or drowned.
Some strange, protecting veil kept the nightmare thought from our minds,
as it did the loss of our friends. Their disappearance struck us as less a
solid blow than a dark shadow which chilled our hearts and passed on.
We seemed already to be living in another world, separate and exalted,

45

where the gulf between life and death had closed and was no longer forbidding.

(Peter Townsend, *Duel of Eagles*, Weidenfeld & Nicolson, 1970)

Exhortation

The simple, underlying faith – personal and unspoken – upon which rested a thousand silent hopes.

Have I not commanded thee? Be strong and of a good courage; be not afraid, neither be thou dismayed: for the Lord thy God is with thee, withersoever thou goest.

(Joshua 1:7)

COMBAT

Royal Air Force victory

We ran into them at 18,000 feet, twenty yellow-nosed Messerschmitt 109s, about 500 feet above us. Our Squadron strength was eight, and as they came down on us we went into line astern and turned head-on to them. Brian Carbury, who was leading the Section, dropped the nose of his machine, and I could almost feel the leading Nazi pilot push forward on his stick to bring his guns to bear. At the same moment Brian hauled hard back on his own control stick and led us over them in a steep climbing turn to the left. In two vital seconds they lost their advantage. I saw Brian let go a burst of fire at the leading plane, saw the pilot put his machine into a half roll, and knew that he was mine. Automatically, I kicked the rudder to the left to get him at right angles, turned the gun-button to 'Fire,' and let go in a four-second burst with full deflection. He came right through my sights and I saw the tracer from all eight guns thud home. For a second he seemed to hang motionless; then a jet of red flame shot upwards and he spun out of sight.

For the next few minutes I was too busy looking after myself to think of anything, but when, after a short while, they turned and made off over the Channel, and we were ordered to our base, my mind began to work again.

It had happened.

My first emotion was one of satisfaction, satisfaction at a job adequately done, at the final logical conclusion of months of specialized training. And then I had a feeling of the essential rightness of it all. He was dead and I was alive; it could so easily have been the other way round; and that would somehow have been right too. I realized in that moment just how lucky a fighter pilot is. He has none of the personalized emotions of the soldier, handed a rifle and bayonet and told to charge. He does not even have to share the dangerous emotions of the bomber pilot who night after night must experience that childhood longing for smashing things.

The fighter pilot's emotions are those of the duellist – cool, precise, impersonal. He is privileged to kill well. For if one must either kill or be killed, as now one must, it should, I feel, be done with dignity. Death should be given the setting it deserves; it should never be a pettiness; and for the fighter pilot it never can be.

From this flight Broody Benson did not return.

(Richard Hillary, *The Last Enemy*, Macmillan, 1942)

Luftwaffe victory

The second phase of the Battle of Britain, lasting from 24 July to 8 August 1940, was essentially a fighter battle. On its opening day I was with my wing for the first time in action over England. Over the Thames Estuary we got involved in a heavy scrap with Spitfires, which were screening a convoy. Together with the Staff Flight, I selected one formation as our prey, and we made a surprise attack from a favourably higher altitude. I glued myself to the tail of the plane flying outside on the left flank and when, during a right-handed turn, I managed to get in a long burst, the Spitfire went down almost vertically. I followed it until the cockpit cover came flying towards me and the pilot baled out, then followed him down until he crashed into the water. His parachute had failed to open.

The modern Vickers Supermarine Spitfires were slower than our planes by about 10 to 15 m.p.h., but could perform steeper and tighter turns. The older Hawker Hurricane, which was at that time still frequently used by the British, compared badly with our Me 109 as regards speed and rate of climb. Our armament and ammunition were also undoubtedly better. Another advantage was that our engines had injection pumps instead of the carburettors used by the British, and therefore did not conk out through lack of acceleration in critical moments during combat. The British fighters usually tried to shake off pursuit by a half-roll on top of a loop, while we simply went straight for them, with wide-open throttle and eyes bulging out of their sockets. During this first action we lost two aircraft. That was bad, although at the same time we had three confirmed kills. We were no longer in doubt that the RAF would prove a most formidable opponent . . .

The German fighter squadrons on the Channel were from now on in continuous action. Two or three sorties a day was the rule, and the briefing read: 'Free chase over south-east England.' The physical as well as the mental strain on the pilots was considerable. The ground personnel and the planes themselves were taxed to the limit.

After the take-off, the formations used to assemble in the coastal area, still over land, at an altitude of 15,000 to 18,000 feet, in order to climb to between 21,000 and 24,000 feet when crossing the English coast. In the attempt to outclimb the opponent, our dog-fights occurred at ever-increasing altitudes. My highest combat at that time took place at 25,000 feet, but at 27,000 feet and more – close to the lower limits of the stratosphere – one could usually see the vapour trails of German or British fighters.

It used to take us roughly half an hour from take-off to cross the English coast at the narrowest point of the Channel. Having a tactical flying time of only eighty minutes, we therefore had about twenty minutes to complete our task, and this fact limited the distance of penetration. German fighter squadrons based on the Pas de Calais and on the Cotentin peninsula could barely cover the south-eastern parts of the British Isles, circles drawn from these two bases at an operational range of 125 miles overlapping approximately in the London area. Everything beyond was practically out of our reach. This was the most acute weakness of our offensive. An operating radius of 125 miles was sufficient for local defence, but not enough for such tasks as were now demanded of us.

(Adolf Galland, *The First and the Last: The German Fighter Force in World War II*, Methuen, 1955)

And at home . . .

It was a golden summer. The sun that shone across the channel on the busy airfields, the battalions solemnly training for landings on a hostile shore, shone too on a London that pursued its daily life with a touch of defiance. Soldiers played civilians at cricket on village greens and *The Times* advertised 'A Good Selection for your Summer Holidays in Scotland'. Women were urged to 'Spend Wisely at Harrods'. Freya Stark's *A Winter in Arabia* pleased the literary critics and that now forgotten figure, *King Carol of Rumania*, was the subject of an authorized biography.

Although they stood in peril, the incurable English were not to be bullied by that peril into accepting any war-time regulations that they thought affronted the things they were fighting for. H. G. Wells complained bitterly to that national forum, the letter column of *The Times*, about the plight of refugees from Nazism who had been interned by the Government and Gilbert Murray wrote magisterially to the same column 'I tremble for any democracy which yields either to party faction or to mob hysteria'. The nation might be prepared for total war, but it was to be a total war in which the English would abide by their own rules.

The theatres and cinemas were full. *Gone with The Wind* was thrilling audiences with its somewhat fanciful record of another war. Stanley Holloway and Cyril Ritchard were in *Up and Doing* and Vic Oliver appeared in *Black Velvet*. As is their custom in times of trial the English spent a good deal of time laughing at the war and their own efforts. Many people, including senior officers of the three services, thought this light-hearted approach a poor preparation for what was to come. The English laughed harder.

Flora Robson opened in *We Are Not Alone*. But they were and no one seemed to mind. The depression that had set in with the fall of France lifted. There was excitement in the air. At Westminster the incomparable voice of the Prime Minister reminded his countrymen both of their peril and their opportunity. The setting sun fell over airfields on which the number of fighters grew steadily, on shaky lines of Home Guards, on divisions perilously short of weapons standing-to near the invasion coast. So the English waited.

Unlike the fighting in France, the Battle of Britain did not open with a sudden, massive attack. All through June the Luftwaffe had launched small, widely scattered attacks, mostly by night, against British targets. Most daylight attacks had been confined to the ports. Gradually in the early days of July the attacks extended inland. They were heavier in scale, more bombers, more fighters. The sirens sounded in Wales and on the east coast. Then the Luftwaffe revisited the ports Dover, Weymouth, Portland, Plymouth and again the attacks were heavier. The convoys moving through the Channel were heavily attacked.

In those days you could lie on the cliffs near Dover and watch the British ships come steadily onward from the north. Against the blue sky there would appear, suddenly, the tight formations of German bombers. Then the dive by the Stuka – the Luftwaffe had not yet recognized its unsuitability for this battle – the high scream, the thud of the explosion, the towering column of water white through the middle and glinting with sunshine at its top and then the column subsiding into the Channel, the rusty old collier ploughing placidly onwards. Then another bomber and another attack and in your ear the high keen whine of British fighters. Very small, they shone against the sun. Then, faintly, the chatter of machine gun fire. Perhaps a puff of smoke from a plane to be followed by a flicker of flame and a long plume of black smoke as the aircraft plunged. It was hard to believe that in that minute of machines in the sky men fought and that in that burning plane one was fighting for his life. There was always a feeling of relief when a parachute blossomed white against the sky. As swiftly as it began the fight would be over. In the Channel the convoy steamed ahead. The anti-aircraft fire dwindled. It was quiet now on the cliffs and the breeze brought all the scents of summer.

(Drew Middleton, The Sky Suspended: The Battle of Britain,
May 1940– April 1941, Secker & Warburg, 1960)

Debriefing

It was the finest shambles I've been in, since for once we had position, height and numbers. Enemy aircraft were a dirty-looking collection.

(Sergeant pilot reporting to his squadron intelligence officer after combat)

C-IN-C'S ROUTINE

The working day for Dowding throughout the battle extended in the same fashion day after day with no breaks for any days off. It started with that nine o'clock arrival in his office, and it went on until all hours of the night, and often on into the early hours of the morning. His time would be taken up with a very great amount of paper work at his desk, with meetings, discussions and conferences, and with quick trips down to the Operations and Filter Rooms. All the time he was also having to make journeys to London for further conferences and meetings; and there were as many visits as he could make to the various Group Headquarters and the aerodromes.

The only breaks in the day were for lunch and dinner, and for these Dowding would return to Montrose. He seldom had anything to drink, and never if he was at lunch or dinner with only his sister in the house, and he would quickly return to Bentley Priory. The time after dinner was usually spent cleaning up the day's paper work. The last thing that he would do at night, no matter how late, would be to pay another visit to the Operations and Filter Rooms for a final check on what was going on.

There were two small features about Dowding at his desk which have remained firmly in my mind as well as Francis Wilkinson's. The first was the use that he made of his spectacles. How old they were nobody knew. It was said that they had been bought off the counter of one of the popular chain stores, but that was a joke of private standing among those of his personal staff. They happened to look so old, and they appeared to be, in fact, no more than magnifying glasses of some mild strength. They were horn-rimmed, and Dowding wore them half-way down the bridge of his nose, and whenever he looked up he peered over the top of them with an inevitable expression of slight surprise.

'And do you remember the pen!' Francis Wilkinson reminded me many years later. It was a fountain pen of an even greater age than the spectacles. Lack of running repairs had long since nullified its usefulness as a fountain pen, but the nib was to Dowding's liking and that was all that mattered. In Wilkinson's words: 'While the rest of us were sporting the most expensive fountain pens, Stuffy worked away with that wonderful old pen of his, dipping it in a simple ink pot.'

(Robert Wright, *Dowding and the Battle of Britain*, Macdonald, 1969)

STRAINING THE QUALITY OF MERCY

Dutch Hugo [Pilot Officer – later Group Captain – Piet Hugo, the exceptional South African] recalled that, after Dunkirk, 615 Squadron flew to Kenley to be brought up to strength with Hurricanes and inexperienced pilots . . . It was a memorable, if hectic, time . . .

Returning from a mission over France on 27 June, the Squadron was surprised to find King George VI waiting on the tarmac to decorate their CO, Squadron Leader Kyall, with the DSO and the DFC, and Flight Lieutenant Sanders with the DFC.

A few days later, after the Squadron had moved forward to Hawkinge, the advance airfield, hard by Folkestone, overlooking the Straits of Dover in East Kent, it was visited by its Honorary Air Commodore, Winston Churchill. Snatching a few hours from Downing Street and the central direction of the war, the Prime Minister had flown down to Hawkinge in an old Flamingo aircraft escorted by a lone Hurricane piloted by none other than the Air Officer Commanding 11 Group, Air Vice-Marshal Keith Park. The AOC's brilliant handling of his squadrons in the weeks ahead was soon to save Fighter Command and Britain from defeat.

To enable him to dine with his pilots, which he much enjoyed, Mr Churchill decided to stay overnight. Keith Park, who did not drink, on the other hand returned to his headquarters . . . Dutch remembered acutely that, during its time at Hawkinge, the Squadron was so close to the enemy that it never had sufficient time to gain adequate height to tackle the 109s. It always seemed to be below the Luftwaffe's fighters and usually heavily outnumbered . . .

On 27 July, with the Battle now well under way, there occurred a particularly controversial incident. Luftwaffe air–sea rescue seaplanes, although carrying the Red Cross emblem and ostensibly searching for missing pilots, were thought (mistakenly in my view) to be spotting for German long-range guns on the French coast firing at shipping in the narrow waters.

On the direct orders of the Prime Minister, these aircraft were to be attacked and on this day Dutch remembered pilots of 615 shooting down a Heinkel 59 floatplane (in pieces) into the sea before landing back at Hawkinge for supper and sleep.

(J. E. [Johnnie] Johnson, personal collection)

The Poles were fed up with me when I admitted that I could not bring myself to shoot the chap in the parachute and they reminded me of events earlier in the month when we were told that one or two pilots of No. 1 Squadron had baled out and had then been shot by German fighters. At the time the Poles had asked me if it was true that this was happening. I had to tell them that, as far as I knew, it was, at which they asked: 'Oh, can we?' I explained that, distasteful as it was, the Germans were within their rights in shooting our pilots over this country and that, if one of us shot down a German aircraft over France and the pilot baled out, then we were quite entitled to shoot him. But this was not so over England as, aside from anything else, he would be out of the war and might even be a very useful source of information for us. They thought about this for a bit and then said: 'Yes, we understand – but what if he is over the Channel?' – to which I had jokingly replied: 'Well, you can't let the poor bugger drown, can you?' This remark was quite seriously thrown in my teeth when they heard about the 109 pilot I had just shot down. There was no doubt about it, the Poles were playing the game for keeps far more than we were.

(Group Captain J. A. Kent,* DFC and bar, AFC, *One of the Few*,
William Kimber, 1971)

THE AIRMAN

He laughed at death, pursued him with a kiss
    Climbed to the skies, pursued him to a star
But death, who never had been wooed like this
    Remained aloof, afar

With spurt and gleam and brightness like the sun's
    He circled death as with a wheel of flame
But death, capricious, sought those other ones
    Who had not called his name

He mocked at death, pursued him into hell
    Mocked him afresh, then crashed to burning space
But death, grown gentle, caught him as he fell
    Nor let him see his face

(Author unknown)

PILOT SHORTAGE

The Cabinet were distressed to hear from you that you were now running short of pilots for fighters, and they had now become the limiting factor ... Lord Beaverbrook has made a surprising improvement in the supply and repair of aeroplanes, and in clearing up the muddle and scandal of the

---

* Flight Lieutenant – later Group Captain – J. A. Kent, the Canadian in the Royal Air Force, was a flight commander in 303, the famous Polish fighter squadron, based at Northolt in the summer of 1940.

aircraft production branch. I greatly hope that you will be able to do as much on the personnel side, for it will indeed be lamentable if we have machines standing idle for want of pilots to fly them.

(Winston S. Churchill to Secretary of State for Air, 3 June 1940)

PEACE OFFERING

Hitler made his famous peace offer to the British Empire on 19 July 1940 from the Reichstag. . . . He started by saying that he had warned Britain and France in his former peace offer of 6 October 1939, and that a small clique of British warmongers were keeping the war alive.

> For this peace proposal I was abused and personally insulted. Mr Chamberlain, in fact, spat upon me before the eyes of the world, and following the instructions of the instigators and warmongers in the background – men such as Churchill, Duff Cooper, Eden, Hore-Belisha and others – declined even to mention peace, let alone to work for it.

With words flowing with sarcasm he poured scorn on the British resolved to fight whatever the consequences.

> In the opinion of British politicians their last hopes, apart from allied peoples consisting of a number of kings without a throne, statesmen without a nation and generals without an army, seem to be based on fresh complications which they hope to bring about thanks to their proven skill in such matters.
>   A veritable 'wandering Jew' among these hopes is the belief in the possibility of a fresh estrangement between Germany and Russia.

He said that any such hope was based on a false premise and he then reverted to his constant theme that it was only this small war clique in Britain which was causing the war, and that the British people were longing for peace:

> Mr Churchill ought perhaps, for once, to believe me when I prophesy that a great Empire will be destroyed, an Empire which it was never my intention to destroy or even to harm. I do, however, realize that this struggle, if it continues, can end only with the complete annihilation of one or other of the two adversaries. Mr Churchill may believe that this will be Germany. I know that it will be different.
>   In this hour, I feel it to be my duty before my own conscience to appeal once more to reason and commonsense in Great Britain as much as elsewhere. I consider myself in a position to make this appeal since I

am not the vanquished, begging favours, but the victor speaking in the name of reason.

I can see no reason why this war must go on. . . .

Possibly, Mr Churchill will again brush aside this statement of mine by saying that it is merely born of fear and of doubt in our final victory. In that case, I shall have relieved my conscience in regard to the things to come.

Winston Churchill regarded Hitler's peace offer as a gross affront, and did not condescend to reply. On 22 July the peace offer was casually rejected out of hand by Lord Halifax in a routine broadcast.

(James Douglas-Hamilton, *Motive for a Mission*,
Mainstream Publishing, 1979)

THE LUFTWAFFE

Reichmarschall *Hermann Göring, Commander-in- Chief*

Of all Hitler's 'Paladins' – those companions from the *Kampfzeit*, the years of struggle, who stayed with him to the end – Hermann Göring was, in every sense, the largest and the most colourful. In the beginning he was the most useful, the nearest thing the Nazis had to a gentleman. For a long time he was the most popular. After the flight of Hess, he was Hitler's designated deputy. And although at the end he was discredited, he made at Nuremberg a remarkable comeback. The inflated, corrupt transvestite and drug addict recovered his old energy and turned the tables on his over-confident prosecutor. Finally condemned to hang, he cheated his gaolers and died at his own time, by his own hand.

(Hugh Trevor-Roper, *Sunday Telegraph*, 20 August 1989, reviewing David
Irving, *Göring: A Biography*, Macmillan, 1989)

The elimination of the RAF was laid down by Göring as the primary task of the three Luftflotten. This was to be done in two phases. First there was to be a sustained offensive against the fighter airfields in England south of a line between Chelmsford and Gloucester. The airfields were to be made unusable for the British fighters and the installations destroyed. The RAF was to be attacked in the air wherever it was found. The whole thing Göring said would take four days. One is reminded of Napoleon on the morning of Waterloo telling his marshals that the battle would be over by lunch. The second phase Göring admitted might take four weeks. This was to be a methodical attack on other RAF bases to the north of the line Chelmsford–Gloucester.

After this attack had been concluded, Göring informed his air generals, there would be no more RAF left to fight. He also ordered that while these two consecutive assaults were mounted against the British bases, there should be day and night attacks on the British aircraft industry.

The offensive would begin, Göring said, on 13 August and the first day's attack would be given the code name Adler Tag (Eagle Day) . . .

The heat lay heavy on the land that summer and the haze sometimes obscured vision. But the young men of the Luftwaffe high over the Pas de Calais in the summer dawn could glance across the Channel to where England lay, ripely green. To them it must have seemed so easy in those last days before the whirlwind caught them up and they plunged into one of the great battles of history.

(Drew Middleton, *The Sky Suspended: The Battle of Britain, May 1940– April 1941*, Secker & Warburg, 1960)

Generalfeldmarschall's *belief*

I was in the Reichstag in Berlin on 19 July 1940. The Reichstag speech, which contained, among other things, my promotion to Field-Marshal, made our minds easy. We regarded Hitler's peace offer as seriously meant, and reckoned with the possibility of England's accepting it. I had no idea at that time that many army officers did not consider the Luftwaffe Field-Marshals as their equals in rank. I am still today firmly convinced that none of us would have been made Field-Marshals after the western campaign if Hitler had not believed in the probability of peace.

I am both an army and an air force officer, in the later course of the war holding both air and Army Group commands; I therefore believe I am in a position to appreciate the tasks of individual commanders in both services. If performance is to be judged by results, there can be no question that the Luftwaffe, both strategically and tactically, played a decisive part in army operations. Naval strategy is the pace-maker for air strategy. In both arms technical problems loom larger than in the army. There can be no doubt that an air operation demands profound knowledge and planning which, although on a different level, is not less complicated than that required by the army. Nor can it be doubted that air operations in the army battle zone or in sea warfare call for a high degree of knowledge and understanding of the rudiments of all three arms.

Results will demonstrate an officer's fitness to be a Field-Marshal, and no one will then ask about origins, whether he came from the army or the Luftwaffe. But one piece of advice I give to all Air Field Marshals: do not become a one-sided technician, but learn to think and lead in terms of all three services.

(Albert Kesselring [Commander of *Luftflotte* 2, 1940], *The Memoirs of Field Marshal Kesselring*, William Kimber, 1953)

BRITISH RADAR

The Luftwaffe attacks

Today, for the first time, the unit's target was not shipping or harbour installations. It was the top-secret 'radar' aerials sticking up at many points along the English coast. These could be seen quite clearly by telescope across the Channel.

By systematic listening-in on the enemy's radio channels it had become known to the Germans that the British fighters were remotely controlled over the VHF by ground stations. It was further known that these stations obtained their information about approaching German air formations by means of a new radio-location system, the visible 'feelers' of which were these same antennae aerials on the coast.

For General Wolfgang Martini, chief of the Luftwaffe's signal communications system, this discovery had come as a shock. He had assumed that his own side was far ahead in this field.

In summer 1940 Germany possessed two types of radar:

(1) The *Freya*. This was a mobile equipment which, sending out impulses on a 240-cm wavelength served for plotting air and sea targets from the coast. One such installation was at Wissant, west of Calais. This located British coastal convoys, which were then attacked by . . . aircraft and by armed speedboats.

(2) The *Wurzburg*. This was only just coming into series production, and was first used by Flak regiments in the Ruhr. Using an ultra-short wavelength of 53 cm its impulses could be sharply concentrated, and sometimes the results were startling. It could read the location, course and altitude of an aircraft with such accuracy that in the previous May a flak battery at Essen-Frintop had shot down a British bomber which, flying above dense cloud, had felt itself quite safe.

From the technical angle, therefore, the discoveries made about the British by Martini's radar and intercept men – who had been rushed to the French coast as soon as it was occupied – were nothing new. The wavelength used was no less than 1,200 cm and British sources have confirmed that, in particular, forecasts of the size of approaching formations were, at the outset, sometimes up to 300 per cent inaccurate. . . .

It was not the enemy's technical, but his evident organizational lead that troubled Martini. The discovery that the whole length of the east and south coasts of Britain were already covered by a protective chain of listening and transmitting posts was a blow indeed. Reports from them would be evaluated in central operations rooms, and the resulting air picture used to guide the British fighter squadrons to their targets.

On the German side such an organization did not exist. Though the 'DeTe apparatus' (such was the cover name*) was there, its likely influence on the course of the war was not considered vitally important.

Now the German command had to think again. If, through the eyes of his radar, the enemy could follow the raiding formations as they approached, or even while they formed up over France, the element of surprise – almost essential for an aggressor – would be entirely lost. The Luftwaffe would, in fact, join battle with the Royal Air Force at a serious tactical disadvantage – unless the locating stations on the coast could first be destroyed. . . .

. . . The teleprinters at the headquarters of *Luftflotten* 2 and 3 tapped out a directive from General Jeschonnek, the Luftwaffe's chief of general staff: 'Known English DeTe stations are to be attacked by special forces of the first wave to put them out of action.'

With the *first* wave! It means that the attack on the coastal radar installations would also be the signal for the Battle of Britain to begin!

Captain Rubensdörffer looked at his watch. By German time it was a few minutes to eleven. With his twelve Me 110s he turned north-west towards the enemy coast. The squadrons split up to make for their individual targets.

1 Squadron, led by First Lieutenant Martin Lutz, sighted the mast of Pevensey radar station, near Eastbourne. The six aircraft climbed slowly, weighed down by their two 1,000-lb bombs. Though they were fighters, they carried twice the bomb load of a Ju 87 dive-bomber.

At last they were high enough. Flicking over, they glided down on to their target. Then, waiting till the lattice-work of the first of the four antenna aerials completely filled his reflector sight, Lutz let go his bombs.

Like a sudden squall of wind the six Messerschmitts swept over the radar station and were gone, leaving eight 1,000-lb bombs to explode on the target. One was a direct hit on an elongated building, a second slashed the main power cable, and the transmitters broke down. Pevensey was off the air.

Five minutes flying time to the east, 2 Squadron, under First Lieutenant Rössigner, went for a similar station at Rye, near Hastings. Their leader reported ten hits on the installations with 1,000-lb and 500-lb bombs. British sources confirm that all the buildings were destroyed, with the important exceptions of the transmitting and receiving blocks and the watch room.

Meanwhile First Lieutenant Hintze, with 3 Squadron, attacked the aerial layout at Dover. Three bombs burst close by them; shrapnel hurtled into the struts, and two aerial masts tottered – but remained standing.

---

* DeTe = Decimeter Telegraphy. English equivalent: RDF – Radio Direction Finding. The term 'Radar', so familiar today, and the German term '*Furimess*', only came into use half-way through the war.

Everywhere it was the same story. As the attackers turned away, their efforts were marked by fountains of flying earth and black smoke, but always the aerials still sticking out above. It had been just the same in Poland during the attacks on the radio transmitting stations. No matter how accurately one aimed, the aerial masts never fell down.

Three hours later the station at Rye, with emergency equipment, was again functioning. In the course of the afternoon other stations followed suit. All broken links in the British radar chain had been repaired – with one exception:

From 11.30 onwards three *Gruppen* of KG 51 and KG 54, totalling sixty-three Ju 88 bombers, had been attacking the harbour works at Portsmouth. But one *Gruppe* of fifteen machines peeled off over the Isle of Wight and dived down on the radar station at Ventnor. Its equipment was so badly damaged that the station became a write-off. Eleven days uninterrupted labour were necessary before a new station could be constructed on the island and the gap in the chain closed.

The English masked the fact that Ventnor was out of action (and deceived the Germans) by sending out impulses from another transmitter. Though these produced no echo, the enemy, hearing them, could only suppose that the station had been repaired.

Disappointment spread. Apparently the 'eyes' of the British early warning system could only be 'blinded' for a maximum of two hours.

(Cajus Bekker, The Battle of Britain: The Luftwaffe War Diaries,
Macdonald, 1967)

AOC's Assessment

The attack on [the] radar stations . . . showed what could be done. Dover, Pevensey and Rye were all put out of action although emergency systems enabled them to resume reporting within six hours. They were difficult targets to destroy, but the Germans failed to realize they were worth the effort. On this occasion a large raid was built up (unseen by the Kent and Sussex radar stations) which hit the Isle of Wight hard and knocked out Ventnor radar station.

(Vincent Orange, Sir Keith Park, Methuen, 1984)

Jamming – German deficiency

[There] . . . had been a remarkable 'squeamishness' on our part regarding technical countermeasures against German radar, as far as the Air side was concerned. . . . Although I repeatedly pointed to [this fact], I encountered a nebulous but strong reluctance against taking technical measures against Luftwaffe radar.

The reluctance went right back to the early days of Bawdsey,* and at the heart of it was Watson-Watt.† No trials of spurious reflectors had been made after I had suggested their use in 1937. . . . In defence of Watson-Watt [, however,] it could be argued that anything that might have thrown doubts on the value of radar, such as the early development of a successful jamming system, might have caused the Air Staff to lack confidence, and thus not to support radar enthusiastically. We might then not have had such an effective system ready in time for the Battle of Britain. But it could equally well be argued that had we been up against a more thorough opponent who had developed a proper system of jamming, our 1940 radar would have been rendered powerless, and we should have been culpably unprepared to deal with such a situation.

(R. V. Jones, *Most Secret War: British Scientific Intelligence*, Hamish Hamilton, 1978)

BUSTING THE ENEMY'S CODE

Enigma

In 1938 a Polish mechanic had been employed in a factory in Eastern Germany which was making what the young man rightly judged to be some sort of secret signalling machine. As a Pole, he was not very fond of the Germans . . . and, being an intelligent observer, he took careful note of the various parts that he and his fellow workmen were making. I expect it was after one of the security checks which were made by the Gestapo on all high security factories that they discovered his nationality. He was sacked and sent back to Poland. His keen observation had done him some good, and he got in touch with our man in Warsaw. The Gestapo in Poland were active, and so he was told to lie low. Meantime, we received the information in London. It was obviously a very delicate matter, and our chief, Admiral Sinclair, decided that the fewer people, even in our office, that knew about it, the better. He therefore put the development of the concept in the hands of his deputy, Colonel Stewart Menzies, and it was decided that only the departmental heads were to be kept in the picture.

In due course the young Pole was persuaded to leave Warsaw and was secretly smuggled out under a false passport with the help of the Polish Secret Service; he was then installed in Paris where, with the aid of the Deuxième Bureau, he was given a workshop. With the help of a carpenter . . . he began to make a wooden mock-up of the machine he had been working on in Germany.

There had been a number of cypher machines invented over the years

* On the Suffolk coast.
† Later Sir Robert Watson-Watt.

and our own backroom boys had records and drawings of most of them. It didn't take them long to identify the mock-up as some sort of improved mechanical cypher machine called Enigma. The name Enigma was given to the machine by the German manufacturers. The Pole had been told not to attempt to make his wooden model to scale. In fact, the bigger the better, because he could then more easily incorporate any details he could remember. The result was rather like the top half of an upright piano, but it was enough to tell us that it would be essential to get hold of an actual machine if we were to stand any chance of [understanding] its method of operation. So, while the Pole was carefully looked after in Paris, we set about working out a scheme with our friends in Poland, who were just as keen as we were to try and grab a complete machine from Germany. We knew where the factory was and all about its security methods, and that there were still some Poles working there under German names. However, the Polish Secret Service thought the scheme might stand more chance of success if we gave them the money and they did the job. They knew the terrain and the people much better than we did, so we gladly agreed.

First fruits

Once France had fallen there was, for a short time, a lull in the signals picked up. Those which were broken mostly concerned the disposition of troops and headquarters for occupational purposes in France and were not of very much interest to us at the moment. It was not long, however, before the Luftwaffe signals started to increase again, and now it began to look more serious for us. In the middle of July Ultra produced the signal we had all been waiting for. It had evidently been delivered in great secrecy from Hitler's headquarters to the Army, Navy and Air Force commanders-in-chief. Göring, however, then put the gist of it on the air to the generals commanding his air fleets. In his signal he stated that, despite her hopeless military situation, England showed no signs of willingness to make peace. Hitler had therefore decided to prepare and, if necessary, to carry out a landing operation against her. The aim of the operation was to eliminate England as a base from which war against Germany could be continued and, if necessary, to occupy it completely. The operation was to be called Sea-lion. I sent the signal over to the Prime Minister immediately. It was the first time the words Sea-lion had been used and it now made it much easier for us to identify any activities connected with the invasion plan. It was certainly this signal that gave Churchill the idea of making his famous speech telling the Germans that we would fight them on the beaches and everywhere else.

By now my teleprinter line from Hut 3 [at Bletchley Park, HQ of the Ultra intelligence] organization to my office was working well. No longer were there scraps of paper of all shapes and sizes, they were now neat sheets about seven by nine inches, and in bold red letters across the top the word Ultra.

> (F. W. Winterbotham, [Chief of the Air Department of the Secret Intelligence Service (MI6) 1930–45], *The Ultra Secret*, Weidenfeld & Nicolson, 1974)

SPECIAL OPERATIONS EXECUTIVE

Clandestine courage

The knots were unravelled by mid-July. Halifax [Foreign Secretary] took the chair at the critical meeting, held in the Foreign Office on 1 July. Three other ministers were present; Hankey, Lord Lloyd, the Colonial Secretary, an old friend of T. E. Lawrence's, and Dr Hugh Dalton, the Minister of Economic Warfare. Cadogan was there, with Gladwyn Jebb, his private secretary, to take the minutes. So was C [Head of MI5], so was the DMI [Director of Military Intelligence] (though there was no one from the Admiralty or the Air Ministry); so was (Sir) Desmond Morton, the Prime Minister's private secretary who handled all Churchill's relations with most secret affairs. They went briefly over ground that was now familiar to most of them. Lloyd summed up the conclusion to which they all agreed: that what was needed was 'a Controller armed with almost dictatorial powers'.

Dalton wrote to Halifax next day in an often-quoted but still requotable letter:

> We have got to organize movements in enemy-occupied territory comparable to the Sinn Fein movement in Ireland, to the Chinese guerillas now operating against Japan, to the Spanish irregulars who played a notable part in Wellington's campaign or – one might as well admit it – to the organizations which the Nazis themselves have developed so remarkably in almost every country in the world. This 'democratic international' must use many different methods, including industrial and military sabotage, labour agitation and strikes, continuous propaganda, terrorist acts against traitors and German leaders, boycotts and riots.
>
> It is quite clear to me that an organization on this scale and of this character is not something which can be handled by the ordinary departmental machinery of either the British Civil Service or the British military machine. What is needed is a new organization to co-ordinate, inspire, control and assist the nationals of the oppressed countries who must themselves be the direct participants. We need absolute secrecy, a certain fanatical enthusiasm, willingness to work with people of different nationalities, complete political reliability. Some of these

qualities are certainly to be found in some military officers and, if such men are available, they should undoubtedly be used. But the organization should, in my view, be entirely independent of the War Office machine.

This document became known to the high command of SOE, once it had been set up, and influenced a good deal of its early thinking about the problems of strategy that lay before it.

(M. D. R. Foot, *SOE: The Special Operations Executive*, 1940–1946, British Broadcasting Corporation, 1984)

Modest beginnings

SOE made several false starts. Section D had an early casualty, when a flying-boat with one of its officers on board disappeared in late June 1940 in an attempt to get Madame de Gaulle out of Brittany. (She arranged her own and her daughter's [evacuation].) Three Frenchmen were sent across the Channel in a small and noisy boat on 1 August, ran into a German coastal convoy, were fired on and turned back; two of them failed to get ashore by sea on 11 October; one – this got more and more like the ten little nigger boys – was sent over by air on 14 November, and was brave enough to refuse to jump. Winter weather then closed in.

Just before it did so, SOE had a hand in operation 'Shamrock', off the mouth of the Gironde. It was run . . . by Martin Minshall, a buccaneering type left over from the great Elizabeth's reign, who had been brought into irregular warfare by his friend Ian Fleming, and had exercised his gift for rubbing people up the wrong way on Fleming's boss, Godfrey, the formidable director of naval intelligence. Minshall established for certain a point the Admiralty did not know – exactly how U-boats entered and left the river-mouth – by commandeering a local fishing smack, watching them do it, and sailing the smack back to Falmouth to report!

(M. D. R. Foot, *SOE: The Special Operations Executive*, 1940–1946, British Broadcasting Corporation, 1984)

IDENTIFICATION

I was returning from Hornchurch to Hendon and had been delayed by an air raid.* By that time the evening was turning to nightfall and the visibility murky, so without night-flying equipment I decided that land was on the whole a more satisfactory location. I settled on a playing field in Cricklewood,† in spite of goal posts and other obstructions which were obligatory at that time.

---

* Group Captain Lord George Douglas-Hamilton (Earl of Selkirk), Chief Intelligence Officer, HQ Fighter Command.
† In north-west London.

Rather satisfied with myself, I was surprised to see a sturdy young man advancing menacingly towards me waving a cricket stump. He was quickly followed by an officer of the police who politely but firmly required my presence at the police station. He was not impressed by my uniform nor by the papers which I carried, so I rang my office at Fighter Command where my voice was recognized. This made no impression on the officer so strict were the instructions issued to the police.

He then asked did I know anyone at Hendon, to which I could only say that I had no reason to believe that I did. However we proceeded to Hendon and there my luck changed: by pure chance I met Squadron Leader Urie whom I had known in Glasgow with 602 Squadron, formerly commanded by my brother, Douglo.* At last the diligent police officer was content. . . . If anyone doubts the value of such strict policies, their views would I believe change following even a cursory glance at the book *Double Cross*, by the late Sir John Masterman. Therein is very convincing evidence how valuable these policies were.

(The Earl of Selkirk in Laddie Lucas (ed.), *Out of the Blue: The Role of Luck in Air Warfare, 1917–1966*, Hutchinson, 1985)

NINETEEN – AND NOT A CLUE?

I am absolutely convinced that people [of] my age hadn't the faintest idea, not a bloody clue, what was going on. It was just beer, women and Spitfires, a bunch of little John Waynes running about the place. When you were nineteen, you couldn't give a monkey's . . .

[But] the Battle of Britain was a great period to have lived through . . . I often wonder what would have happened if the German fighter 'Ace', Adolf Galland, and his merry men had had long-range jettison tanks fitted to their [109s] to allow them rather more than 15 minutes' combat time over London. Together with their superior numbers, this would certainly have given them an even greater advantage, and the outcome of the Battle of Britain might have been very different.

Today, I would propose that the epic aerial campaign of 1940 should be restaged, only this time the 109s should have gleaming drop tanks so that *they* would win and be poor, and *we* could lose and get rich . . . instead of slowly becoming what Prince Charles has recently described as a fourth-rate nation.

(Paddy Barthropp, *Paddy: The Life and Times of Wing Commander Patrick Barthropp*, DFC, AFC, Howard Baker, 1986)

* Group Captain the Duke of Hamilton, 14th Duke, eldest of the four Douglas-Hamilton brothers.

SECURING THE BASE

In the early days, we had orders to stop everybody we saw after dusk on the Downs and ask for their identity cards. I wonder if in any other part of the country so many lovers were disturbed as in that real lovers' paradise. On our first night, we came across a couple in a car – this was before the ban on pleasure motoring – and as they stole furtively away on the approach of our armed party, our leader held them up, demanded their identity cards, and said to the man, 'Do you know that you have been in a prohibited area?' 'No, he hasn't.' snapped the girl.

A big shot from Halsham came down one day to ginger us up. I was asked to pass on to the troops his somewhat bloodthirsty picture of what was to happen when the Germans came, explaining the roadblocks and tank traps – a sort of 'general idea' of the coming battle. We villagers were to 'contain' the Germans till the arrival of the real soldiers from the rear. 'Of course, none of you chaps will probably be alive when they get here and drive the Huns back into the sea.'

(Charles Graves, Daily Mail columnist, in The Home Guard of Britain,
Hutchinson, 1943)

LAUGHING STOCK!

The opening phase of the Battle, like the fighting over France and Dunkirk before it, brought its inevitable tactical revelations. One of the first was the pilots' realization that the set-piece, textbook Fighter Command Attacks, which the Service had worked out and practised with such assiduity in the 1930s, were totally impracticable in modern war, an echo from peacetime Hendon Air Displays in front of 100,000 applauding spectators.

Fighter Attack No. 6 [From Dead Astern] [see diagram on page 205] was probably the most anachronistic of them all. The sequence of instructions, a summary of which will be found in Appendix B, represented a recipe for disaster. Douglas Bader, now leading 242 Squadron, saw things differently.

He had never ceased to mistrust the stereotyped, textbook approach to combat to which, for years, the Royal Air Force had blindly adhered. He preferred to rely on history. The time he had spent as a cadet at Cranwell studying the writings, experiences and tactical doctrines of heroes like Ball, Mannock, McCudden, Bishop, Richthofen, Boelke and others had persuaded him that the principles upon which they had rested their combat faith must still apply.

The speeds of the aircraft they flew were very slow by comparison with those of the latter-day Spitfires and Hurricanes. But that, he felt, was irrelevant. Speed, after all, was only relative. Tightly circumscribed manoeuvres flown at 100 or 120 m.p.h. simply became wider patterns traced at indicated airspeeds of 225 to 250 m.p.h. The lessons and methods hadn't changed in twenty years: they had just been forgotten in the clamour for progress and a uniform system.

After [the opening exchanges] he was certain that the three basic articles of a First World War fighter pilot's faith had been reaffirmed. . . . He could still recite them like a piece of catching doggerel:

He who has the height controls the battle.
He who has the sun achieves surprise.
He who gets in close shoots them down.

If the [early] fighting . . . had proved his point, the [later stages of the] Battle [would] provide the double check.

(Laddie Lucas, *Flying Colours: The Epic Story of Douglas Bader*,
Hutchinson, 1981)

PROPER CHARLIES!

In the opening encounters the British were at a considerable disadvantage because of their close formation. Since the Spanish Civil War we had introduced the wide-open combat formation, in which great intervals were kept between the smaller single formations and groups, each of which flew at a different altitude. This offered a number of valuable advantages: greater air coverage, relief for the individual pilot, who could now concentrate more on the enemy than on keeping formation, freedom of initiative right down to the smallest unit without loss of collective strength, reduced vulnerability as compared to close formation, and, most important of all, better vision. The first rule of all air combat is to see the opponent first. Like the hunter who stalks his prey and manoeuvres himself unnoticed into the most favourable position for the kill, the fighter in the opening of a dog-fight must detect the opponent as early as possible in order to attain a superior position for the attack. The British quickly realized the superiority of our combat formation and readjusted their own. At first they introduced the so-called 'Charlies' – two flanking planes following in the rear of the main formation and flying slightly higher and further out on a weaving course. Finally, they adopted our combat formation entirely. Since then, without any fundamental change, it has been accepted throughout the world. Werner Mölders was greatly responsible for these developments.

(Adolf Galland, *The First and the Last: The German Fighter Force
in World War II*, Methuen, 1955)

NIGHT MUST FALL

Nachtjagdgeschwader 2's first flights over England bore little relation to what would come. Herbert Thomas [a 22-year-old night fighter pilot from Bochum] was right:

> The aim of our first [night] flights over England was simply to stir the defences into action. We wanted to test the RAF's reaction and get used to the idea of flying over enemy territory . . . When our crews returned after four or five hours over England [there was nothing] to report . . . To goad the RAF into the air, we later took flares and incendiary bombs with us. I made one such flight sitting in the Bola, the underslung gondola, of a Do 17, with a canister of incendiary bombs beside me . . .
> Eventually we saw some smoke rising from a chimney and I prepared for action. I armed the bombs and pushed them out through the door. This was crazy – just like the bombers of the First World War . . . Our Bordfunker called out that he could see lights and we took evasive action to lose the British fighter, but the lights he had seen were only our own flares igniting! It was lucky for us the defences were still inexperienced . . .
>
> (Simon W. Parry, *Intruders over Britain: The Luftwaffe Night Fighter Offensive*, 1940–1945, Air Research Publications in association with Kristall Productions Ltd, 1987)

THE PRIME MINISTER DIRECTS

Meanwhile, as July blended into August and the battle for control of the daylight air moved into high gear, Churchill remained the dominant national figure at the head of the great wartime Coalition. A future incumbent of No. 10 recalled two directives to Ministers:

I have preserved two records of this heroic period, both characteristic of the author. The first was a notice issued in similar terms to that of 29 May 1940, and circulated to all Ministers of whatever rank:

On what may be the eve of an attempted invasion or battle for our native land, the Prime Minister desires to impress upon all persons holding responsible positions in the Government, in the Fighting Services, or in the Civil Departments, their duty to maintain a spirit of alert and confident energy. While every precaution must be taken that time and means afford, there are no grounds for supposing that more German troops can be landed in this country, either from the air or across the sea, than can be destroyed or captured by the strong forces at present under arms. The Royal Air Force is in excellent order and at the highest strength it has yet attained. The German Navy was never so weak, nor the British Army at home so strong as now. The Prime Minister expects all His Majesty's servants in

high places to set an example of steadiness and resolution. They should check and rebuke expressions of loose and ill-digested opinion in their circles, or by their subordinates. They should not hesitate to report, or if necessary remove, any officers or officials who are found to be consciously exercising a disturbing or depressing influence, and whose talk is calculated to spread alarm and despondency. Thus alone will they be worthy of the fighting men, who in the air, on the sea, and on land, have already met the enemy without any sense of being out-matched in martial qualities.
Winston S. Churchill 4 July 1940

The second, sent round . . . in the middle of the Battle . . . is equally typical. It ran as follows:

To do our work, we all have to read a mass of papers. Nearly all of them are far too long. This wastes time, while energy has to be spent in looking for the essential points.

    I ask my colleagues and their staffs to see to it that their Reports are shorter.

(i) The aim should be Reports which set out the main points in a series of short, crisp paragraphs.

(ii) If a Report relies on detailed analysis of some complicated factors, or on statistics, these should be set out in an Appendix.

(iii) Often the occasion is best met by submitting not a full-dress Report, but an *Aide-mémoire* consisting of headings only, which can be expanded orally if needed.

(iv) Let us have an end of such phrases as these: 'It is also of importance to bear in the mind the following considerations . . .', or 'Consideration should be given to the possibility of carrying into effect . . .'. Most of these woolly phrases are mere padding, which can be left out altogether, or replaced by a single word. Let us not shrink from using the short expressive phrase, even if it is conversational.

    If the great war messages have their honoured place in history, this last admonition will always be relevant. I still like to think of Churchill sitting down on that August day, while the fate of Britain was in the balance, to remind us of the value of brevity.

(Harold Macmillan [Earl of Stockton], *The Blast of War, 1939–1945*,
Macmillan, 1967)

Part Two

1 AUGUST–6 SEPTEMBER 1940
Crisis Days

On 8 August 1940 the RAF Fighter Command
took off to save everything and between then and
the end of September they saved it all.

(General Henry H. [Hap] Arnold,
United States Army Air Force)

The Luftwaffe – the Formidable Enemy

The Führer's contention

Come what may, Great Britain will collapse. I know no other end than this.

When people are very curious in Great Britain and ask, 'Yes, why don't you come?', we reply, 'Calm yourselves, we shall come.' The world will be set free. Once and for all we must do away with the absurd state of affairs that one nation is in a position at its own sweet will to blockade an entire continent. I prefer to fight till a definite and final decision is reached.

We are prepared for everything, we have the will and determination to act at any time. Above all, nothing can make us afraid. We German national-socialists have been schooled in the hardest school that can be imagined. Nothing can intimidate us, nothing can surprise us.

When England entered the war a year ago she said, 'We have an ally called General Revolution.' She had no idea of national-socialist Germany. The revolution did not take place. Then she said she had another ally – General Hunger. We knew in advance that the great friend of humanity, as in the Great War, would attempt to starve women and children, and we prepared ourselves for it.

Thus this general was only a bad speculation. Now England has discovered a third general. It is General Winter. But the British should not forget to raise their most important general to the rank of Field-Marshal of the Empire. I mean General Bluff. That is their only reliable ally. But they cannot beat us any longer with this general. Therefore we can, perhaps, make fools of them.

The German people have now got really to know Great Britain. The British will not win the war by this method; and the other methods are, thank God, in our hands, and will remain in our hands. When the hour has come we shall place General Fact in the place of General Hunger, or Revolution, or Winter, or Bluff. That is what we are going to do; and then we shall see who is the better man.

The Nazi Chancellor then turned his guns on the British Prime Minister alleging that he had ordered the bombing of civilians. The reply, when it came, he said, would bring 'unending misery and suffering' upon the [British] people –

Believe me . . . I feel a deep disgust for this type of unscrupulous politician who wrecks whole nations and states. It almost causes me pain to think that I should have been selected by fate to deal the final blow to the structure which [Churchill has] already set tottering. It never has been my intention to wage war, but rather to build up a state with a new social order and the finest possible standard of culture. Every year that this war drags on is keeping me away from this work, and the cause of this [is] nothing but a ridiculous nonentity. . . . Of course, the German reply [will not affect] Mr Churchill, for he no doubt will already be in Canada.

(Adolf Hitler addressing the German people: speech extracts August/September 1940

The Führer and Supreme Commander　　　　Führer Headquarters,
of the Armed Forces　　　　　　　　　　　　　　August 1940
　　　　　　　　　　　　　　　　　　　　　　　　　10 copies

War Directive No. 17
For the conduct of air and sea warfare against England

In order to establish the necessary conditions for the final conquest of England I intend to intensify air and sea warfare against the English homeland. I therefore order as follows:

(1) The German Air Force is to overpower the English Air Force with all the forces at its command, in the shortest possible time. The attacks are to be directed primarily against flying units, their ground installations, and their supply organizations, but also against the aircraft industry, including that manufacturing anti-aircraft equipment.

(2) After achieving temporary or local air superiority the air war is to be continued against ports, in particular against stores of food, and also against stores of provisions in the interior of the country.

Attacks on south coast ports will be made on the smallest possible scale, in view of our own forthcoming operations.

(3) On the other hand, air attacks on enemy warships and merchant ships may be reduced except where some particularly favourable target happens to present itself, where such attacks would lend additional effectiveness to those mentioned in paragraph 2, or where such attacks are necessary for the training of air crews for further operations.

(4) The intensified air warfare will be carried out in such a way that the Air Force can at any time be called upon to give adequate support to naval operations against suitable targets. It must also be ready to take part in full force in 'Undertaking Sea-lion'.

(5) I reserve to myself the right to decide on terror attacks as measures of reprisal.

(6) The intensification of the air war may begin on or after 5 August. The exact time is to be decided by the Air Force after the completion of preparations and in the light of the weather.

The Navy is authorized to begin the proposed intensified naval war at the same time.

(Adolf Hitler)

The reality . . .

Oberst *Theo Osterkamp* [commander of* Jagdgeschwader *51 – soon to be taken over by Major Werner Mölders] was an unusually observant and reflective commander, who learnt much from these early encounters with the 'Lords' as his men called their English opponents. . . . On the same day (1 August) that Hitler issued Directive No. 17, Göring held a great conclave of Luftwaffe commanders at the Hague. Osterkamp's account is vivid and revealing.*

A big conference of the Luftwaffe command with its Supreme Commander Hermann Göring. Place of action – The Hague, at the headquarters of General Christiansen, the commander in Holland. I have the honour to join this illustrious company as the representative of the fighter forces.

Everybody of rank and name is present. Because of the good weather the festival takes place in the garden. The 'Iron One' [Göring] appears in a new white gala uniform.

At first he praised extravagantly the lion's share of the Luftwaffe in the defeat of France. 'And now, gentlemen, the Führer has ordered me to crush Britain with my Luftwaffe. By means of hard blows I plan to have this enemy, who has already suffered a decisive moral defeat, down on his knees in the nearest future, so that an occupation of the island by our troops can proceed without any risk!'

Then the matter of orders and directives for the execution of the plan was taken up. According to the information of the intelligence service. Britain disposed in its southern sector – the only one which came into question for us – of, at the most, 400–500 fighters. Their destruction in the air and on land was to be carried out in three phases: during the first five days in a semicircle starting in the west and proceeding south and then

---

* Later, *Generalleutnant* Theo Osterkamp, 'Onkel Theo', commander of the fighter arm in Kesselring's *Luftflotte* 2, a First World War ace and protégé of Oswald Bölcke and friend of Manfred von Richthofen. Forty-eight years old, Osterkamp had been in combat since 1939 and had added six kills to his First World War total of 32. Ed.

east, within a radius of 150 to 100 kilometres south of London; in the next three days within 50 to 100 kilometres; and during the last five days within the 50-kilometre circle around London. That would irrevocably gain an absolute air superiority over England and fulfil the Führer's mission!

I think that I must have made a terribly stupid face, but in my case that should scarcely attract any attention. Udet told me later that I shook my head in shock, but I do not remember.

At any rate I saw Udet leaning down to Göring and whispering something to him. Göring looked up, saw me and said, 'Well, Osterkamp, have you got a question?'

I explained to him that during the time when I alone was in combat over England with my *Geschwader* I counted, on the basis of continuous monitoring of the British radio and of air battles during which the distinctive marks of the units [to which the British fighters belonged] were ascertained, that at that time about 500 to 700 British fighters were concentrated in the area around London. Their numbers had increased considerably if compared with the number of planes available at the beginning of the battle. All new units were equipped with Spitfires, which I considered of a quality equal to our fighters.

I wanted to say more, but Göring cut me off angrily: 'This is nonsense, our information is excellent, and I am perfectly aware of the situation. Besides, the Messerschmitt is much better than the Spitfire, because, as you yourself reported, the British are too cowardly to engage your fighters!'

'I shall permit myself to remark that I reported only that the British fighters were ordered to avoid battles with our fighters – ' 'That is the same thing,' Hermann shouted: 'if they were as strong and good as you maintain, I would have to send my *Luftzeugmeister* [Udet] before the firing squad.'

Udet smiled and touched his neck with his hand. I still could not hold back and said, 'May I ask how many fighters will be used in the combat against Britain?' Hermann answered, 'Naturally, all our fighter squadrons will be used in the struggle.' I now knew as much as I had known before and thought, after a careful appraisal, to be able to count on some 1,200 to 1,500 fighters. In this too I was to be bitterly disappointed.

The disappointment with the bombers came sooner. Both of the *Luftflottenchefs*, General Sperrle and General Kesselring, hesitated to stage bomber attacks before the destruction of the British fighter force.

They proposed, with reason, first to destroy, with continuous night bomber attacks, the ground organization, the airfields, etc., of the fighters, as well as the fighter-producing industry centres. Only after the British fighter force had been decisively weakened should mass [day bomber] attacks on the fighter fields around London take place. Göring declared that these objections were ridiculous. 'Jagdgeschwader 51, which alone is at the Channel, has downed over 150 planes. That is enough of a weakening. And besides, considering the number of the bombers of both *Luftflotten*, the few British fighters will be of no consequence!'

Göring's assertion to the effect that my *Geschwader* had downed over 150 planes was correct, to be sure, but he forgot that that number included also all planes which we had destroyed both in the air and on land during the French campaign.

But he was already continuing: 'Count how many bombers alone we can put into the sky for this campaign!'

On the basis of the fact that our industry had concentrated on bomber production for a long time, and having deducted the losses suffered in France, I was counting on at least 1,500 to 2,000 bombers. Göring often spoke publicly of 4,500, but I considered that his estimates were exaggerated about one hundred per cent. Therefore I was completely staggered when the two *Luftflotten* reported that they had not even 700 bombers ready for combat duty. But Göring, too, was sitting there completely staggered, and his consternation seemed genuine. Looking around, shocked and as if in search of help, he murmured, 'Is this my Luftwaffe?'

(Quoted by Telford Taylor in The Breaking Wave,
Weidenfeld & Nicolson, 1967)

'Age hath yet his honour . . .'

Onkel Theo Osterkamp was by no means the only First World War veteran to fly in the Battle of Britain on the German side JG 2's *Kommodore*. Harry von Bulow-Bothkamp was credited with no less than eighteen victories, to add to the six he had earned in the First World War. He was 45 years old. Commanding his *III Gruppe* there was 41-year-old Erick Mix. He had shot down three Allied planes in the First World War and was now on his way to the thirteen more that he downed in the Second World War.

Added to these must be several veterans who flew in the bomber units. The amazing *Oberstleutnant* Joachim Huth had lost a leg in the First World War but now led the Bd 110's of ZG 76. Oldest of all was Eduard Ritter von Schleich who'd won thirty-five victories in the previous war when his all-black Albatross DV 2 earned him the nickname 'Black Knight'. He'd flown in Spain and had only recently been ordered off combat flying with JG 26 at the age of 51.

(Len Deighton, Fighter: The True Story of the Battle of Britain,
Jonathan Cape, 1977)

NCOs

The Luftwaffe also had NCO pilots making reputations as air fighters. One of the most famous was Siegfried Schnell of 11/JG 2, the *Richthofen Geschwader* (where his name was being mentioned even in comparison with *Hauptmann* Helmut Wieck, a fast-rising star of the fighter force and soon to lead the *Geschwader*).* Both the *Hauptmann* and the young NCO were on their way to getting the twenty confirmed kills that almost automatically brought the Knight's Cross. And that decoration, conspicuously worn at the collar, granted the holder the sort of respect and adulation that pop stars and footballers win. It meant the best seat in restaurants, a place at the head of the line, deference from even the most senior officers, pictures in the newspapers, and hugs from the girls.

Kurt Bühligen was also in the *Richthofen Geschwader*. A young NCO who was eventually to get the very highest awards for valour and become one of the few aces to shoot down over 100 machines while fighting on the western front. There was another such NCO flying alongside the famous Mölders in JG 51 (a unit that was in later years to bear the name Mölders, just as JG 2 was named Richthofen); this was Heinz 'Pritzl' Bär.

Born near Leipzig in 1913, the son of a farmer, Bär had flown gliders, and then powered gliders, to get his pilot's licence in 1930. But no matter how he tried, he could not get a job flying for Lufthansa. In 1937 he joined the Luftwaffe. He scored his first aerial victory in France within a month of the start of the war. During the Battle of Britain period, Bär was credited with seventeen victories and was soon commissioned. By the end of the war Bär was to become one of the top German aces, having fought on every front, won the Knight's Cross with oak leaves, swords, and diamonds, flown the Me 262 jets, and been credited with 220 victories. He was the highest scoring ace of the fighting in the west, and the most successful ace with jets (sixteen victories).

At this stage of the war it was hard to predict which of the fighter pilots would become top aces. Some pilots such as Georg-Peter Eder (who ended the war with seventy-eight victories) went through the summer of 1940 without scoring even one victory.

(Len Deighton, *Fighter: The True Story of the Battle of Britain*, Jonathan Cape, 1977)

---

* Helmut Wieck, then *Kommodore* of JG 2, was shot down on 28 November by John Dundas, elder brother of Hugh, who was then himself shot down and killed in the same engagement. Ed.

Born to lead

Major Hartmann Grasser served as [Werner] Mölders' adjutant in
Jagdgeschwader 51 during the Battle of Britain . . . Himself an ace with
103 kills, Grasser retains a warm . . . recollection of his former CO.

Mölders was a very well-educated and highly intelligent man with an
exceptionally good character. His character was such that it guaranteed
everything else about him. He had a direct line of thought, was brilliantly
analytical, and he was especially a man with good leadership. He had an
ear and an eye for everybody in his *Geschwader*. He had a good discipline
without harshness, and an understanding for the mistakes of others – but
he had no understanding of anything that went against discipline in
fighting the war.

He was an outstanding teacher and instructor. He could teach you to
fight in the air. His special personal attention was given to every new pilot
who came to the wing. He would take these young men to himself and
introduce them to the conditions and demands of aerial fighting. His
credo was, 'The most important thing for a fighter pilot is to get the first
victory without too much shock.'

He had a gift for tactics, an outstanding tactical imagination. He was
mature beyond his years . . . a thinker, a practical man and, with it all, a
humanist. I owe my life entirely to Werner Mölders. He not only showed
me how to fight in the air, he showed me how to stay alive and come back
from a fighter operation. His men were devoted to him.

I think that [had] Mölders . . . lived [his] character and intellectual
capacity [would have enabled] his ideas [to prevail] against the leadership
– against the politicians.*

(Trevor J. Constable and Raymond F. Toliver, *Horrido*, Macmillan, 1968)

The prime aim

We have reached the decisive period of the air war against England. The
vital task is to turn all means at our disposal to the defeat of the enemy Air
Force. Our first aim is the destruction of the enemy's fighters. If they no
longer take the air, we shall attack them on the ground, or force them into

---

* Mölders' great Luftwaffe contemporary, Adolf Galland, has written of his friend and
competitor: 'His sudden and unexpected death [in an aeroplane accident in 1941] came as a
hammer blow . . . The Heinkel 111, in which he was being flown by *Leutnant* Kolbe, an
experienced pilot, who had served with the Condor Legion in Spain, developed engine trouble *en
route* to Germany from the Crimea. Having feathered one engine, the pilot decided to attempt a
single-engine landing at Breslau in appalling weather . . . Finding that he was undershooting, he
at once opened the throttle, but then the 'good' engine [failed] and the aircraft crashed, killing
Mölders and the flight engineer instantly. The pilot died on the way to hospital, but Werner's aide
. . . and the radio operator survived . . . to describe the terrible circumstances. (Laddie Lucas
(ed.), *Thanks for the Memory: Unforgettable Characters in Air Warfare*, Stanley Paul, 1989).

battle by directing bomber attacks against targets within the range of our fighters. At the same time, and on a growing scale, we must continue our activities against the ground organization of the enemy bomber units. Surprise attacks on the enemy aircraft industry must be made by day and by night. Once the enemy Air Force has been annihilated, our attacks will be directed as ordered against other vital targets.

(Extract from Directives issued by Hermann Göring after a conference held at Karinhall on 19 August 1940)

Luftwaffe Order of battle

Strength of Forces used in the Battle of Britain as at 10 August 1940

	Establishment	*Strength*	*Serviceability*
Close recce.	120	95	80
Long-range recce.	126	100	71
S.E. fighters	1,011	934	805
T.E. fighters	301	289	224
Bombers	1,569	1,481	998
Dive-bombers	348	327	261
Ground attack	40	39	31
Coastal	94	93	80
Total	3,609	3,358	2,550

Source: AHB6, Air Ministry, 20 August 1947.

SOUTHWARDS INTO BATTLE

At ten o'clock we were back at Turnhouse. The rest of [603] Squadron were all set to leave; we were to move down to Hornchurch, an aerodrome 12 miles east of London on the Thames Estuary . . . We took off at four o'clock, some five hours after the others, Broody leading, Pip and I to each side, and Colin in the box, map-reading. Twenty-four of us flew south that tenth day of August, 1940: of those 24 eight were to fly back.

(Richard Hillary *The Last Enemy*, Macmillan, 1942)

MISSING

Less said the better.
The bill unpaid, the dead letter,
No roses at the end
Of Smith, my friend.

Last words don't matter,
And there are none to flatter.
Words will not fill the post
Of Smith, the ghost.

For Smith, our brother,
Only son of loving mother,
The ocean lifted, stirred,
Leaving no word.

(John Pudney)

'GENIUS IN THE ART OF WAR'

The continuous heavy air fighting of July and early August had been directed upon the Kent promontory and the Channel coast. Göring and his skilled advisers formed the opinion that they must have drawn nearly all our fighter squadrons into this southern struggle. They therefore decided to make a daylight raid on the manufacturing cities north of the Wash. The distance was too great for their first-class fighters, the Me 109s. They would have to risk their bombers with only escorts from the Me 110s, which, though they had the range, had nothing like the quality, which was what mattered now. This was nevertheless a reasonable step for them to take, and the risk was well run.

Accordingly, on 15 August, about a hundred bombers, with an escort of forty Me 110s, were launched against Tyneside. At the same time a raid of more than eight hundred planes was sent to pin down our forces in the south, where it was thought they were already all gathered. But now the dispositions which Dowding had made of the Fighter Command were signally vindicated. The danger had been foreseen. Seven Hurricane or Spitfire squadrons had been withdrawn from the intense struggle in the south to rest in and at the same time to guard the north. They had suffered severely, but were nonetheless deeply grieved to leave the battle. The pilots respectfully represented that they were not at all tired. Now came an unexpected consolation. These squadrons were able to welcome the assailants as they crossed the coast. Thirty German planes were shot down, most of them heavy bombers (Heinkel 111s, with four trained men in each crew), for a British loss of only two pilots injured. The foresight of Air Marshal Dowding in his direction of Fighter Command deserves high praise, but even more remarkable had been the restraint and the exact measurement of formidable stresses which had reserved a fighter force in the north through all these long weeks of mortal conflict in the south. We must regard the generalship here shown as an example of genius in the art of war. Never again was a daylight raid attempted outside the range of the highest class fighter protection. Henceforth everything north of the Wash was safe by day.

(Winston S. Churchill, *Their Finest Hour*, Curtis Brown on behalf of the Estate of Sir Winston Churchill, C & T Publications, 1949)

A PARROT ON HIS SHOULDER

10th August. It has been quite a day!

It started quietly though with the squadron stood down for the morning when I was able to do some work in the office and take a look at the airmen's billets, which are far from satisfactory and smell of dogs. It was as we sat down for lunch the fun and games started.

We were surprised to be given the order to scramble from a state of 'released', but the reason was all too apparent as we rushed helter-skelter from the mess to see thirty Ju 87 dive-bombers screaming vertically on to Tangmere. The noise was terrifying as the explosions of the bombs mingled with the din of ack-ack guns which were firing from positions all round us. We could hear the rattle of spent bullets as they fell on the metal-covered nissens where we hurriedly donned our flying kit. Chunks of spent lead fell about us as we jinked out to our aircraft. Our crews, wearing steel helmets, had already started the engines and sped us on our way with the minimum of delay. It was a complete panic take-off, with Spitfires darting together from all corners of the field and it was a miracle that none collided in the frantic scramble to get airborne.

I called the boys to form up over base at Angels 2. A Flight was already with me, but there was no sign of B Flight. However, there was no time to stop and look for them! The air was a kaleidoscope of aeroplanes swooping and diving around us, and for a moment I felt like pulling the blankets over my head and pretending I wasn't there! I had no idea it could be as chaotic as this. Selected a gaggle of 110s and dived to attack. Out of the corner of my eye I caught sight of a Spitfire having a go at another 110 and blowing the canopy clean off it. A Hurricane on fire flashed by and I was momentarily taken aback when the pilot of the aircraft in front of me baled out, until I realized he had come from the 110 I had been firing at! Then it was all over. No one else was about.

I drove over to Tangmere [from Westhampnett, 602 Squadron's satellite airfield], in the evening and found the place in an utter shambles, with wisps of smoke still rising from shattered buildings. Little knots of people were wandering about with dazed looks on their faces, obviously deeply affected by the events of the day. I eventually tracked down the Station Commander standing on the lawn in front of the officers' mess with a parrot sitting on his shoulder. Jack [Boret] was covered in grime and the wretched bird was screeching its imitation of a Stuka at the height of the attack! The once immaculate grass was littered with personal belongings which had been blasted from the wing which had received a direct hit. Shirts, towels, socks, a portable gramophone – a little private world exposed for all to see lay in profusion around our feet. However, the bar had been spared and was doing a brisk trade!

Tommy Thomson, the Station Adjutant took me over to the airfield to see the damage. Rubble was everywhere and all three hangars had been wrecked. I managed to crawl under the tangled remains of one of them as I wanted to find out how my aircraft had fared. Alas, a heavy girder had crashed on top of Q, breaking her back and severing one of the mainplanes. I feel very sad about this, for I had grown to love that aeroplane and it was patently obvious that she was only fit for the scrap heap.

Tommy then showed me the remains of the neighbouring hangar, and, pointing to its massive door lying flat on the ground, remarked wistfully, 'My Triumph Dolomite is under that little lot. I only bought it last week!'

What could I say?

Four of our aircraft had been in the hangars at Tangmere, and we have lost the lot. The remains of Billy Fiske's Hurricane was still smouldering in the middle of the airfield when I left and Billy himself is in the station hospital, gravely injured. Max Aitken and his 601 boys have been having a hard time of it since they came to Tangmere.

Already stories are going around of how the fellows reacted during the aerial onslaught – some patently numbed by the force of it, whilst others seemed to become spurred to greater action by the terrifying enormity of the moment. And the heroes were often those whom one would least expect to stand out among their fellow men. Such a man has been our medical officer, Doc Willey, who apparently was doing great deeds throughout the blitz.

The Germans launched heavy attacks against many sites along the south coast today. Biggin Hill, Kenley, Manston and North Weald have all been thumped.

(Air Vice-Marshal A. V. R. Johnstone, *Enemy in the Sky: My 1940 Diary*, William Kimber, 1976)

EARLY WARNING?

From the very beginning the British had an extraordinary advantage which we could never overcome throughout the entire war: radar and fighter control. For us and for our command this was a surprise, and a very bitter one. Britain possessed a closely knit radar network conforming to the highest technical standards of the day which provided Fighter Command with the most detailed data imaginable. Thus the British fighter was guided all the way from take-off to his correct position for attack on the German formations.

(Adolf Galland, *The First and the Last: The German Fighter Force in World War II*, Methuen, 1955)

FRUSTRATED

It is doubtful whether there is any point in continuing the attacks on radar sites, in view of the fact that not one of those attacked has been put out of action.

(Hermann Göring at a Conference held at Karinhall on 15 August 1940)

THE BATTLE'S ONLY VICTORIA CROSS

The Victoria Cross has been won only three times in Britain, by Lieut. Leefe Robinson of the Worcester Regiment and Royal Flying Corps, who shot down a Zeppelin over Hertfordshire in 1916; by Acting Leading Seaman Jack Foreman Mantle, RN, in Portland Harbour on 4 July 1940, in HMS *Foylebank*; and Flt Lt. J. B. Nicholson, [of No. 249 Squadron], RAF, who remained in his blazing [Hurricane fighter] during a dog-fight over Southampton on 16 August 1940, and although badly wounded shot down an enemy fighter before baling out . . . Nicholson's plane was hit by four cannon shells, two of which wounded him while another set fire to the gravity tank. When about to bale out from his burning aircraft he sighted an enemy fighter which he attacked and shot down as a result of which he sustained serious burns.

(Brigadier the Rt Hon. Sir John Smyth, Bt, VC, MC, MP, *The Story of the Victoria Cross*, Frederick Muller, 1963)

DEFIANT IN NAME, BUT . . .

Mölders often fought over Dunkirk, where the Defiant, a two-seater fighter, gave him a nasty shock because it had a four-gun power-operated turret which had a good arc of fire on either flank. At a range of half a mile the Defiant looked not unlike a Hurricane and when, during its first combats, the Germans allowed it to come alongside, it gained a spectacular but short-lived success. But the turret proved little compensation for the Defiant's indifferent performance, the Germans soon had its measure and, like the Lysander and the Battle, it was fought out of the sky.

(J. E. [Johnnie] Johnson, *The Story of Air Fighting*, Hutchinson, 1985)

If these few days in mid-July showed the first hints of vulnerability of the Ju 87 Stuka, they also tragically proved the unsuitability of the Defiant for front-line fighter duties. These turret fighters of 141 Squadron were unblooded until 19 July, when they were moved down to Hawkinge from West Malling. The day had dawned clear, vulnerable convoys were numerous and trouble was expected.

All nine serviceable Defiants were ordered off soon after midday to patrol south of Folkestone. They were carrying out this duty in a model manner when, without warning from the controller, a *Staffel* of Me 109s fell upon them. Unmanoeuvrable and at a hopeless disadvantage, the gunners valiantly attempted to spin their turrets to get a bead on the swooping 'snappers'. Another *Staffel*, eager to join the massacre, added to the one-sidedness of the dog-fight. One after the other the Defiants fell from the sky, some in flames, the gunners at a hopeless disadvantage in struggling to get out.

Only the belated arrival of John Thompson's Hurricanes of 111 Squadron saved the last of 141 Squadron. Three pilots got back to Hawkinge, one of them without his gunner and in an aircraft that could never fly again.

> (Richard Hough and Denis Richards, *The Battle of Britain: The Jubilee History*, Hodder & Stoughton, 1989)

When 264 Squadron was posted down from Lincolnshire to Hornchurch toward the end of August, we faced the tragedy almost immediately of losing our CO, Philip Hunter. He was last seen going out over the Channel in pursuit of planes that had bombed the town of Ramsgate. We never found out what happened to him. It did our morale not much good. . . .

The fact was our Defiants were outturned, outclimbed, and outgunned by the Me 109s. In the last week in August, we lost nine gunners and five pilots. We'd lost a CO dead, the acting CO shot down injured, both flight commanders shot down injured . . .

When we went back up to Kirton-in-Lindsey in Lincolnshire, we were led by our most experienced surviving pilot, Samuel Richard Thomas, only a pilot officer and not yet twenty-one years old.

> (Norman Gelb, *Scramble*, Michael Joseph, 1986)

HONESTY

There were some expert and well-tried pilots on the squadron [615]. We were well led and we needed it for we were a mixed bunch, of mixed and usually inadequate skills. Like many squadrons, we were sent a number of foreign pilots, in our case some Czechs and quite a large proportion of French.

Typically, the latter were very much individuals. Many of them had escaped by their own initiative from the French Desert Air Force (one learnt with fascination that, during their lonely tours of duty in remote North African stations, their personal and officially supplied equipment had included full-sized inflatable rubber ladies, a sound precaution no doubt against undesirable local involvements, homosexuality or cafard). Of the half dozen Frenchmen on the squadron, the one to make the greatest name for himself later was René Mouchotte, handsome, charming and debonair, but a most courageous and determined fighter; he was eventually killed leading the Biggin Hill Wing. The only survivor among them was Henri Lafont, now one of the brains behind the Paris Air Show.

I was bitterly disappointed but should perhaps not have been surprised to find that my personal success on fighters was not much better than on Lysanders [in the Battle of France]. Indeed success is quite the wrong word – by the time I left Fighter Command after eight or nine months I had inflicted no confirmed damage on the enemy and had cost the country two Hurricanes; one crashed overshooting at West Malling after a battle; one shot down in flames from which I parachuted from a great height, landing near Ashford in Kent and enjoying the quite common experience at the time of being identified by the intrepid locals as a German. On recovering from a heavy and painful landing, I was surprised to be almost frog-marched away at the point of a pitchfork; only when a police car turned up and the driver was told 'Got one of the bastards here for you', did I appreciate the lie of the land and dispel the misunderstanding with some hauteur.

The frequency of such incidents was not surprising. The greater proportion of those descending by parachute were in fact German; and by the time our propaganda machine had got to work on that proportion, it was quite natural for the good people of south-east England to presume that a downed pilot was a Luftwaffe pilot. Whether any of them ever learned to recognize Al Deere after he had baled out eight or nine times I cannot say. Perhaps the worst recorded case was that of Flight Lieutenant Nicholson, who, baling out badly burnt after the epic fight that won him his Victoria Cross, was duly shot by a member of the Home Guard as he descended.

My failure to distinguish myself in the Battle was by no means as uncommon as many people would imagine. Particularly, one's shooting was haphazard and untutored, most of us having been thrown into the Battle quite without adequate training in that highly scientific art. We did not often get into an attacking position and when we did, we missed, firing at too long ranges and without enough deflection. Those who survived eventually learnt by experience; but in 1940 the successes went to the few old hands, the naturally gifted and lucky. It is a statistical fact that on both sides more than three-quarters of the aircraft destroyed were shot down by less than a third of the pilots.

At least we weaker brethren, with non-existent or even minus scores, had no cause to search our consciences when the postwar publication of actual German losses indicated that some exaggeration had been made in those claimed.

> (Christopher Foxley-Norris,* *A Lighter Shade of Blue: The Lighthearted Memoirs of an Air Marshal*, Ian Allan, 1978)

FORGET-ME-NOTS FOR PILOTS, 1940

Reporting of enemy

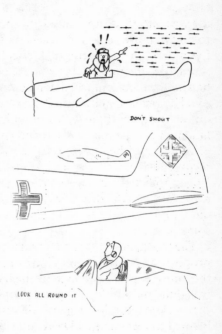

DON'T get excited, and DON'T shout. Speak slowly and into the microphone. Report ALL hostile aircraft, not one group, and then a few minutes afterwards another one below or above.

If you see a formation of enemy aircraft look all round it, and report its escorts at the same time, using the clock system, and giving their height above or below you.

It is also quite a good idea when you have finished, to put your R/T set on to receive.

Remember that ACK-ACK bursts are often a useful indication of the whereabouts of enemy aircraft.

A LIFE IN THE DAY OF . . .

For me, 11 August 1940 was . . . A Day.

Before breakfast . . . we [74 Squadron] intercepted some Me 109s approaching Dover and I attacked one, which fell into the Channel. Then I closed on another 109 which, after a short burst from close range, exploded in mid-air. I chased two more . . . one of which dived away shedding pieces, but I did not see it crash.

---

* Later Air Chief Marshal Sir Christopher Foxley-Norris, Chairman of the Battle of Britain Fighter Association.

My second mission was abortive because my radio telephone was unserviceable.

On my third sortie, we spotted about forty Me 110s approaching a convoy about twelve miles east of Clacton. As we drew nearer the German planes formed into a circle with the object of guarding each other's tails.

One flight dived into the middle of the circle and then our squadron leader turned into the opposite director of the circling 110s. Within a few seconds the Germans split us in all directions and I attacked one with a long burst, which spiralled down in flames. Then I attacked another and after some violent turning and twisting I got in a burst which sent the 110 into the Channel. . . . I attacked a third Me 110 and scored several hits, but lost contact on breaking away to discover both fuel and ammunition were running low.

On my fourth and last sortie of this epic day, our CO led us into a flight against ten Ju 87s escorted by some twenty Me 109s near Margate. Our flight went for the fighters and after a few moments I managed to get on the tail of a 109 which dived away. I followed, firing short bursts, and eventually the German baled out and his aeroplane crashed in flames immediately to the west of Ramsgate. The pall of smoke from this crash was seen from Manston airfield.

(Pilot Officer [later Wing Commander] H. M. Stephen,
Profiles, Military Gallery, Bath)

PRESERVING THE BASE

I was much concerned on visiting Manston Aerodrome* yesterday to find that although more than four clear days have passed since it was last raided, the greater part of the craters on the landing ground remained unfilled and the aerodrome was barely serviceable. When you remember what the Germans did at the Stavanger Aerodrome and the enormous rapidity with which craters were filled, I must protest emphatically against this feeble method of repairing damage. Altogether, there were 150 people available to work, including those that could be provided from the air force personnel. These were doing their best. No effective appliances were available, and the whole process appeared disproportionate to the value of maintaining this fighting vantage ground.

(Winston S. Churchill to Secretary of State for Air, CAS and
General Ismay, 29 August 1940)

* Forward airfield in East Kent.

CANDID MOMENTS

Flight Lieutenant Alan Deere

Our morale was getting a bit low because there were only three of us – George Gribble, Colin Gray, and me – left in the squadron who had any combat experience. We had been there the whole time and were pretty tired. Each time we went up, there seemed to be more and more Germans up there. We'd gone through two squadron commanders. The new pilots who came in – they just went up and came down! You'd say to them, 'Now, look, don't get yourself lost. Stick with us. Don't bother about shooting to start with.' But of course they couldn't resist peeling off, and some of them didn't come back and some had to crash-land. . . .

   You never could tell. Some of the least likely chaps turned out to be best and sometimes you got things wrong in sizing men up. I had a pilot who came to me one day and said, 'I can't fly today. I'm not feeling well.' I said, 'You've got to fly. We're short of men.'

   He said, 'I just can't.'

   I called the doctor and told him, 'Take a look at this chap. I think he's lost his nerve.'

   It turned out he had malaria. I was unable to judge because I was so tired myself.

(Norman Gelb, Scramble, Michael Joseph, 1986)

Pilot Officer John Ellacombe

There were fourteen, fifteen hours of daylight each day. You were on duty right through. Chaps were being lost all the time. We had seventeen out of twenty-three killed or wounded in my squadron in less than three weeks. We had another eight aircraft shot down with the chaps unhurt, including myself twice. It was a fight for survival. There was tremendous 'twitch'. If somebody slammed a door, half the chaps would jump out of their chairs. There were times when you were so tired, you'd pick up your pint of beer with two hands. But no one was cowering, terrified, in a corner. My greatest fear was that I'd reach the stage where I'd show fear. But it took me years after the war to get rid of my twitch.

(Norman Gelb, Scramble, Michael Joseph, 1986)

PER ARDUA

(To those who gave their lives to England during the Battle of Britain and left such a shining example to we who follow, these lines are dedicated.)

They that have climbed the white mists of the morning,
They that have soared, before the world's awake,
To herald up their foemen to them, scorning
The thin dawn's rest their weary folk might take;

Some that have left other mouths to tell the story
Of high, blue battle, – quite young limbs that bled;
How they had thundered up the clouds to glory
Or fallen to an English field stained red;

Because my faltering feet would fail I find them
Laughing beside me, steadying the hand
That seeks their deadly courage – yet behind them
The cold light dies in that once brilliant land . . .

Do these, who help the quickened pulse run slowly,
Whose stern remembered image cools the brow –
Till the far dawn of Victory know only
Night's darkness, and Valhalla's silence now?

(Pilot Officer John Magee* [RCAF], United
States citizen)

CANNON TROUBLE

During this period the armament experts at Fighter Command had been trying to improve the weight of fire-power of the Spitfire and had decided that two 20-mm cannons plus four machine guns would be an ideal mixture. 19 Squadron – the first squadron of all to have Spitfires – were the unlucky recipients of these first cannons.

I well remember the occasion when 19 Squadron's Spitfires were fitted with these cannons, since we were in the same sector, Duxford. The cannons would fire about two rounds and then stop. The reason was that the wings had been adapted to accept cannons instead of being built *for* cannons. The stoppage occurred on recoil. After a couple of sorties with no cannons working in close combat with the enemy, the pilots were not best pleased. The armament 'experts' at 12 Group and Fighter Command tried to insist that the 19 Squadron armourers did not know their job.

---

* John Gillespie Magee, a classicist at Rugby before moving to the USA, ostensibly to complete his education and enter Yale, was born in Shanghai on 9 June 1922 of an American father, the Rev. John Magee, an Episcopalian missionary in China, and an English mother. After training in Canada, Magee joined 412 (Canadian) Squadron in England and was killed, sadly, in an aircraft collision on 11 December 1941. His friends in the squadron had no idea that he wrote poetry, still less that he would be remembered as one of World War II's best-known poets. Ed.

'Stuffy' Dowding heard about this and came, with his armament 'experts' to see for himself.

I was present on this occasion. Sandy Lane was the 19 Squadron Commander, an old chum. Dowding said: 'Hullo, Lane, I hear you're in trouble with your cannons. Tell me.' Sandy replied: 'They fire one round, sir, and that's all.' At this point one of the armament 'experts' mistakenly intervened to say: 'There's nothing wrong with the cannons, sir. I think the armourers do not fully understand them.' Courteously, Dowding turned to him and said: 'I want to hear what Squadron Leader Lane thinks.' He looked at Sandy and said: 'What do you recommend?' Without pause, Sandy answered: 'Remove the cannons and put back the machine guns, sir.' Stuffy said: 'Thank you, Lane.' He then turned to his staff and said: 'You will arrange that straight away, please.'

That was typical of the C-in-C, Fighter Command in 1940. I was present once when he told one of his staff officers: 'Our job in his Headquarters is to look after the squadrons in the field.' The following year when the Spitfire Vb was in production the wing had been designed to take cannons and they worked perfectly.

(Douglas Bader, *Fight for the Sky: The Story of the Spitfire and the Hurricane*, Sidgwick & Jackson, 1973)

GUY GIBSON, FIGHTER PILOT

It was a simple trip and although we were laying mines very close to the shore the flak did not bother us much, and the whole squadron did a good job of work. Afterwards we looked around for some E-boats which we were told were operating in that area. We turned out to sea and stooged around with our navigation lights on so as to lull all and sundry into believing us to be friendly aircraft. Suddenly, in the long silver reflection of the moon in the calm water we saw one going at a rate of knots for a small harbour in the Île d'Eu; and Houghton pressed the button. However, at times like this when bombing wasn't a highly organized affair, we weren't sure of our height and Houghton certainly wasn't sure of our level, and so the two 250-pound bombs fell within a few yards but did not hit him; whether we damaged him or not we couldn't say, but there was some happy chatter on board as we turned for home.

But even better was to come. As we crossed over Cherbourg on the way home an aircraft passed us going in the opposite direction with his navigation lights on. This must have been a Hun which had been bombing England. Quickly we whipped around and by pushing the old Hampden to the limit so that she shuddered and quivered at the unknown horsepower she was developing, we at last caught him up just near to Lorient. For a while we flew in formation, about fifty yards away, trying to make out what type of aircraft it was, but the night was dark. At last, through the welcome beam of an enemy searchlight we identified it as a Dornier 17. Moreover, both pilots on board seemed very happy; they had their full cockpit lights on and we could see them inside sitting motionless as they, no doubt, thought of the ersatz coffee and bacon and eggs they were going to get in a few minutes' time.

In the rear both my bottom and top guns slid slowly over to the starboard side and I told Mac to take careful aim. Then I counted slowly.

'One – two – three,' and then I yelled: 'Let him have it, Mac.'

There was a quick staccato roar as all four guns belched out tracers and the Dornier dived to the ground with one engine on fire. In doing so he flew low right over Lorient Docks where his own flak, no doubt thinking he was one of ours, gave him a pretty good pasting, and the last we saw of him was a flaming mass going down behind some trees. Bomber Command credited us with a probable when we got home.

(Guy Gibson, VC, *Enemy Coast Ahead*, Michael Joseph, 1946; Goodall Publications, 1986)

FOUR-LETTER ENGLISHMAN?

The sea was waiting for me. It was the minute of truth: life or death. It occurred to me that to survive was only to run the chance of dying all over again a week, or a month later. Faced with the simple alternatives of death or survival, instinct takes over from reason and the mind works with clarity and precision. I was surprised to feel so calm about the whole thing, perhaps because neither death nor life was yet certain. The sea would decide.

As I stood in the cockpit to dive out into space there came to my mind a story I had read as a boy: a German airman of the First World War, grabbing vainly at the rip cord ring, had crashed to death. I crossed my arms in front of me, my right hand firmly on the vital ring. Then I dived out head first, and down to the sea. I was falling on my back, in total silence, my feet pointing at the sky, when I pulled the ripcord. The parachute canopy clacked open and the harness wrenched my body violently from its headlong fall. Far below I could see Hurricane VY-K diving vertically towards the sea to disappear in an eruption of spume and spray.

Swinging there high above the sea I felt safe for the moment. Having first attached the ripcord ring to the microphone wire, I took off my helmet and dropped it. That rid me of one encumbrance. Clad as I was only in a light sweater and trousers, there remained but one more thing, my flying boots. Oddly enough I preferred to stick to them. If necessary I would kick them off in the sea.

When the big splash came I hit the harness release knob and sank, it seemed fathoms deep, into green obscurity. The harness was gone and long seconds followed while I thrashed out vigorously with arms and legs. When at last I broke the surface I saw the little ship lying less than a mile away. Luckily they had seen me and were lowering a boat. I kicked off my boots and feeling tiny and impotent in that immense sea swam around rather relaxed, supported by my Mae West. The bulbous yellow life-jacket filled with kapok could be inflated only by mouth. I blew through the pink tube, but swallowed mouthfuls of sea water. So I took to swimming again and steered towards my helmet, a small dark blob floating a hundred yards away, with the ripcord ring still firmly attached. This precious souvenir more than compensated for my boots.

When the little boat, rowed by four stalwart sailors, approached, a fifth stood up in the stern brandishing a boat-hook and shouted, 'Blimey, if he ain't a fucking Hun.' Only one answer was possible: 'I'm not, I'm a fucking Englishman.' I shouted back, and the boat hook was quietly lowered. A moment later brawny arms were around me and a warm Yorkshire voice was speaking. 'Come on lad, we've got you. It's all right.' And they hauled me into the boat. Unknown, willing hands had saved me from certain death.

(Peter Townsend, Duel of Eagles, Weidenfeld & Nicolson, 1970;
Corgi Books, 1972)

THE SUSPENSE OF IT!

I have no idea how many loops the Spitfire did before I was finally able to slide back the hood. But it was not a moment too soon, because by then the oil tank was on fire and the flames were spreading back from the engine. I threw off my seat harness and stood up, but found I could go no further because I still had my helmet on and it was attached firmly to the aircraft. By now I was getting pretty desperate and I wrenched the helmet off with all my strength. Afterwards I found the helmet in the wreckage and saw that I had actually torn it across the leather; I was amazed at the force I must have summoned to do that.

The next thing I knew I was falling clear of my aircraft, head-down and on my back, at an angle of about forty-five degrees. I had no idea how high I was, so I pulled the D-ring right away. I knew it was a mistake, as soon as I did it.

When the parachute began to deploy, I was in just about the worst possible position. I remember watching, an interested spectator, as the canopy and the rigging lines came streaming out from between my legs. One of the lines coiled itself round my leg and when the canopy developed I found myself hanging upside down. I had never parachuted before, but from my sketchy prevous instruction I was fairly certain that head-first was not the position to be in when I hit the ground! So I grabbed a handful of slack rigging lines on the opposite side to my entangled leg and started to climb up hand over hand. After a lot of kicking and pulling I managed to get my leg free; with a sigh of relief I sank back into my harness, right way up.

Now I had time to think about what was happening around me. The first thing that struck me was the quietness: the only sounds were the spasmodic bursts of cannon and machine gun fire and the howls of the engines coming from the battle still in progress high above; it seemed an age since I had been part of it. But my own troubles were not over yet.

Gradually it began to dawn on me that the straps leading up from my harness, instead of being comfortably clear of my head on either side, were tangled together and chafing my ears and face. And higher up the rigging lines were also tangled, preventing the canopy from developing to its fullest extent. That meant that I was falling much faster than I should have been; and struggle as I might, I could not get the lines untangled. I went down past a cloud and it seemed to whizz by; it was not going to be a very pleasant landing. The only time I had ever needed a parachute and this had to happen!

Gradually I got lower, and I could make out trees and farmhouses and curious faces raised skywards. At about 500 feet the wind carried me across some high tension cables and even though I was hundreds of feet above the wires I could not resist the instinct to lift my feet up. Still I was coming down much too fast. The one thing I needed most of all was a nice soft tree, to break my fall. And there in my line of drift, in answer to my prayer, was a wood full of them.

Just before I hit I covered my face with my arms and came to rest amid the crack of breaking twigs. When the noise stopped I cautiously lowered my arms and looked around. My parachute canopy was draped across a couple of trees and I was bouncing up and down between the trunks like a yo-yo. I was about twenty feet up, suspended above an asphalt road.

At about my level, just out of reach was a small branch. By doing a sort of Tarzan stunt, swinging back and forth from side to side, I was able to get closer and closer until in the end I was able to grab hold of it. Gingerly I pulled myself up and on to a thicker bough, before letting go of my harness. By this time quite a crowd had begun to collect underneath the tree: at first there seemed to be some doubt about my nationality but the vehemence of my Anglo-Saxon demands for help soon satisfied everyone that I was, in fact, British. Some Home Guard men made a human ladder by sitting on each others' shoulders and with their aid I managed to clamber down to mother earth. It had indeed been a memorable day.

(Alfred Price, *Spitfire at War*, Ian Allan, 1974)

Bob Tuck, Squadron Commander

Third party

267 Squadron (Hurricanes), which, until now, had not enjoyed the highest morale, lost a pilot on Saturday 31 August and another on 3 September, with two wounded. 'We were a very demoralized squadron until Bob Stanford-Tuck arrived. He vitalized us and we soon went to the top.'

> (Jack Ryder, an instrument repairer of 257 Squadron, quoted in Richard Hough and Denis Richards, *The Battle of Britain: The Jubilee History*, Hodder & Stoughton, 1989)

Comparisons can be invidious, but few would deny that in Bob Stanford-Tuck (Wing Commander Robert R. Stanford-Tuck) of Britain, and Colin Gray (Group Captain C. F. Gray), of New Zealand, the Allies possessed two of the most enlightened examples of the fighting art . . . When Bob Tuck was [eventually] shot down by flak in northern France and taken prisoner after no more than two years of actual combat, he had twenty-nine enemy aircraft credited to his guns. God knows what he would have collected had he been able to engage in the last three full seasons of the war. But by the time he left the stage [a year after the Battle of Britain] he was a principal figure in the cast.

> (Laddie Lucas, *Wings of War: Airmen of All Nations Tell Their Stories, 1939–1945*, Hutchinson, 1983)

I first met [Bob Stanford-Tuck] in May 1940 on Martlesham airfield when we were both Flight Lieutenants in different Spitfire squadrons . . . He looked like a matador and subsequently proved to be a pretty good one in the air. Strangely he nearly failed his flying course when he joined the Royal Air Force a year or two before the war. He was a fine shot, and this I think was the main reason for his great successes at Dunkirk, during the Battle of Britain, and in the subsequent operations over northern France in 1941. Like many, Bob had his lucky escapes but undoubtedly the most fortunate one was . . . [when he] was drinking with some chums in a local pub in Norfolk [during the Battle] and decided to leave early. No one else would come with him. A matter of minutes after he left, the pub was hit by an enemy bomb and everyone inside was killed.

> (Douglas Bader, *Fight for the Sky: The Story of the Spitfire and the Hurricane*, Sidgwick & Jackson, 1973)

Strictly personal

I did my flying training at Grantham in 1935 in company with my great friend, 'Sailor' Malan, who turned out to be probably one of the greatest fighter leaders of the war. Like me, he had been a cadet in the Merchant

Service and it became obvious to both of us that if one was not flying accurately, it was no good pushing the firing button and hoping for the best. If you opened fire with your 'bank and turn' indicator showing a bad skid either way, your bullets would go nowhere near where you thought you were aiming as you looked through the graticule of your gunsight, just in front of your face. Hence, accurate flying was essential at the moment of opening fire.

When attacking large formations of bombers, the ideal situation was to have the sun behind and be in a shallow dive with good overtaking speed. The tactic then was to pass slightly below the bombers, climb fast, and, when well within range, shoot up into the belly of the aircraft where there was little, if any, protective armour plate. If you were not shot down in the process of delivering an attack of this sort, it always produced instant results. . . .

Air fighting, often at great heights, is a 'cat and mouse', stark and brutal business, but all I can say is that I would not have missed it for all the rice in China. However, I would certainly not [have wished] to repeat it!'

(Robert Stanford-Tuck, in Laddie Lucas, *Wings of War: Airmen of All Nations Tell Their Stories, 1939–1945*, Hutchinson, 1983)

. . . I was still with 92, during the first half of the Battle of Britain, when I was posted to take over command of 257 (Hurricane) Squadron, which, until this time, had suffered heavy casualties. I commanded this squadron until half-way through 1941, when I was given command of the Fighter Wing at Duxford . . .

At the end of the war, I was credited with 29 victories, but, in 1978, the Aircraft Recovery Group excavated the remains of an Me 109 22 ft deep in the marshes (sadly, still containing the remains of the pilot, Lt. Werner Knittle). Subsequently, after considerable research at the MOD, it was decided that it was an aircraft that I had shot down [during the Battle of Britain] but had only claimed as a 'probable' at the time. It was credited to me, bringing my total to 30.

(Robert Stanford-Tuck, *Profiles*, Military Gallery, Bath, 1981)

SHOOTING TO KILL – A NEW ZEALAND SECRET

I learned my lesson in deflection shooting early on during the Battle of Britain . . . when attacking an Me 109 over the Thames Estuary. The pilot started to turn and, being somewhat excited, I overreacted and pulled through to more than twice the angle off which I'd originally intended (and which I thought was overgenerous in the first place). To my surprise the aircraft burst into flames and the pilot jumped out!

The lesson was simple – double the number you first thought of and add a bit for good measure. I think it was an art some pilots instinctively acquired; there wasn't much chance to practise.

But the overriding factor in success was the range of opening fire and the determination to press home the attack as close as possible. After all, we only had a total of 14 seconds fire-power with machine guns and even less with cannons. If you were right up the back-end of an enemy aircraft even quite large errors didn't matter.

(Colin Gray, in Laddie Lucas, *Wings of War: Airmen of All Nations Tell Their Stories, 1939–1945*, Hutchinson, 1983)

UNITED STATES SPOTLIGHT ON BRITAIN

The Royal Air Force – England's shield

. . . Germany is preparing for invasion. Several thousand young men stand between Hitler and his dreams of conquest of this island. They are giving him considerable trouble in completing his preparations. They are the men of the RAF. On them has fallen one of the greatest tasks in history. Their young bodies are literally the first wall Hitler must penetrate to put foot on this island. The RAF must be mastered before invasion by troops can start. Therefore, RAF aerodromes must be bombarded. Hitler is trying to put RAF aerodromes out of commission. British aeroplanes must be destroyed, pilots must be put out. Hitler has superiority in numbers, both machines and men. But the RAF resistance must surprise him. For he is paying a heavy toll. The RAF destruction of German machines and pilots is so heavy that the final verdict of the battle of the air for Britain depends upon what resources Hitler has, or is prepared to throw in. He must know now that the Luftwaffe must pay a high percentage in any assault on Britain.

The Luftwaffe renewed mass attacks on this island today. After a dramatic pause, Hitler launched his planes on Sunday in three mass attacks. It is estimated that 600 aircraft came over in attacks on airdromes and harbours in the south and south-east. It is stated authoritatively that German air losses on Sunday were well over 100. Sixteen British fighters were lost.

(Bill Hillman, NBC Broadcast to the US from London, 00.15 BST, 19 August 1940)

The ordinary people

This is London . . .

. . . I spent five hours this afternoon on the outskirts of London; bombs fell there today. From what I saw I am convinced that the Germans were after military objectives. Hours of driving and walking, plus the production of innumerable passes, failed to secure admission to those military areas. Therefore, you will understand that I am talking now of the people and the damage done in civilian areas. Bombs behaved in a most unpredictable manner. Several fell in a working-class district – cheap flimsy houses jammed one against the other. One tenant had constructed a sort of lean-to and in it he had a bathroom. That pitiful little bathroom had been sheared away from the house as though by a giant meat cleaver. Windows had been blown in over a wide area, but the window just above the lean-to was intact. A red sponge was still in the soap dish.

[But] it's about the people I want to talk [tonight] – the little people who live in those little houses, who have no uniforms and get no decorations for bravery. Those men whose only uniform was a tin hat who were digging unexploded bombs out of the ground this afternoon. The two women who gossiped across the narrow strip of tired brown grass that separated their two houses – they didn't have to open their kitchen windows in order to converse. The glass had been blown out. The little man with a pipe in his mouth who walked up and looked at a bombed house and said, 'One fell there and all.' These people were calm and courageous. About an hour after the all clear had sounded men were sitting in deck chairs on their lawns reading the Sunday papers. The girls in light cheap dresses were strolling along the streets. There was no bravado, no loud voices, only a quiet acceptance of the situation. To me, these people were incredibly brave and calm. They are the unknown heroes of this war.

This afternoon I saw a military manoeuvre that I shall long remember. A company of women dressed in Royal Air Force blue, marching in close order. Most of them were girls with blonde hair and plenty of make-up. They marched well, right arms thrust forward and snapped smartly down after the fashion of the Guards. They swung through a gate into an aerodrome that had been bombed only a few hours before.

Some of them were probably frightened, but every head was up, the ranks were steady and most of them were smiling. They were the clerks, cooks and waitresses going on duty. I was told that members of the Women's Auxiliary Air Force were killed in that earlier raid.

After watching and talking with those people this afternoon, I am more than ever convinced that they are made of stern stuff. They can take what is coming – even the women with two or three children clustered about them were steady and business-like. A policeman showed me a German machine gun bullet he had picked up near his feet. He said, 'I was certainly frightened. Look at my hand, it's still shaking.' But it wasn't shaking and I doubt if it had been.

Now there is room for many opinions about the diplomatic, economic and military policy of the British Government. This country is still ruled by a class, in spite of Miss Dorothy Thompson's broadcast to this country the other night in which she informed Mr Churchill that he was the head of a socialist state. If the people who rule Britain are made of the same stuff as the little people I have seen today, if they understand the stuff of which the people who work with their hands are made, if they trust them, then the defence of Britain will be something of which men will speak with awe and admiration so long as the English language survives. Politicians have repeatedly called this a people's war. These people deserve well of their leaders.

(Edward Murrow, CBS Broadcast to the US from London,
00.07 BST, 19 August 1940)

The white cliffs

I have loved England, dearly and deeply,
Since that first morning, shining and pure,
The white cliffs of Dover I saw rising steeply
Out of the sea that once made her secure.

I had no thought then of husband or lover,
I was a traveller, the guest of a week;
Yet when they pointed 'the white cliffs of Dover',
Startled I found there were tears on my cheek.

I have loved England, and still as a stranger,
Here is my home and I still am alone.
Now in her hour of trial and danger,
Only the English are really her own.

(Alice Duer Miller, *The White Cliffs*, Methuen, 1941)

Women

There are in the world today not only men fighting in planes but women behind them, if not literally then figuratively, in the back cockpits. Women who love and watch and wait eternally.

(Anne Morrow Lindbergh, Preface, *The Steep Ascent*,
Chatto & Windus, 1945)

Virtuoso before a microphone

On Sunday nights the BBC had a forum often used by Churchill or other national figures. Called the 'Postscript to the Nine O'clock News', it was listened to on every ship at sea, in every army encampment, and in every home in the country. The Prime Minister was a virtuoso when he sat before a microphone. If he said something funny, you could hear him chuckling, and the chuckle was infectious. When he referred to Hitler, there was loathing and contempt in his voice, and always there was his dogged confidence that communicated itself to the millions of listeners. One Sunday night I was in a noisy Fleet Street pub as the 'Postscript' came on. The place fell silent as Churchill began to speak. I watched the faces of the listeners. It has been said that the man in the pub is England herself. At that moment, certainly, the idea did not seem strained. All eyes were glued on the loudspeaker, almost as if the listeners believed that by concentrating they could see Churchill's face. 'Little does Hitler know the spirit of the British nation,' the familiar voice rasped, and each man seemed to tighten his jaw. One of Churchill's secrets was that he never talked down. He often used extraordinary language, but only to create verbal images that anyone could understand. As I listened to him and watched his rapt audience, I realized that England had the leader that France had lacked. Churchill was not only speaking to his people; he was speaking for them. When he finished with the thought that the Old World and the New would eventually join hands to rebuild the temples of man's freedom and man's honour, the pub rang with enthusiastic yells – from an audience that was half blasé reporters and editors and half truck drivers and shopkeepers.

'I don't know how in hell we're going to win this war,' Frank Owen of the *Evening Standard* told me after the cheering died down, 'but if the Old Man says we can, I guess we can.'

When Colebaugh* got a story from me entitled 'England Can't Lose', he cabled: YOU ARE PROBABLY CRAZY BUT CALL SHOTS AS YOU SEE THEM. WE WILL PRINT EVERYTHING YOU WRITE. And *Collier's* continued to do so, in spite of the sometimes abusive letters it received from its readers.

(Quentin Reynolds, By Quentin Reynolds, Heinemann, 1964)

Special 'Sailor'

There were four squadrons of fighter planes at the base I visited, and, of the squadron leaders, the one who immediately stood out for me and became the central figure of my story was A. G. Malan, a South African called 'Sailor' because he had spent most of his short life as a seaman. Six months later, after the worst of the Channel fighting was over, Sailor Malan was generally acknowledged to be the greatest of all RAF fighter pilots. Much later, when the American Eighth Air Force came to England, they borrowed Sailor as an instructor. When I met him he was still just another squadron leader, though with an enviable record of twelve enemy planes shot down. At thirty, he was older than the other pilots, but it was not simply his seniority that made the younger men look up to him. There was something compelling about the stocky South African's calmness. He

---

* Editor of *Colliers*.

was almost phlegmatic. My first revealing experience with him was in the matter of some books. I had half a dozen paperback mysteries in my bag and I asked Malan if he would like to borrow a couple of them. 'No, thanks,' he said, then added, 'I've never read a book in my life for pleasure. To enjoy reading, it seems to me a man requires a lot of imagination. I have no imagination at all. Maybe that's why I'm still alive.'

He had pitched me a curve. I asked him what he meant.

'When you're up there fighting, you've got to be realistic,' he said, 'and when you come back, you've got to put it all out of your mind. A lot of these youngsters go to bed at night and refight the scrambles. Thank God I'm not the worrying kind. They're the first to go.'

I soon found that Malan's simple division of the pilots into the worriers and the non-worriers was not enough. Some were exuberant believers in the idea that 'The Jerries may get everyone else but they'll never get me.' Others knew that the death rate in the RAF was high and felt that they had virtually written themselves off by joining up. It was this group that went to the village pubs at night to drink quietly, a bit sullenly. Some of the pilots felt a fierce hatred towards the Germans. Others looked with detachment upon the dirty business of killing them. Each time I talked with another of these men, I found a new combination of the basic attitudes that in effect made him a special case. Malan was simply more special than the rest.

(Quentin Reynolds, *By Quentin Reynolds*, Heinemann, 1964)

> I am American bred
> I have seen much to hate here – much to forgive,
>   But in a world where England is finished and dead,
> I do not wish to live.
> (Alice Duer Miller, *The White Cliffs*, Methuen, 1941)

Before Pearl Harbor

On this day the first of a small but select and highly colourful band of Americans reached an operational Fighter Command unit with the arrival of Pilot Officer W. M. L. Fiske on 601 Squadron at Tangmere. This was an extraordinary group of young men, who had travelled all manner of strange and often exciting routes to find themselves dressed in Air Force blue and wearing the thin sleeve band of Pilot Officer's rank and the RAF's pilot brevet. Some were accomplished pilots, others possessed no more experience than that which Training Command had been able to give them; but those American pilots – volunteers as they were – possessed no less determination to fight Nazi Germany than their British colleagues. They were universally popular on the squadrons –

affectionately being regarded as considerably larger than life! Of the seven who fought with Fighter Command during the Battle, six were to lose their lives in the defence of Britain.*

(Francis K. Mason, Battle over Britain, McWhirter Twins, 1969)

Billy Fiske

Pilot Officer William Meade Lindsley Fiske, RAF, an American citizen, who died that England might live.

(Inscription on the plaque erected in Fiske's memory
in St Paul's Cathedral. Ed.)

[On 16 August] a warning was received in the control room at Tangmere that a large number of enemy bombers and fighters were approaching the aerodrome at a height of twenty thousand feet.

601 Squadron at once took off to engage them. And the action that was fought high above the aerodrome was one of the fiercest that took place during that autumn of fierce actions.

Billy, in the thick of it, got an incendiary bullet through his petrol tank which immediately exploded it. His plane caught fire; with smoke and flames pouring from the engine and the cockpit become a blazing inferno, he yet managed to keep sufficient control to bring it down and crash-land on a corner of the aerodrome.

Terribly burned, his spirit remained unbeaten; when the ambulance party reached him he was trying to climb out of the burning wreckage on legs which were charred to the bone. He died in hospital twelve hours later, having remained conscious for long enough to grin at his wife in his own inimitable way.

They buried him in a country churchyard from which you can see the planes land and take off from the aerodrome on which he died; his friends in the squadron felt that this was the spot which he himself would have chosen. And in the crypt of St Paul's Cathedral on 4 July 1941, anniversary of American Independence Day, a marble tablet dedicated to his memory was unveiled by Sir Archibald Sinclair, Minister of Air, in the presence of the American Ambassador and a host of British and American people who had gathered to pay homage to the first American pilot to be killed while fighting voluntarily for Britain.

(Derek Tangye, Went the Day Well, Harrap, 1942)

---

* Apart from Pilot Officer 'Billy' Fiske (who died of wounds on 17 August 1940), the other American pilots were Pilot Officer A. G. Donahue, DFC (64 Squadron, killed since the Battle); Pilot Officer J. K. Haviland, DFC (151 Squadron, survives); Pilot Officer V. C. ('Shorty') Keogh (609 Squadron, killed since Battle); Pilot Officer P. H. Deckrone (616 Squadron, killed since Battle); Pilot Officer A. ('Andy') Mamedoff (609 Squadron, killed since the Battle); Pilot Officer Q. ('Red') Tobin (609 Squadron, killed since the Battle).

There had been talk in the early summer of 1940 that William Mead Lindsley Fiske III, of London, a popular transplanted American sportsman with a number of highly placed British friends, might head up an interceptor squadron of US pilots if one were formed. Fiske, the son of an international banker living in Paris, was a scratch golfer at Cambridge, had set a record for the Cresta bobsled run at Saint-Moritz, and had captained the team that won the Olympic bobsled championship at Lake Placid, New York, in the early 1930s. At the age of nineteen, he had driven the first Stutz car to be entered in the twenty-four hour race at Le Mans.

'Billy Fiske should have been our first squadron leader, and it had all been arranged with the Air Ministry,' Bobby Sweeny recounted. 'Unfortunately, he was killed – the first American to die in active service against the Nazis.'

Charles Sweeny* agreed: 'Undoubtedly, Billy Fiske had all the qualities of leadership which would have made him an outstanding officer if he had lived. I talked over with him my ideas for an Eagle Squadron and he was very receptive.'

(Vern Haugland, *The Eagle Squadrons: Yanks in the RAF, 1940–1942*, Ziff-Davis Flying Books, New York, 1979)

US Eagles' sacrifice

Lord, hold them in thy mighty hand
Above the ocean and the land
Like wings of Eagles mounting high
Along the pathways of the sky.

Immortal is the name they bear
And high the honour that they share.
Until a thousand years have rolled,
Their deeds of valour shall be told.

In dark of night and light of day
God speed and bless them on their way.
And homeward safely guide each one
With glory gained and duty done.

(Anonymous)

---

* Founder, with his brother, Bobby, of the three US Eagle Squadrons in the Royal Air Force in the summer and autumn of 1940. As Vern Haugland has written: 'The 240 US pilots who enrolled as Eagles . . . did so voluntarily, determined to fight and fly in a war that was not really their own . . . One Eagle in every three did not live to see the United States again . . .' Ed.

THE WAY IT WAS . . .

1. *With the replacement CO*

. . . The mere fact that you had a lot of flying hours under your belt, all of which had been done in peacetime or in Training Command, didn't qualify you to lead a fighter squadron right in the middle of the Battle of Britain. We had an awful lot of experienced pilots, but not many experienced *fighter* pilots.

There was a very nice chap who came to take over our squadron. One of the first mornings he came down to dispersal, he had some oil on the sleeve of his tunic. He got a rag, dipped it in some 100-octane fuel and rubbed it on the sleeve of his tunic to get the oil off. He then lit a cigarette and, of course, burst into flames. He had to be carried off to hospital, so I became acting CO of the squadron, though only a flight lieutenant.

I led the squadron for two or three weeks and then we got another CO, a squadron leader who had a decoration for activity on the Northwest Frontier in India. His operational experience was chasing Pathan tribesmen in that part of the world. He'd dropped notes on villages where people had misbehaved, saying, 'We're going to bomb you rotters at twelve o'clock on Tuesday. So get the hell out.' And then at twelve o'clock on Tuesday, they'd drop a couple of bombs and afterward the people would go back and carry on as before. That was the operational experience of our new CO. He decided to fly on my wing for a few days for experience. On the second flight, he was shot down. Not killed – the bullet came up through the floor of his cockpit, took skin off his ankles, the inside of his knees and the tip of his tool, the tip of his nose, and went out through the top. So I continued as CO.

Two or three weeks later, we got another CO, a very nice chap who had lots of flying hours under his belt but only as a flying instructor. He also flew as my number two to get the hang of it. He was shot down, too, off my wing tip, his third or fourth flight. So I continued as CO until I was shot down.

(Flight Lieutenant [later Group Captain] Brian Kingcome)

2. *With the Spitfire spares*

Westhampnett, the satellite field where we landed when we came south from Scotland in mid-August, was just three large fields knocked into one. There were no airfield buildings at all on it. The place still looked like three fields . . .

We'd been told we were coming south for only a short period, so we hadn't brought much stores with us. It was a blow when the station commander at Tangmere, who was in charge of Westhampnett, too, came across to see me and said, 'By the way, I hope you brought plenty of stores with you. We've got nothing but Hurricane squadrons so we don't

ver in the field of human conflict was so much owed by so many to one man. The Honorary Air
mmodore of 615 (County of Surrey) Squadron, Auxiliary Air Force

Above left Field Marshal and Master Tactician: Luftwaffe's Albert Kesselring, C-in-C of Luftflotte 2 and Werner Mölders, *Kommodore* of *Jagdgeswader* 51, at the Channel coast, July 1940. *Right* Adolf Galland, exceptional *Kommodore* of *Jagdgeswader* 26; Göring would in time promote him to be General of the Fighters

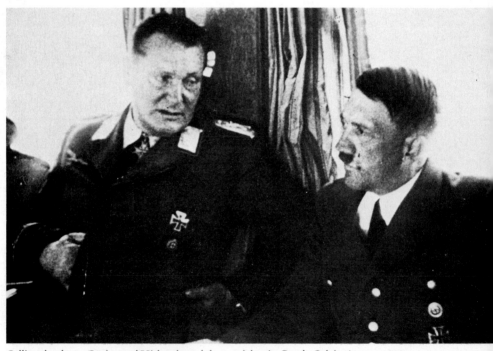

Calling the shots: Göring and Hitler aboard the special train, Pas de Calais, August 1940

ove left Sector Commander, Duxford, briefing the Secretary of State. Wing Commander A.B. Woodhall
th Sir Archibald Sinclair, autumn, 1940. *Right* Air Vice-Marshal and Flight Lieutenant: W. Sholto
ouglas, Deputy Chief of the Air Staff, with Brian Kingcome, acting CO of 92 Squadron

ecision makers: Air Council in session — facing camera left to right: Captain Harold Balfour,
nder-Secretary of State, Sir Archibald Sinclair and Air Chief Marshal Sir Cyril Newall, Chief of the Air
aff

Right Director of
Plans, Air Ministry,
1940: (then) Air
Commodore J.C.
Slessor, later CAS

Far right
Outstanding staff
officer: (then) Air
Vice-Marshal D.C.S.
(Strath) Evill, Senior
Air Staff Officer,
Fighter Command
HQ

Below Big Wing
champion: (then) Air
Vice-Marshal
Trafford
Leigh-Mallory,
AOC, 12 Group,
during the Battle. He
would become
AOC-in-C, Fighter
Command after
Sholto Douglas

Above Rugged Wing and
Station Commander: Wir
Commander Harry
Broadhurst, on the way u
Left Winner of the tactica
battle: Air Vice-Marshal
Keith Park, Air Officer
Commanding, 11 Group,
keeping in touch

mily victors: dynamic father, courageous son – Lord Beaverbrook, Minister of Aircraft Production, and e Hon Max Aitken, CO of 601 (County of London) Squadron

termath of triumph: Air Chief Marshal Sir Hugh (later Lord) Dowding (centre in civilian clothes), C-in-C o shaped the victory, with some of the Few

Left Fleet Street's Battle pin-up: Harbourne M. Stephen, Volunteer Reservist, with a wartime tally of 23 enemy aircraft destroyed, became managing director of the *Daily Telegraph*

Below Glittering New Zealand star and stalwart: Alan C. Deere, natural leader, who rose to head the Biggin Hill Wing

Above Scottish auxiliary: A.V.R. (Sandy) Johnstone, spirited leader of the City of Glasgow's 602 Squadron

Right Battle immortal and one of the best shots in the business: the irrepressible Robert Stanford Tuck – Bob Tuck to one and all – CO of 257 Squadron

Left Born to fly and to lead: Michael Robinson, flight commander of 601 and then CO of 609, who was later to fall leading the Biggin Wing

Below left Colin Gray, New Zealand maestro, of 54 Squadron. He and his compatriot, Al Deere, achieved, between them, a battle total of more than 30 aircraft destroyed

Below Genius from Cape Province: Piet ('Dutch') Hugo, who combined with 'Sailor' Malan, Fighter Command's most successful leader (*see front cover*), to head South Africa's contributors to victory

ith a 'First' in classics, scholar, essayist and poet, David Scott-Malden, made his mark with 603 (City of inburgh) Squadron before advancing to lead the Norwegians' North Weald Wing

Below left Etonian leader, Michael Crossley, who blended 32 Squadron's Polish, Czech, Belgian and British mix into one of the Battle's most successful units. *Below right* United States' trio who made Britain's cause theirs: Pilot Officers Gene Tobin of Los Angeles, Andrew Mamedoff of Connecticut and Vernon Keough of Brooklyn

Douglas Bader (third from right, hands in pockets), controversial leader of 242 (Canadian) Squadron. Pilot Officer (later Air Marshal Sir Denis) Crowley-Milling (extreme left) and Flying Officer (later Group Captain) Stanley Turner (third from left) all became successful leaders

Duxford Sector, September, 1940: 616 (South Yorkshire) Squadron at 30 minutes. Hugh Dundas (left) would soon become a flight commander

Below Dogs were a feature of squadron life – not least of 92: the masters here were Pilot Officers Bob Holland (left) and Tommy Lund (right)

Foot The unrelenting story: pilots at five minutes' readiness at Biggin Hill, autumn 1940

Top Medway scramblers: Hurricanes of 501 (County of Gloucester) Squadron airborne from Gravesend. Sergeant J.H. ('Ginger') Lacey was the Squadron's star. *Above* Playing the tables: plotters at work in Fighter Command's HQ Operations Room, Stanmore, Middlesex

p Hornchurch Sector, 15 September, 1940. 'Trebble Two's' Spitfire 1A's scramble. *Above* One confirmed
stroyed! Dornier 17Z half-a-mile east of Biggin Hill: the crew were made prisoners of war

Germany expects: Reichsmarschall Hermann Göring gives it to the JU 88 crews straight, Northern France, September 1940

Serviceable! Messerschmitt 109E being run up, Wissant, September, 1940

allmarks of success: starred German trinity — Major Lutzow, Hauptmann Balthasar and Leutnant Troha,
s de Calais, October 1940

left Fatal switch! 7
September, 1940: German
High Command turns away
from the airfields and goes for
London's docks

below left London can take it!
People prepare for the night in
the Underground

right St. Paul's rises above the
City's flames. 30 September
1940

below Manchester's turn:
King George VI, with
Herbert Morrison, Home
Secretary, at his side and the
Queen following, sees for
himself, autumn, 1940

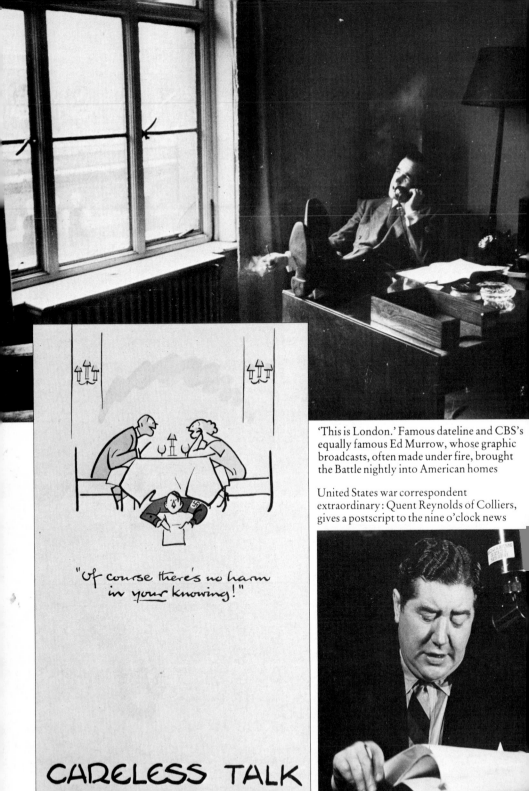

'This is London.' Famous dateline and CBS's equally famous Ed Murrow, whose graphic broadcasts, often made under fire, brought the Battle nightly into American homes

United States war correspondent extraordinary: Quent Reynolds of Colliers, gives a postscript to the nine o'clock news

"Of course there's no harm in *your* knowing!"

CARELESS TALK COSTS LIVES

No comment!

carry any Spitfire spares.' Middle Wallop was the nearest airfield that had Spitfires operating from it. I rang the Sector commander, a chap named Roberts, and told him our predicament. I asked him if he could let us have a few spares to keep us going. He said, 'Certainly. Send over a lorry and we'll see what we can do for you.' We were jolly busy and I couldn't spare an officer so I picked a young corporal, Murphy, by name, a tough little Glasgow keelie, and three other chaps, and sent them over, with Murphy in charge. It was the first time he'd been in charge of anything. He was cock-a-hoop.

I gave them strict instructions. They were not to dally. They were to get there, make themselves known, get as much spares as they could, and come straight back. They were two miles short of the airfield at Middle Wallop when it came under attack. They suddenly saw the German aircraft diving on the field. Murphy stopped the lorry and got all his chaps out and into a ditch. A Messerschmitt 110 flashed over their heads, on fire, and disappeared over a hill and crashed. Suddenly, they saw a parachute coming down close to them. They rushed over, collared the German, tied him up, and put him in the back of the lorry . . .

[Then] . . . a sergeant appeared, took charge of the prisoner, locked him up in the cells, and told our fellows how to get to the equipment station.

They drove off with fires going on all around them, backed [the lorry] up to the stores section and, just as at the guardroom, found that all the senior people had gone off to help. They had left the place in charge of a couple of inexperienced airmen who didn't know our fellows weren't from their station. When they heard they'd come for Spitfire spares, they began bundling the stuff out. We got enough stuff almost to build two new Spitfires, including wings and everything. We were delighted. When I rang up Roberts to thank him, he said, 'What for?' I said, 'All this stuff you gave us.' He was amazed. Nobody in charge had even known Murphy had been there.

(Squadron Leader [later Air Vice-Marshal] A. V. R. [Sandy] Johnstone)

FIGHTING ALLIES

I must confess that I had been a little doubtful of the effect which their experience in their own countries and in France might have had upon the Polish and Czech pilots, but my doubts were soon laid to rest, because all three Squadrons swung [into] the fight with a dash and enthusiasm which is beyond praise. They were inspired by a burning hatred for the Germans which made them very deadly opponents.

(Air Chief Marshal Sir Hugh Dowding, Battle of Britain Despatch, 20 August 1941)

Honoured Czech

The outstanding fighter pilot on the British side in 1940 was a member of 303 (Polish) Squadron; he was a Czech, Sergeant Pilot Josef Frantisek.

> (Wing Commander H. R. [Dizzy] Allen, *Fighter Squadron: A Memoir, 1940–42*, William Kimber, 1979)

One of our best pilots was Sergeant (Pilot) Frantisek, who had patented a special tactic of his own. After the first onslaught by the whole squadron, he would profit by the confusion to slip away and hang about over Dover, where he kept a patient vigil for homeward-bound raiders. There were always a few of these – planes which had run out of ammunition or (were) short of fuel. He placidly put paid to them. The CO kept telling him off for breaking formation, but Frantisek went on adding the black crosses to his scoreboard.

> (Jean Zumbach, *On Wings of War: My Life as a Pilot Adventurer*, André Deutsch, London, 1975)

Josef Frantisek was the son of a carpenter and car-body repairer in Otaslavice, near Prostejov in Moravia. From childhood his interest was in motor cars. This led him to an engineering apprenticeship and he qualified as a mechanic. Immediately afterwards, he joined the Czechoslovak Air Force as a student pilot. After qualifying he was posted to 5 Squadron of the 2nd Air Regiment in Olomouc.

Lance Corporal Frantisek was a good looking, pleasant young man. He was particular about his dress and his personal appearance. He laughed heartily and was a friendly man. He did not like discipline, but he loved flying. He lived his life to the full and he was often absent from military barracks when he should have been in his billet. His many friends covered up for him, but this did not always stop him from being reported as a defaulter.

The real problem for Frantisek was his friendship with another pilot named Kokes. People tended to tease Kokes because he was so short of stature. They called him names like 'Small Beer'. This greatly annoyed Frantisek and it led to fights, often involving a crowd in a pub. It was all the same to him whether he faced one or twenty opponents – he would fight, disregarding danger or damage. His CO warned him that this might lose him his lowly rank or even cause grounding. Josef wasn't bothered about the prospects of demotion, but permanent grounding was something else.

When a new CO took over he called the eternal lance corporal in and said: 'Frantisek, I command you to stop being a lance corporal and become corporal!' He added an aside which surprised the young pilot. 'For Christ's sake at least behave for six weeks so I can promote you.' Josef came sharply to attention. 'Understood, sir,' he said, saluting smartly.

When Frantisek came to England in 1940, he travelled mainly with Poles. The Czechoslovak Air Force didn't reclaim him so he flew with 303, the Polish fighter squadron, in the Battle of Britain. The environment of the brave and generous Poles was greatly stimulating. After warnings from the considerate CO about leaving the squadron to attack by himself, he eventually came to be regarded as a kind of guest performer with the right to hunt on his own.

He was a brilliant pilot and marksman. His ability to shoot from an angle and altitude was matched by his thirst for combat. His victories mounted. When he was killed, aged twenty-seven, on 8 October 1940, in a mysterious landing accident, he had shot down 17 enemy aircraft during twenty-seven days' operations with 303. Some Polish and British sources claim that to this total should be added the 10 or 11 aircraft he was believed to have shot down during the fighting in France.

Once Josef Frantisek decided to serve with the Poles, he did not wish to change, but he was never a renegade; he did not become alienated from his own country. The squadron respected him for it.

His name is at the top of the pilots who fought for the freedom of the Czechoslovak Republic. Granted, posthumously, the rank of flying officer, Frantisek will always be the pride of Czechoslovak military aviation.

(Frantisek Fajtl, *Vzpominky na Padlé Kamarády*, Mlada fronta edice Třináct, Prague, 1980)

Dammit, Sir, hardly cricket!

At Elham [in south-east Kent], a burning Hurricane flew low down the valley and suddenly flicked on its back, allowing the pilot to drop out and open his parachute. Arthur Wootten said 'It was one of the neatest things I've ever seen.' The pilot hit the ground heavily in a cornfield at Ottinge, the silk canopy settling over the prostrate figure. After a pause, the hump sprang into life and a flailing man, cursing in Polish, struggled to get into the sunlight. Being Sunday, people appeared very quickly until there were about a hundred attending the tall Pole who spoke very little English and gesticulated wildly in an endeavour to explain that he'd baled out over the district the previous day. When a car came to take him back to Hawkinge, the local people formed a passage for him to reach the car and spontaneous clapping broke out – just as if he were a batsman returning to the pavilion after a spirited innings.

(Dennis Knight, *Harvest of Messerschmitts: The Chronicle of a Village at War*, Frederick Warne)

THE CRITICAL SHORTAGE

I was worried daily from July to September by a chronic shortage of trained fighter pilots and it was not until the battle was nearly lost that Air Staff of the Air Ministry assisted by borrowing pilots from Bomber Command and from the Royal Navy. Incidently, in December 1940 when I was posted to Flying Training Command, I found that the flying schools were working at only two-thirds capacity and were following peace-time routines being quite unaware of the grave shortage of pilots in Fighter Command.

Finally, when the German Air Force had concentrated on bombing my fighter aerodromes, I could get such little help from Air Ministry to repair the bomb damage that I had to borrow some thousands of troops from the British Army to fill in the bomb craters to keep the aerodromes serviceable. For doing so I was severely criticized by the Air Ministry at the time for accepting Army assistance. Had my fighter aerodromes been put out of action, the German Air Force would have won the battle by 15 September 1940.

(Air Vice-Marshal Keith Park, *The Battle of Britain*, Icare, Paris, 1965)

THE FLEET AIR ARM'S PART

I lost my first young pilot on 20 August – Midshipman Patterson, shot down into the sea on a convoy patrol. With Fighter Command short of pilots in the frantic build-up after Dunkirk, the Royal Navy seconded to us fighter pilots from the Fleet Air Arm. They were without exception well-trained, disciplined and great characters. I had three in 242 Squadron – Midshipman Patterson, and Sub-Lieutenants Cork and Gardner. The first two were RN while Jimmy Gardner (the sole survivor of the war) was 'Wavy-Navy' (RNVR). The part played by pilots of the Royal Navy in the Battle of Britain is never forgotten by the rest of us.

Dickie Cork ... flew alongside me throughout ... [this] period. Towards the end of the battle, he was awarded the Distinguished Flying Cross, the first naval pilot to be so decorated. We received the usual telegram from the Air Ministry to the effect that His Majesty the King, on the recommendation of the Commander-in-Chief, had been graciously pleased to award the Distinguished Flying Cross to Sub-Lieutenant R. Cork, RN. We celebrated, and pinned the ribbon on his chest. A couple of days later a second telegram was received, this time from the Admiralty. It said: 'For Distinguished Flying Cross read Distinguished Service Cross.' The latter is the Royal Navy's equivalent to the Army's Military Cross (MC) and the Royal Air Force's DFC. Through the proper channels we firmly expressed non-comprehension. The King had given him the DFC;

only His Majesty could change it. Corky continued to wear his DFC. While this exchange continued, we received a visit from the Air Minister, Sir Archibald Sinclair, to whom we told our tale. He assured us of his support, declaring that we were absolutely right.

After the Battle of Britain, Dickie Cork and Jimmy Gardner (our splendid 'Wavy Navy' pilot) were posted back to a Fleet Air Arm unit at Barrow-in-Furness. During his time with us Corky had acquired four buttons from the tunics of fellow pilots in the Duxford Wing. These he wore as the left row of his double-breasted naval tunic. From top to bottom they were an RAF button, a Royal Canadian Air Force button, a Czech Air Force button, and a Polish Air Force button. The last named was in silver and particularly conspicuous, as all the rest on his tunic were golden.

A week or so after his departure, Corky flew in to see us. As he walked towards us we noticed with horror that he was properly dressed, and worse still he was wearing the ribbon of the DSC instead of our DFC.

He told us that soon after his arrival at Barrow, he encountered an Admiral whom he saluted, intending to pass on. The Admiral stopped him, pointed at the purple and white diagonal stripes of his DFC ribbon and asked, 'What's that?' Respectfully, Sub-Lieutenant Cork told him. The Admiral's gaze shifted to his tunic with its row of exotic buttons. His face suffused, then became empurpled. There was, Corky assured us, 'an unparalleled scene'. Since then he had been correctly dressed as an officer of the Royal Navy.

The last time I saw him was in the summer of 1941 at Tangmere. He had flown in with a bearded friend called 'Butch'. The Tangmere Wing was due over northern France two hours later. We put them each in a Spitfire and took them with us. Like old times, Corky flew alongside me.

Dickie Cork died later in an accident at night over Trincomalee (Sri Lanka). In his confidential report when he left 242 Squadron I had written: 'He is one of the finest young officers I have ever known.'

(Douglas Bader, *Fight for the Sky*, Sidgwick & Jackson, 1973)

FOR JOHNNY

Do not despair
For Johnny-head-in-air;
He sleeps as sound
As Johnny underground.

Fetch out no shroud
For Johnny-in-the-cloud;
And keep your tears
For him in after years.

Better by far
For Johnny-the-bright-star,
To keep your head,
And see his children fed.

(John Pudney)

BATTLE INTERLUDE:
DAVID NIVEN AND 'THE WAAF'

We were having a late supper on the balcony of the Café de Paris . . . I stared gloomily down on the dancers . . .

Suddenly, the orchestra leader stopped the music and Poulsen, the owner, stepped forward . . . 'Ladies and gentlemen, in case anyone is interested, the air raid warning just sounded.' Such was the effect . . . that this announcement was greeted with cheers, hunting cries and cat-calls . . . in ten seconds it was forgotten.

Less than a year later . . . a bomb shrieked through the roof and exploded on the dance floor, killing Poulsen, nearly all the orchestra and a tragic percentage of the dancers . . .

David [Kelburn] got up to speak to some friends and I was left looking jealously at a table of RAF pilots and their girls immediately below me. Although I was sitting unobtrusively in the balcony, they noticed me and raised their glasses, perhaps mockingly, perhaps not, but I was so self-conscious about the blaring publicity of my arrival in the country that I preferred not to speculate. One girl had her back to me. She, too, was in the powder-blue uniform of the RAF. She turned and looked up. Long blonde hair fell away and I found myself gazing into a face of such beauty and such sweetness that I just stared blankly back.

Her complexion was so perfect that the inevitable description, 'English Rose', would have been an insult. Her eyes were the merriest and the bluest I had ever seen. She looked at me for a long moment and when she got up to dance, I saw that she was tall with a divinely willowy figure.

I had a funny feeling that I would never forget her and in my mind, she became marked down as 'the WAAF'. . . .

The Battle of Britain was now in full swing as Göring tried to break the back of the RAF as a prelude to invasion . . .

London was being heavily bombed and moves were made to take the minds of the civilians off their increasing discomfort. At the National Gallery, for instance, as an inducement to relax and forget what was happening over one's head, eminent musicians gave free lunch-time concerts.

I took advantage of this and one day, I walked there from the War Office and wandered round a couple of galleries. From a third, I heard a cello being played by an expert. I watched her complete concentration and bathed myself in the haunting sounds for several minutes before I realized that a few feet away, and totally engrossed, stood – 'the WAAF'.

Almost guiltily, I stared at her. At close quarters and under the overhead lighting of the gallery she was even more beautiful than I had remembered and so sweet looking and gentle.

When the music ended she did not move: she stood quite still, lost in the beauty of what she had heard. People applauded and the cellist picked up her things and left. Still the WAAF did not move. When there was only two of us left in the gallery, she looked up and noticed me.

'Hello,' she said, 'wasn't that wonderful?'

I persuaded her to have a sandwich with me at a nearby coffee shop . . . we were both on the point of being late back to work.

I discovered her name, the fact that she was the cypher clerk at the RAF Reconnaissance Squadron at Heston just outside London and that she was billeted on a family friend who lived in the middle of Regent's Park.

There was never a shadow of doubt in my mind that this was the one, but with the whole world flying apart at the seams, there was no time for the niceties of a prolonged courtship. That night I called at the house in Regent's Park and passed in a note saying that I was outside the door, was considering buying the Park from the King and would like some advice on the dredging of the lake.

She appeared giggling deliciously and invited me in.

Two days later I was invited to luncheon to meet her mother and by the end of the week, I found myself shaking and sweating and being introduced to her father who lived apart. My mission was to persuade him to allow his daughter to become my wife.

Bill Rollo was an angel. Nobody has ever been able to say a word against him and this despite the fact that he was a famous divorce lawyer.

When I met him he was, though over fifty, also in the uniform of the RAF . . . on his chest an impressive row of ribbons from World War I.

He worked all day at his law office and did night duty in a special war room where on a wall map the Prime Minister could see at a glance the latest disposition of flotillas, brigades and squadrons.

He protested mightily: 'But, Primmie darling, you *can't* put me in this position because I don't know how to behave!'

'Don't be nervous, papa,' said she, 'leave everything to us.'

He handed me an enormous drink and helped himself liberally. 'Oh, God!' he said, 'this is agony, isn't it? I ought to ask you all sorts of questions . . . Do you have any prospects? . . . Well, that's bloody silly for a start because the air raid warning has just gone.'

It was the night of a particularly heavy 'blitz' and bombs were soon raining down. It had been arranged that we would go out to dinner but there was so much shrapnel flying about that we decided against it.

'I can't think why you want to marry her,' said Bill, 'she can't cook and she can't sew.'

'You're a big help,' said his daughter.

We opened some wine, some cans of beans and some cheese and as a particularly heavy bombardment made the high old building shudder and sway, with the three of us huddling under the kitchen table, Bill Rollo gave his consent.*

(David Niven, *The Moon's a Balloon: Reminiscences*,
Hamish Hamilton, 1971)

THE ROMANTIC CHARTER†

I am not fighting for the Poles or Czechs,
    And only indirectly for the Rex –
I do not greatly love the Slav or Greek,
    I cannot bear the way Colonials speak –
I loathe efficiency and Nissen huts,
    And as for 'bonhomie', I hate its guts –
I am not fighting Germans just to get
    My democratic share of 'blood and sweat'.

        Dear Sir
                I feel that you may get the gist
Of all *my* WAR AIMS from the following list:

. . . Georgian houses, red replicas of heaven,
    Split pediments, breakfast at eleven,
Large white peonies in big glass bowls,
    Asparagus au beurre, whitebait in shoals,
Close cropped grass, huge trees and cawing rooks,
    A sunny breakfast room, a library with books,
Clean white housemaids in new print frocks,
    Coachmen turned chauffeur, footmen on the box,

* Six years, and two sons later, Primmie Niven, daughter of the Hon. William and Lady Kathleen Rollo, was dead – victim of a lethal fall in their home in Hollywood. The couple's friends were devastated. Ed.

† Ken Davison, the author of these lines, was a successful night fighter pilot (starting with Blenheims in 1940), a decorated officer and leader. He rose, in time, to command 85 (Mosquito) Squadron in 100 Group in support of Bomber Command's great night offensive against the Third Reich. His special talents pointed him, in peace, to the Royal Opera House and to the appointment of Organizing Secretary of the Friends of Covent Garden. This engaging piece of doggerel – a play upon The Atlantic Charter (The Romantic Charter!) – was read in High Places with a scowl, but in 10 Downing Street with a broadening smile. Ed.

Dinner parties all in evening dress,
   Glamorous women drenched in 'Mary Chess',
Charades and paper games, hot houses with heat on,
   Superficiality and Cecil Beaton –
Shrimps from Morecambe Bay, port that is tawny,
   Claret and Beaujolais, soles that are Mornay,
Hot scones for tea, thick cream, the smell of logs,
   Long country walks, thick shoes and spaniel dogs,
Ducks in the evening, swishing swans in flight,
   Fires in bedrooms flickering at night –
And of those 'autrefois' all those 'moeurs'
   Which are epitomised in 'Valse des Fleurs' –
Fresh shiny chintzes, an herbaceous border
   DEATH and DESTRUCTION
                to this damned
                   NEW ORDER.

                      (Ken Davison)

THAT INDEFINABLE QUALITY . . .

On 20 August, Douglas Bader's 'Big Wing' was scrambled to counter large enemy formations, but, like Drake with his bowls, the Wing Leader had found time to arrange a game of squash.

The masterful voice started firing comments over the RT with such assurance that pilots could not help feeling confident. His remarks, by design or accident, so often took the nervous sting out of the business ahead. . . . [This day], for instance, a lanky, nineteen-year-old boy called Cocky Dundas flew with the wing for the first time. Exactly a month earlier Dundas had been with 616 Squadron at Kenley; they were waiting at readiness for an evening visit from Winston Churchill when they had been scrambled and run into a flock of 109s over Kent. It was Dundas's first fight and a 109 had 'jumped' him, shot his controls to bits and put bullets in his engine and glycol tank. Smoke and glycol fumes filled the cockpit and he could not get his hood open. He spun out of control from 12,000 feet till finally he was able to jettison the hood and baled out at 800 feet, breaking his collar-bone at the same time. Now only two of the old pilots were left in the squadron, and Dundas, still shaken, shoulder still weak, was going back for more. They were scrambled in a great hurry and, being young and human, he had 'the twitch', dry mouth, butterflies in the stomach and thumping heart. Then in his ears as they climbed, that odd, legless leader's voice:

'Hey, Woody, I'm supposed to be playing squash with Peters in an hour's time. Ring him up, will you, and tell him I won't be back till later.'

(Dear God. Legless! Playing squash!)

Woodhall's voice: 'Never mind that now, Douglas, Vector one-nine-zero. Orbit North Weald. Angels twenty.'

'Oh, go on, Woody. Ring him up now.'

'Haven't got time, Douglas. There's a plot on the board heading for the coast.'

'Well, can't you make time? You're sitting in front of a row of phones. Pick up one and ring the chap.'

'All right. All right,' said the philosophical Woodhall. 'For the sake of peace and quiet I will. Now would you mind getting on with the war.'

Dundas flew on with lifted heart, like all the others.

(Paul Brickhill, *Reach for the Sky*, Collins, 1954)

The fortunes of war flow this way and that and no prudent fighter holds his enemy in contempt.

(Goethe)

DUMMY RUN

[Göring] . . . ordered the bomber squadrons to move against Britain in individual daylight operations. 'Impossible,' Sperrle objected. The monocled, big-boned, tough-looking Field-Marshal was no great friend of Göring. As a senior officer in the First World War he had once rebuked the exuberant fighter pilot, Lieutenant Göring, for an act of indiscipline. Göring could never forgive him; he always felt that Sperrle was still addressing the young lieutenant in him and not the senior Marshal of the Reich and Commander-in-Chief of the Luftwaffe. 'What's the matter? Why impossible?' he asked.

It took Sperrle, supported by Kesselring, only a few minutes to explain. Daylight raids in big style were impossible in the face of determined British defence. Owing to the limited fighter range, attacks would have to be restricted to targets near the coast. Göring, who had only a rudimentary knowledge of night operations and only a short personal experience of night flying, was not happy as he approved a switch to night operations which were started with an attack on Portsmouth. Two days later a raving Göring was calling his staff together. They came forward with great reluctance. His own ADC, Colonel Brauchitsch, kept away as long as he could. Göring was in a state of almost maniacal fury: 'Didn't I tell these fools,' he shouted. It appeared that the Luftwaffe's crack squadrons had unloaded their bombs on a dummy replica of Portsmouth harbour. The first major night operation was a complete flop.

(Willie Frischauer, *Göring*, Odhams Press, 1951)

THE BATTLE OF THE BARGES

Bomber Command steps in . . .

Meanwhile, although everything wasn't going dead according to plan for the Hun, he hadn't been exactly defeated in the air. No doubt Göring thought that in a few weeks' time we would come to our last reserves, and then Hitler could establish his headquarters in Buckingham Palace and the Marshal himself could take over the Savoy Hotel. In other words, the plans for the invasion of England were still on.

All the military strategists in Germany knew very well that the first thing on the programme was to obtain complete and absolute air superiority over the Channel ports. Then it would be possible to launch an invasion force, consisting of many thousands of 2,000-ton barges which would sail across one dark night, covered on either side by submarines, minesweepers and E-boats . . .

By the beginning of September unusual activity was noticed on the canals in Germany. Barges of all kinds began to make their way to most of the invasion ports; many of these were ocean-going barges with 200-horsepower engines, capable of ploughing through the seas at 10 knots. They were laden with high explosives, tanks, field- and anti-aircraft artillery; troops stood by in the dockyards, waiting for the order to set sail. Everything was ready. Every port from Antwerp to Dieppe was packed like lumber floating in a river with thousands of these invasion barges. The Huns knew, of course, that our meagre bomber force would attack them. Light flak guns were brought from far and wide to put up a cordon of steel which would ensure that no bombs could be dropped within miles; flak towers were erected, balloon barrages were put up . . .

[The raids] went on day and night, Blenheims, Hampdens, Wellingtons all taking part in low-level attacks which not only destroyed many barges on the spot, but also killed many troops whose billets were in the warehouses nearby.

On one of these raids on Antwerp I flew for a while alongside an aeroplane which was on fire. It was a nasty sight because I could see it was one of our own. As flames and sparks came out like the wrong end of a rocket hanging in the air, I saw one chap bale out and land in the river, and I remember hoping that he could swim.

When we got back I asked young O'Connor, a Canadian boy, what sort of a trip he had had. He did not say much except that he had caught fire over the target and had got hell from the light flak. Later, I heard that Hannah, of our squadron, had been awarded the VC for his attempt to stamp out the flames with his bare hands.

Two nights later we went again to Antwerp, and this city, with its heavy flak defences, shot down one of the few left. I saw him flying straight and level over one of the basins; taking his time about his run, making sure that all his bombs went into the right spot. Then he blew up – and Pitcairn-Hill had gone to join his forefathers . . .

These raids on the invasion ports were organized to destroy as many barges as possible. Each squadron was given a port which was to be considered its own particular port and the pet baby of all concerned; each crew was given a basin; in each basin there were so many barges, sometimes 200, sometimes even 400. . . .

After each raid a reconnaissance was made, and the CO would call all crews together.

'I have got some pictures of C Basin at Antwerp. Yesterday there were 400 barges there; today's reconnaissance shows 350. Who is on C Basin?'

Some pilot would shuffle to his feet.

'Well, you sank sixty, you and the rest, but that is not enough. You have got to put all your bombs in that basin, not a stick starting on the edge and then doing its job, but every single bomb. Otherwise those bastards over there are going to come and invade us and then you will have to fight with your bare hands . . .'

(Guy Gibson, VC, *Enemy Coast Ahead*, Michael Joseph, 1946;
Goodall Publications, 1986)

AIRCREW

Fighter trail etched white on blue
   Bomber pilot, seaplane crew;
These men, like Gods, though wrought as we
   Are brushed with immortality.
Their youth, not lost as years go by
   But grandly, in a moment – soaring high
Through conquered sky.

(Harold Balfour)

PROEM

September 3 dawned dark and overcast, with a slight breeze ruffling the waters of the Estuary. Hornchurch . . . wore its usual morning pallor of yellow fog, lending an added air of grimness to the dimly silhouetted Spitfires around the boundary. From time to time a balloon would poke its head grotesquely through the mist as though looking for possible victims before falling back like some tired monster.

We came out on to the tarmac at about eight o'clock . . . I was worried. We had been bombed a short time before, and my plane had been fitted out with a new cockpit hood. This hood unfortunately would not slide open along its groove; and with a depleted ground staff and no tools, I began to fear it never would. Unless it did open, I shouldn't be able to bale out in a hurry if I had to. Miraculously, 'Uncle George' Denholm, our Squadron Leader, produced three men with a heavy file and lubricating oil, and the corporal fitter and I set upon the hood in a fury of haste.

[By] . . . ten o'clock, when the mist had cleared and the sun was blazing out of a clear sky, the hood was still sticking firmly half-way along the groove; at ten-fifteen, what I had feared for the last hour happened. Down the loud-speaker came the emotionless voice of the controller: '603 Squadron take off and patrol base; you will receive further orders in the air: 603 Squadron take off as quickly as you can, please.'. . .

. . . Uncle George and the leading section took off in a cloud of dust; Brian Carbury looked across and put up his thumbs. I nodded and opened up, to take off for the last time from Hornchurch. I was flying No. 3 in Brian's section, with Stapme Stapleton on the right: the third section consisted of only two machines, so that our Squadron strength was eight. We headed south-east, climbing all out on a steady course. At about 12,000 feet we came up through the clouds: I looked down and saw them spread out below me like layers of whipped cream. The sun was brilliant and made it difficult to see even the next plane when turning. I was peering anxiously ahead, for the controller had given us warning of at least fifty enemy fighters approaching very high . . .

Then . . . I saw what I had been praying for – a Messerschmitt climbing and away from the sun. I closed in to 200 yards, and from slightly to one side gave him a two-second burst: fabric ripped off the wing and black smoke poured from the engine, but he did not go down. Like a fool, I did not break away, but put in another three-second burst . . .

At that moment, I felt a terrific explosion which knocked the control stick from my hand, and the whole machine quivered like a stricken animal. In a second, the cockpit was a mass of flames: instinctively, I reached up to open the hood. It would not move. I tore off my straps and managed to force it back; but this took time, and when I dropped back in to the seat and reached for the stick in an effort to turn the plane on its back, the heat was so intense that I could feel myself going. I remember a second of sharp agony, remember thinking 'So this is it!' and putting both hands to my eyes. Then I passed out.

When I regained consciousness I was free of the machine and falling rapidly. I pulled the rip-cord of my parachute and checked my descent with a jerk. Looking down, I saw that my left trouser leg was burnt off, that I was going to fall into the sea, and that the English coast was deplorably far away. About twenty feet above the water, I attempted to undo my parachute, failed, and flopped into the sea with it billowing round me. . . .

The water was not unwarm and I was pleasantly surprised to find that my life-jacket kept me afloat. I looked at my watch: it was not there. Then, for the first time, I noticed how burnt my hands were: down to the wrist, the skin was dead white and hung in shreds: I felt faintly sick from the smell of burnt flesh. By closing one eye I could see my lips, jutting out like motor tyres. The side of my parachute harness was cutting into me particularly painfully, so that I guessed my right hip was burnt. I made a further attempt to undo the harness, but owing to the pain of my hands, soon desisted. Instead, I lay back and reviewed my position: I was a long way from land; my hands were burnt, and so, judging from the pain of the sun, was my face; it was unlikely that anyone on shore had seen me come down and even more unlikely that a ship would come by; I could float for possibly four hours in my Mae West. I began to feel that I had perhaps been premature in considering myself lucky to have escaped from the machine. After about half an hour my teeth started chattering, and to quiet them I kept up a regular tuneless chant, varying it from time to time with calls for help. . . .

The water now seemed much colder and I noticed with surprise that the sun had gone in though my face was still burning. I looked down at my hands, and not seeing them, realized that I had gone blind. So I was going to die. It came to me like that – I was going to die, and I was not afraid. This realization came as a surprise. The manner of my approaching death appalled and horrified me, but the actual vision of death left me unafraid: I felt only a profound curiosity and a sense of satisfaction that within a few minutes or a few hours I was to learn the great answer. I decided that it should be in a few minutes. I had no qualms about hastening my end and, reaching up, I managed to unscrew the valve of my Mae West. The air escaped in a rush and my head went under water. It is said by people who have all but died in the sea that drowning is a pleasant death. I did not find it so. . . . I lay back exhausted, and then I started to laugh. By this time I was probably not entirely normal and I doubt if my laughter was wholly sane, but there was something irresistibly comical in my grand gesture of suicide being so simply thwarted. . . .

It is often said that a dying man re-lives his whole life in one rapid kaleidoscope. I merely thought gloomily of the Squadron returning, of my mother at home, and of the few people who would miss me. Outside my family, I could count them on the fingers of one hand. . . .

. . . I took it for granted that I must soon become delirious, and I attempted to hasten the process: I encouraged my mind to wander vaguely and aimlessly, with the result that I did experience a certain peace. But when I forced myself to think of something concrete, I found that I was still only too lucid. I went on shuttling between the two with varying success until I was picked up. I remember as in a dream hearing somebody shout: it seemed so far away and quite unconnected with me. . . .

Then willing arms were dragging me over the side; my parachute was taken off. A brandy flask was pushed between my swollen lips; a voice said, 'OK, Joe, it's one of ours and still kicking'; and I was safe. I was neither relieved nor angry: I was past caring.

It was to the Margate lifeboat that I owed my rescue. We were then fifteen miles east of [its base] . . .

While in the water I had been numb and had felt very little pain. Now that I began to thaw out, the agony was such that I could have cried out. The good fellows made me as comfortable as possible, put up some sort of awning to keep the sun from my face, and phoned through for a doctor. It seemed to me to take an eternity to reach shore. I was put into an ambulance and driven rapidly to hospital. Through all this I was quite conscious, though unable to see. At the hospital they cut off my uniform, I gave the requisite information to a nurse about my next of kin, and then, to my infinite relief, felt a hyperdermic syringe pushed into my arm.

(Richard Hillary*, *The Last Enemy*, Macmillan 1942)

Was it so hard, Achilles,
So very hard to die?
Thou knowest and I know not –
So much the happier I.

I will go back this morning
From Imbros over the sea;
Stand in the trench, Achilles,
Flame-capped, and shout for me.
(Patrick Shaw-Stewart)

BIGGIN, THE TARGET

The second [attack] – against Biggin Hill, – took place during the early evening, when a small force of some nine Junkers 88s, escorted by a dozen 109s, detached itself from other formations milling about the Straits and lost height over the Channel to get below a layer of cloud at 5,000 feet, where visibility was excellent. The leader made a landfall near Dover, flew across Kent to the Isle of Sheppey, where he swung left, lost more height, and made a fast, low run to the airfield on the hill. While the 109s

* Educated at Shrewsbury and Trinity, Oxford, Hillary wrote *The Last Enemy* during a long period of surgery and convalescence. It has rightly come to be regarded as a classic of World War II. Sadly, no more manuscripts of similar length flowed from the author's pen. He was killed, flying at night, at an Operational Training Unit early in 1943 as he was converting on to night fighters – the dreadful result of a persistent and almost pathological agitation to be allowed to return to operations. His friends, who had previously been serving with him at Fighter Command HQ, had tried in vain to dissuade him from such a course. He had already given his all . . . Ed.

strafed, each bomber dropped two weapons so that eighteen bombs wrecked workshops, the MT yard, the armoury, the meteorological office and the NAAFI. The sergeants' mess, the WAAF quarters and the airmen's barracks were made uninhabitable. Most of the transport was badly damaged: two Spitfires were burned out, all electricity, water and gas mains were cut, most telephone communications were out, and thirty-nine personnel were killed. Six Spitfires fell in with the Junkers as they retired, and a Spitfire squadron engaged near the coast. Four Spitfires were brought down, while the cost to the Germans of the most successful attack yet carried out against a Fighter Command station was one Messerschmitt.

(J. E. [Johnnie] Johnson, *The Story of Air Fighting*, Hutchinson, 1985)

THE MANIFESTATION OF CHRONIC FATIGUE

The cry for more pilots, give us more pilots, was being echoed by all squadron commanders at about this time. There was a desperate shortage throughout the Command. Not so fighter aircraft. The miracles worked by Lord Beaverbrook at the Ministry of Aircraft Production were being felt at squadron level where replacement aircraft arrived on virtually the same day as the demand was sent. This achievement was due in no small measure to the sterling work of the Maintenance Unit which serviced the Spitfires allotted to operational units. On-the-spot repairs of damaged aircraft were carried out by our own ground crews, who were magnificent. All night long, lights burned in the shuttered hangars as the fitters, electricians, armourers and riggers worked unceasingly to put the maximum number on the line for the next day's operations. All day too they worked, not even ceasing when the airfield was threatened with attack. A grand body of men about whom too little has been written but without whose efforts victory would not have been possible.

. . . Not only was the replacement problem serious, but this growing strain on those who had been in action continuously, with only brief rests, was also beginning to tell. Small things which earlier would have been laughed off as irrelevant, now became points of bitter contention. At this stage of the Battle pilot losses far outstripped the replacements and it was only a question of time before the serious position became a grave one. Referring to this aspect of the Battle, the History of the Royal Air Force says:

The replacement of casualties* was the most serious aspect of the pilot problem, but it was not the only one. There was also the growing strain on those who

---

* 154 pilots had been killed, missing or severely wounded in 10 days' fighting and only 63 new fighter pilots were produced in the same period.

118

survived. . . . The long hours at dispersal, the constant flying at high altitudes, the repeated combats, the parachute descents, the forced landings – all took their toll, even where the harm was not at once apparent. The growing tiredness of those who had been most actively engaged was a factor which Dowding could neglect no more than his casualties. Fighter Command was still successfully resisting the enemy. Its own strength was being steadily sapped in the process.

. . . .

Further along the [dining room] table George [Gribble] had dropped off to sleep and, with his head nodding lower and lower, was gently swaying to and fro in his seat, his bacon and egg untouched in front of him. As we watched, his face pitched forward into his eggs, much to the amusement of the assembled pilots.

'Hi, George, you are meant to eat those eggs, not put your face in them,' shouted Colin [Gray] across the table.

George sat erect with a start and looked around with hostility before departing in silence to his room. This action was most unlike George, but indicative of the state of fatigue reached by the over-worked leaders, and the effect of strain on even the most forbearing of chaps. . . .

. . . .

Four times 54 Squadron entangled with the enemy and four times returned without loss of pilots or aircraft. Operating at great altitudes under the new scheme of drawing off the escort, we destroyed or probably destroyed fourteen enemy fighters, an achievement which was to mark the peak of the squadron's efficiency in the Battle of Britain. From this day onwards our efficiency gradually deteriorated, as we grew more and more tired, until in the end we were but a token force in the air. The turning point had been reached. . . .

This was the time when 54 Squadron should have been moved out of the line for a rest. Without a squadron commander, only four survivors with any experience of leading a flight, and no other pilot really up to the standard required to lead a section, the squadron was in an extremely bad way. It was a grim situation not made any easier to bear by the move out, on that very day, of 65 Squadron to a northern airfield for a rest. Once again 54 Squadron was to act as guinea pig for the blooding of the new squadrons being brought into the Battle.

. . . .

In the twenty-one days since our return, I had not been off the airfield, except for the one unhappy night in hospital, nor had any of the four leaders on whom the squadron now depended. . . . The strain had almost reached breaking point. The usually good natured George was quiet and irritable; Colin, by nature thin-faced, was noticeably more hollow-cheeked; Desmond, inclined to be weighty, was reduced to manageable proportions; and I, although I had no way of knowing how I appeared to

119

the others, was all on edge and practically jumped out of my skin when someone shouted unexpectedly over the RT. But still we continued to operate – there was no alternative.

(Air Commodore Alan C. Deere, DSO, OBE, DFC, *Nine Lives*,
Hodder & Stoughton, 1959)

Postscript – forty-odd years on

[Looking back] I thought toward the end of August [1940] that we were on a bit of a loser. Each time we went up, there seemed to be more and more Germans up there.

(A. C. D.)

THE BATTLE'S (AND WORLD WAR II's) MOST FAMOUS QUOTE?

The gratitude of every home in our Island, in our Empire, and indeed throughout the world, except in the abodes of the guilty, goes out to the British airmen who, undaunted by odds, unwearied in their constant challenge and mortal danger, are turning the tide of the world war by their prowess and by their devotion. Never in the field of human conflict was so much owed by so many to so few.* All hearts go out to the fighter pilots, whose brilliant actions we see with our own eyes day after day; but we must never forget that all the time, night after night, month after month, our bomber squadrons travel far into Germany, find their targets in the darkness by the highest navigational skill, aim their attacks, often under the heaviest fire, often with serious loss, with deliberate careful discrimination, and inflict shattering blows upon the whole of the technical and war-making structure of the Nazi power. On no part of the Royal Air Force does the weight of the war fall more heavily than on the daylight bombers who will play an invaluable part in the case of invasion and whose unflinching zeal it has been necessary in the meanwhile on numerous occasions to restrain.

(Winston S. Churchill, House of Commons, 20 August 1940)

NEAR THE END OF THE TETHER

. . . Towards the end of the Battle I had taken just about as much as I could bear. My nerves were in ribbons and I was scared stiff that one day I would pull out and avoid combat. That frightened me more than the

---

* The pilots said, with a self-deprecating twinkle, that the Prime Minister must have been referring to their Mess bills! Ed.

Germans and I pleaded with my CO for a rest. He was sympathetic but quite adamant that until he got replacements I would have to carry on. I am glad now that he was unable to let me go. If I had been allowed to leave the squadron, feeling as I did, I am sure that I would never have flown again. As it was, the Battle of Britain [eventually] fizzled out, the squadron moved back to Bristol for the winter, and when sweeps started over occupied France in the spring of 1941 I was as keen again as the newest replacement.

(James H. [Ginger] Lacey, *The Battle of Britain*, Icare, Paris, 1965)

If the airfields had got another heavy thumping, I'm not sure we could have stood it . . .

(Air Vice-Marshal A. V. R. (Sandy) Johnstone)

LUFTWAFFE REPORT

At the beginning of September reports from the German formations indicated that for the first time the violence of the British fighter defence was slackening. That of II/KG 1 ('Hindenburg'), which on 1 September attacked the Tilbury docks on the Thames, read for instance: 'Slight enemy fighter resistance easily countered by own escort.'

The eighteen Heinkel 111s were in fact covered by no fewer than three fighter *Geschwader*: JGs 52, 53 and 54. On 2 September Major Walter Grabmann, commander of ZG 76, reported to his chief, General Osterkamp, after successfully escorting KG 3 to Eastchurch: 'There's not much doing over there any more.' Even the twin-engined Me 110 could once more maintain its place in the English sky!

The struggle had been hard, but now it seemed that the Luftwaffe's crucial task – the subjugation of the British fighter arm – was all but fulfilled.

(Cajus D. Bekker, *The Luftwaffe War Diaries*, Macdonald, 1967)

THE DARKEST HOUR

Holding by a thread

During this intense late August – early September period, the battle on the ground was against the damage caused to the body corporate of Fighter Command. When ops rooms were destroyed, as at Kenley and Biggin Hill, existing emergency rooms were rushed into service. These, however, could not accommodate a full staff or provide all the landlines necessary for the control of the full quota of their squadrons. Improvisation was the order of the day, while at the same time the rushed construction of fully equipped alternative ops rooms within five miles of the sector station was put in hand.

Those who carried out this repair work were among the unsung heroes of the Battle, like the ground staff, anti-aircraft gunners, ARP workers and members of the Observer Corps. Operational landlines were the responsibility of the GPO (War Group) and these were among the hardest worked people on the ground, often working right through nights, doggedly tackling the repair to vital lines which they had reconnected perhaps only twenty-four hours earlier. Equally busy were the station signals men and members of the Royal Corps of Signals who dealt with internal station lines.

Sir Keith Park in mid-September made no bones about the extremity of the situation between 28 August and 5 September:

> Contrary to general belief and official reports, the enemy's bombing attacks by day did extensive damage to five of our forward aerodromes and also to six of our seven sector stations. There was a critical period when the damage to sector stations and our ground organization was having a serious effect on the fighting efficiency of the squadrons, who could not be given the same good technical and administrative service as previously. . . . The absence of many essential telephone lines, the use of scratch equipment in emergency operations rooms, and the general dislocation of ground organisation, was seriously felt for about a week in the handling of squadrons by day to meet the enemy's massed attacks, which were continued without the former occasional break of a day.
>
> (Richard Hough and Denis Richards, *The Battle of Britain: The Jubilee History*, Hodder & Stoughton, 1989)

THE BALFOUR DECLARATION

I do declare that from my first-hand knowledge, even though on the Air Ministry side of the fence, the margin for victory in terms of aircraft and pilots was knife-edged.

I do declare that if there had been no Beaverbrook and no MAP I do not believe the balance would have been tipped in our favour.

(Harold Balfour [Lord Balfour of Inchrye, PC, MC], *Wings over Westminster*, Hutchinson, 1973)

WOULD THE DAWN EVER BREAK?

When, two months back, the Channel fighting had begun, the Command had been some two hundred pilots short of its establishment. Serious losses during mid-August had made it necessary to reduce the already dangerously low hours at the operational conversion units, and hastily to train volunteers from Bomber Command, Coastal Command and Army Cooperation Squadrons. On paper these measures made good some of the deficiencies, but the newcomers lacked experience and were mere passengers on their first few missions. Moreover they were up against men with more air and combat experience, for German crews averaged between three and four years' service.

Towards the end of August the controller knew that the pilot position had worsened as a result of the bigger enemy fighter escorts. During the first three days of September ninety of the enemy had cost eight-five fighters. The total wastage in fighter pilots was about 120 a week and, since the output of the operational training units was some sixty-five inexperienced replacements a week, it was quite apparent that Fighter Command was fighting a battle of diminishing returns.

The Command was wasting away. If the Luftwaffe kept up the pressure against the sectors the delicate instrument of control and reporting would gradually disintegrate, and it would only be a question of time before the Germans dominated the air over southern England.

Was there a chance to hold the fort for another month? Until this shining summer gave way to the silver-grey skies of autumn and prevented the daily assembly of the big gaggles? This would depend on the Germans. If they took out the radars and came low it could be over very quickly. If they continued against the sector stations it would be a close finish. The controller knew all about the striking increase in the number of barges between Ostend and Le Havre; and there could only be one reason why the Stukas had gathered together in the Pas de Calais. Thank goodness for the Channel . . .

> Which serves it in the office of a wall,
> Or as a moat defensive to a house,
> Against the envy of less happier lands . . .
> (J. E. [Johnnie] Johnson, *The Story of*
> *Air Fighting*, Hutchinson, 1985)

Part Three

7 SEPTEMBER–31 OCTOBER 1940
Autumn Deliverance

Never succumb. It is a struggle for your existence as a nation. If you must die, die with the sword in your hand. But I have no fear whatever for the result. There is a salient living principle of energy in the public mind of England, which only requires proper direction to enable her to withstand this, or any other ferocious foe. Persevere, therefore, till this tyranny be overpast.

(Edmund Burke)

THE FATAL SWITCH – TARGET LONDON!

At this fateful moment – on 7 September to be exact – the Luftwaffe was ordered from the highest quarter to make a drastic change in the nature of its operations. From now on the target was to be London!

This alteration in tactical policy is viewed by the British, from Churchill downwards, as a fundamental German mistake that saved the defences from destruction. The fighter bases at last had a breathing space and could now recover from the serious damage they had received. . . .

During the whole of August . . . Hitler, for political reasons, had forbidden any attack on the capital. Unfortunately, owing to a regrettable lapse in navigation on the part of a few bomber crews, it had happened. On the night of 24/25 August some isolated bombs, destined for the aircraft works at Rochester and oil tanks on the Thames, had descended over the London areas, and this had sparked off a whole chain reaction. . . .

The forbidden had happened. Churchill demanded from a reluctant Bomber Command, who saw no military advantage to be gained by it, an immediate reprisal raid on Berlin. The following night, accordingly, eighty-one British twin-engined bombers made the 600-mile each-way flight to the German capital. Of these twenty-nine claimed to have reached it, though according to German observations less than ten bombers, hindered as they were by heavy cloud, managed to drop their bombs at random on the target area. Military damage was nil. It was the first of four British raids within ten days. . . .

For Hitler it was too much. He abandoned his restraint. With angry disillusionment he proclaimed: 'Since they attack our cities we shall wipe out theirs.'. . .

On the afternoon of 7 September Göring stood with Kesselring and Lörzer* on the coast at Cape Blanc Nez and watched his bombers and fighters droning overhead. He had, as he told radio news correspondents, 'taken over personal command of the Luftwaffe in its war against England.'

This time it was no fewer than 625 bombers which, in the late afternoon and through the night, headed for London. The daylight formations were protected by 648 single and twin-engined fighters. They

* General Bruno Lörzer, World War I comrade of Göring and now commanding Flieger Korps II.

127

flew in several waves and in tight formations stepped up between 14,000 and 20,000 feet. . . .

[. . . The final phase of the Battle had now begun]

(Cajus D. Bekker, *The Luftwaffe War Diaries*, Macdonald, 1967)

'GENERAL DER JAGDFLIEGER' REFLECTS

I put the question to Adolf Galland in the garden of Withers Farm, Sir Douglas and Lady Bader's country home at Marlston, in Berkshire, a few miles from Newbury. My wife and I, and Germany's best-known fighter leader of the Second World War, were staying the weekend.

It was 7 September 1980. The autumn sun was shining down, warm and strong, out of a sky of dusty powder blue. The fields, recently harvested, rolled away across the valley and up the hill to the trees beyond. The English countryside, quiet and still, was at peace with the world.

Forty years ago, on this very day, the German High Command, with Hitler and Göring pressing down upon it, had, in a fatal blunder, switched the direction of its attack from Fighter Command and the Essex and Kentish airfields to London and other major cities. The decision, politically quite as much as militarily motivated, was an undisguised consequence of Bomber Command's attacks on Berlin and the heart of the Third Reich. To appease their own population, the Nazi leaders had been stung into retaliation. The precipitate deviation of aim was to cost Germany the Battle of Britain and, with the invasion of Russia which followed, eventually the whole war.

'Tell me, Dolfo,' I asked (it was Douglas's nickname for this dark, heavily built and dignified man), 'why did your High Command allow itself to be diverted from the attacks upon our airfields in September 1940, when it just about had the battle "made"? Looking back, now, it seems an incredible misjudgement.'

Galland, with his suave courtesy and impressively good manners, threw up his hands and lifted his big round eyes to the heavens. A shrug of his broad shoulders and a slow shake of the head made an answer superfluous . . .

The steady flow of Spitfires and Hurricanes which Lord Beaverbrook, with extraordinary zeal and drive, was prising out of the factories into the squadrons, was not being matched by the supply of pilots. This, and not aircraft, had now become the paramount concern. With death, injury and battle fatigue, the wastage had taken its toll. Another month – even a fortnight – of the August attrition and the end of the game would be in sight.

It was at this agonizing juncture, when all hung tenuously in the balance, that the enemy, doing 'everything by starts, and nothing long', turned away and altered course. For Churchill's War Cabinet, it came like a blessed shift in the wind in some hard-fought, eighteenth-century engagement at sea.

(Laddie Lucas, *Flying Colours: The Epic Story of Douglas Bader*,
Hutchinson, 1981)

THE ISLAND RACE, CLIFTON CHAPEL

> To set the Cause above renown,
>   To love the game beyond the prize,
> To honour, while you strike him down
>   The foe that comes with fearless eyes:
> To count the life of battle good,
>   And dear the land that gave you birth,
> And dearer yet the brotherhood
>   That binds the brave of all the earth.

(Sir Henry Newbolt)

LUNCHEON INTERLUDE

I flew to Hendon by Hurricane [from Tangmere] and from there drove by car to Whitehall.

It was very quiet, I remember, in the courtyard of Admiralty House which was watched by armed Marines. In the entrance hall was a burly naval petty officer with a big revolver strapped to his waist. I went up in the lift and found the Prime Minister, as calm and cherubic as usual. Without undue waste of time he led the way into the dining room.

Lunch was very good. We ate lamb although this was at a time when food rationing was beginning to be severe. Churchill explained: 'This lamb was very unfortunate, Max,' he said solemnly. 'It broke its leg. Otherwise, of course, it would not be here.'

Naturally I knew that I had not been ordered to London in the middle of a battle simply in order to be given a good meal. Before I knew where I was I was being subjected to a severe cross-examination. The Prime Minister wanted to know how things were going with the fighter squadrons. He was not a man to be satisfied with official stories filtered through the various levels of the Air Ministry. I told him that things were going well. This was true although, as the Prime Minister knew even better than I did, we were in . . . [for] a long battle. . . . In answering as confidently as I did, however, I was only expressing the absolute belief of the fighter squadrons. It simply did not occur to us that we could be defeated.

The Prime Minister's next question was, as he showed, backed by considerable technical knowledge. 'Are the German fighters better than ours?' I told him they were certainly not and he seemed to be satisfied with the evidence I gave him. . . . Then, quite suddenly, he got up from the table saying, 'Now I'm going to sleep.' The interview was at an end.

(The Hon. Max Aitken [Group Captain Sir Max Aitken], *The Aitken Papers*)

Nazi Propaganda Broadcasts

'Germany calling, Germany calling'

During the past weeks, events have been moving rapidly, and no event received so much attention as the sustained bombardment of London by the German Air Arm. This subject tends to exclude all others from the newspapers of neutral countries. London, the city of power, majesty and glamour, is being reduced to dust and ashes in accordance with the formula invented by Churchill, even before any invasion of Britain has taken place. How short-sighted was the boast of this incompetent and conceited politician, that he would see London reduced to ruins and ashes, rather than in the hands of the enemy! It seems he has no choice in the matter.

Umbrellas for rifles!

England is feverishly preparing for a war of armed civilians. While waiting to be called up, the gentlemen of England are exercising with umbrellas for want of rifles, and are training for anti-parachutist defence. In addition, innumerable football and polo clubs have suddenly discovered that they had military possibilities and have placed their playing grounds at the disposal of their fatherland. Here the Home Guard are learning to march with their broomsticks on their shoulders. The BBC tells us . . . that this amateur army is drawn from all classes . . . and will be the greatest surprise Hitler has ever had. Radio London, continuing its report on 'England in Arms', tells us the All-England Lawn Tennis Club at Wimbledon will also contribute to the defence of the country by slaughtering pigs. Who, after hearing this, will dare to say that England will fail to do its duty?

Invoking neutral Sweden: Radio Zeesen calling

The correspondent of Stockholm's *Tidningen* admits that he cannot describe adequately with words the most terrible air raids in history . . . Aircraft dived down on London from all directions. There were swarms of German planes in the clouds, and then a deafening roar of fighters attacking barrage balloons. I saw five balloons go down in flames in a minute or so. Then came the bombers. Squadron after squadron attacked, in wave after wave, and dropped their bombs on the Port of London. The attack was directed on industrial installations along the Thames and on the docks themselves. Power stations and other vital spots were seriously damaged. When we drove towards the East End, it looked as if a single huge wall of fire divided the sky in two in front of us. The most serious stage of war in the air has begun. The day of decision is near.

Come off it, Adolf!

Must we remind . . . [the British] of the fact that it was Britain who declared war on Germany, who started to wage it on women and children by preparing the hunger blockade? Must we remind them of the *Altmark* incident, when defenceless German seamen were murdered in cold blood? Must we recall to their memories the air raid on Freidburg when children were killed in an attack on an undefended town in broad daylight, with no military objective even in the vicinity? For months the German people and their Führer have suffered indiscriminate bombing of non-military objectives. Time and again the Führer has offered the hand of understanding and even friendship to the very nation which starved the German people after the peace was concluded in 1919.

Time and again the Führer has warned Britain of the necessary consequences that these brutal attacks might have. Last week he uttered what was his last warning in no uncertain terms. Now, just retribution has befallen Britain, . . . Misery thus caused is not to be laid at Germany's door. Those who . . . drove their nation into senseless war in order to perpetuate an injustice, just to save the interests of a small group of Jewish financiers and inveterate warmongers with Winston Churchill at their head – those men are responsible, not Germany.

'Useless' Radar!

Another feature of Churchillian propaganda received our attention last night – a mysterious scientific device which locates aeroplanes and tells gunners where they are to be found. As we stated, the plans of this contraption were found in the West after the glorious retreat. It proved to be a Heath Robinson thing, but we examined it and rejected it as useless.

Göring over London?

An officer of high rank on Göring's staff has just revealed that the *Reichsmarschall* flew over London last night in one of the new German Junkers 88 bombers. He acted as his own pilot and was accompanied by only two fighter bombers. Impressed by the extraordinarily great effects of the German raids on the British capital, Göring said on his return: 'I am glad to have made my Luftwaffe such a formidable weapon. In Poland, Norway and the West, the Luftwaffe was the decisive factor, and it will also be Germany's sharpest sword in the battle of Britain.'

Churchill, the butt

Churchill yesterday made a broadcast speech which was clearly influenced by the strong German attacks against the heart of the Empire. He gave vent to his fury in abuse of the Führer which was so infamous that even Reuter had to discuss at a conference, which lasted half an hour, whether it could issue these utterances to the public. . . .

. . . Churchill even stated that the British Air Force had almost every time repulsed the German Air Arm. He probably did not [realize] that the whole world will ask how it comes that the Port of London, from the Thames to London Bridge (!) is one sea of fire. The report of the bomb explosion in Buckingham Palace also fits in very badly with the lying boasts of the British Premier. . . .

. . . The inventor of night raids against the German civilian population then told the English that the German Air Arm would wear out, obviously seeking to arouse some hope that the German reprisal raids would slacken. . . . This attrition theory is another favourite of Mr Churchill. . . . If one must talk about attrition at this stage of the war, what about the British Air Force, which can no longer prevent the daily break-through of masses of German planes?

'From somewhere inside England!'
Fifth Column on the air!

. . . If only Hitler's peace offer had been accepted, how much better off we should be! Why was it rejected? Because the men who rule us stood to gain by continuing the war.

The privileged plutocracy!

We have learned with horror and disgust that while London was suffering all the nightmares of aerial bombardment a few nights ago, there was a contrast between the situation of the rich and the poor which we hardly know how to describe. There were two Londons that night. Down by the docks and in the poor districts . . . people lay dead, or dying in agony from their wounds. But, while their countrymen were suffering only a little distance away, the plutocrats and the favoured lords of creation were making the raid an excuse for their drunken orgies and debaucheries in the salons of Piccadilly and at the Café de Paris. Spending on champagne in one night what they would consider enough for a soldier's wife for a month, these moneyed fools shouted and sang in the streets, crying, as the son of a profiteer baron put it, 'They won't bomb this part of town! They want the docks! So fill up the glasses, boys, fill 'em up!'

(Extracts from broadcasts by the German Propaganda Ministry by William Joyce [alias Lord Haw-Haw] and others, September 1940)

SEA-LION* POSTPONED

September 7 is a great day in my memory, for then we were told that the invasion was imminent. The signal 'Cromwell' was given, and with this password flying from mouth to mouth and the church bells ringing, the Army came to instant readiness and the Home Guard stood to arms. We waited for the great moment. But the Germans shrank from the test. On 17 September, as we now know, Hitler postponed invasion 'until further notice'. Yet the danger of invasion continued for a long time, and Churchill and the Chiefs of Staff had to take the necessary precautions for many months to come. But whatever military experts might advise, the public felt that the moment was over, and that whatever might happen Britain would never be forced to her knees by a foreign invader landing on her shores. . . . [However] the heroic combats in the air . . . [continued] between the champions on either side . . . We still keep 15 September – and I hope will always keep it – in commemoration of our victory.

(Harold Macmillan, *The Blast of War, 1939–1945*, Macmillan, 1967)

I am forced to agree with the opinion of the British military historian, Fuller,† when he writes that Sea-lion* was often contemplated, but never planned.

The air battle for England also suffered from the muddle-headedness of the Sea-lion programme. It was clear to every discerning person, including Hitler, that England could not be brought to her knees by the Luftwaffe alone. It is therefore no good talking of the failure of the German air force to reach an impossible goal. It was likewise clear to us Luftwaffe commanders that, although we might gain a temporary ascendancy in the air, permanent air supremacy was impossible without the occupation of the island, for the simple reason that a considerable number of British air bases, aircraft and engine factories were out of range of our bombers. For the same reason only a few of their ports were open to our attack. The range limitations of our fighter aircraft increased the difficulty. We were thus not exactly pleased to hear talk of Sea-lion being washed out or postponed, rumours to which effect were already current

---

* Sea-lion – the High Command's code word for the proposed German invasion of Britain.
† General J. F. C. Fuller.

at the beginning of September. Our disgust will be understood when it is realized that henceforth the whole burden of the battle for England would have to be carried, under aggravated conditions, by the Luftwaffe.

(Albert Kesselring [Field Marshal commanding *Luftflotte* 2 on the Western Front, 1940], *The Memoirs of Field Marshal Kesselring*, William Kimber, 1953)

CAESAR HULL OF 43 SQUADRON

Caesar Hull* took over the command [of 43 Squadron] on September 1, a fulfilment to his career which meant more to him than all his victories. He didn't live long enough to have the third stripe sewn on his sleeve. He led 43 through a succession of combats for only seven days. On September 8 he was found dead, beside his aircraft, in a field in Kent. He had been killed by a bullet during the Battle of the London Docks. The Huns had come over in continuous waves all day, and Caesar had led the squadron in to attack a formation of Dornier bombers. He was never seen alive again.

John† was resting his ankle and shoulder in Cornwall . . . [when] he wrote to me . . . [about the Squadron's loss]:

For two days I have been thinking of Caesar. I loved him as I would a brother. He was more than a rare person in the RAF, and there can never be anyone to replace him in character, charm and kindliness. We came to 43 together and grew up in it together. We knew each other from A to Z and it was a privilege no one else could share.

This hell cannot go on for ever. And reassure yourself with the feeling and knowledge that we do the same to them. I was glad I was here, in a quiet, calm place when the news came. I swim and fish with the wonderful old fishermen, and I walk . . . [in] the woods every day. They are full of giant hydrangeas and wild orchids.

I had a wonderful letter from Mummy. My God, her courage is astounding. . . . I have received my golden caterpillar for the parachute jump. . . .

Your letter about Caesar. I don't know what to say. I thought I was

---

* Caesar Hull, a fine character from Southern Rhodesia, joined the Royal Air Force in the mid-1930s and at once endeared himself to his comrades. He fought in the Norwegian campaign as a flight commander with 263 Squadron before being hit and wounded. After recovery he rejoined 43, his original squadron. Hull's tally of enemy aircraft destroyed had reached double figures by the time he was killed. Ed.

† John Simpson, who also joined 43 Squadron before the war and fought with it at Dunkirk and in the Battle of Britain when he was shot down and wounded. With thirteen aircraft confirmed destroyed, he was awarded the DFC and bar and later served as a Group Captain in North Africa. Ed.

quite used by now to people dying. Do you realize that there are only three of us who were with the squadron when the war began . . . still alive and serving with the squadron? . . . I went for a long walk in the woods when the news came and I cried for the first time since I was little.

Poor 43. But we can take it. We will have to begin all over again. New CO. New pilots. But the squadron spirit is safe. Dear old Caesar. He commanded the squadron he began in as a pilot officer. I would have loved to fly with him as my CO.

It seems funny to think that I shall never see him shaking that left foot of his as he used to do when he was excited. And how he used to rub his nose between his thumb and forefinger when he was nervous. And that laugh!

He had a good life and I think that he loved every minute of it. I never heard anybody say an unkind thing about Caesar and I never heard him say an unkind thing about anybody else. One can't say more than that, can one?

(Hector Bolitho, *Combat Report: The Story of a Fighter Pilot*,
Batsford, 1943)

LOSSES

All the key men fighting with 43 were shot down or killed within eight days. Tubby Badger* was shot down on 30 August. Tony Woods-Scawen† was killed on 2 September. Tom Morgan was shot down on 6 September and Caesar Hull and Dickie Reynell on 8 September. Dickie Reynell, one of the finest pilots in the country, was a Hawker Test Pilot and he had been attached to 43 for only two weeks to gain combat experience with a Hurricane.

(Hector Bolitho, *Combat Report: The Story of a Fighter Pilot*,
Batsford, 1943)

You could not be successful in such an action without a large loss. We must make up our minds to affairs of this kind sometimes, or give up the game.

(Duke of Wellington)

---

* Squadron Leader J. V. C. Badger, DFC, died a year later.
† Flying Officer A. Woods-Scawen was shot down on 2 September and he crashed near an aircraft of 85 Squadron which had also been shot down, in the same battle. Unknown to Tony Woods-Scawen, the aircraft was flown by his brother. They were killed within a few minutes of each other and fell side by side.

A QUESTION OF LUCK?

The Orchard at Ruislip

The haven of our [Polish] dreams materialized when we found the Orchard Inn. Of course there may once have been an orchard near by, but it wasn't the rustic memory that attracted us. First, it was in easy walking distance – not much more than a mile away [from Northolt] in the Ruislip area, so there were no transport problems.

The Jewish landlord was a very friendly man, and the prices of his drinks were as attractive as the girls who frequented the place. Another attraction was that the counter-intelligence officer who kept an eye on our comings and goings did not pull a sour face when we mentioned the Orchard. Every time the question of visiting London had come up he had swamped us with lectures on the perils of the capital. To hear him tell it, London was crawling with spies, especially the female kind. Which left us with the Orchard Inn and its cheerful welcome.

In any case, the landlord knew all there was to know about our exploits. We could hardly cross the threshold before he was toasting the victors of the day and analysing our latest mission. 303 Squadron's score was kept right up to date, and applauded by the beer-drinking regulars and most of all by the girls, whose resistance showed a day-by-day decline.

Every Pole who was based at Northolt has warm memories of that landlord who never forgot to send a basket of fruit to the bedside of a wounded comrade. Discipline may be an army's first driving force, but morale is certainly the second. From the day we discovered the Orchard Inn, our nervous depressions vanished; the part it played in lifting our spirits gives it a vital place in any story of the Polish airmen in Britain. That the memory stayed alive was proved by the many who came to lay their wreath of gratitude on the landlord's grave twenty years later in the local cemetery . . .

. . . Our host never resented having his daily routine and quiet atmosphere disrupted by our riotous lust for life. He knew that some of us were running out of time.

Of course, it was the girls who, before anything else, kept us coming back to the Orchard Inn. They were pretty, easy-going and affectionate. They knew us all by our first names and cried real tears when one of us went missing.

Every night they waited for us in the big saloon bar with its miniature dance floor. Every night the party spirit was kept going by a band who made up for their lack of technique with their eagerness to please. The girls preferred dancing with the foreign airmen, but there was never any friction between ourselves and the British contingent at Northolt. They generously admitted that being foreign gave our embraces the spice of the unknown. Wars, with the chance encounters they bring in their wake, have always had a liberating effect on women, and sexual freedom was long overdue in a country where Victorian respectability had outlived its usefulness. We must have come as a welcome change, at a time when change was in the air.

(Wing Commander Jean Zumbach, *On Wings of War: My Life as a Pilot Adventurer*, André Deutsch, 1975)

Canterbury hospital

Soon after tea . . . we were put on thirty minutes' notice and told that a little later we would be released until dawn next day. Back in the officers' mess we changed into our best uniforms and planned a night out in the West End of London. But no sooner were we ready to go than the tannoy called us back to readiness. Cursing our luck, we drove round the perimeter track to dispersal, lugged our parachutes out to our planes, put on Mae West life-jackets over our tidy tunics and awaited developments.

It turned out that the reason for our recall was a surprise visit to the station by the Prime Minister, Winston Churchill. That, at least, made the sudden and enforced change in our evening plans seem worthwhile. A small procession of cars drove round the taxi track and stopped outside our hut, where we lined up to meet the great man, the lion who roared for England.

Just a few seconds later I had shaken hands with Churchill, Corporal Durham appeared on stage to produce one of his more spectacular performances. Racing out of the hut, he shouted to us to scramble. I remember thinking as we sprinted out to our planes and streamed down the runway in the fastest take-off of the squadron's history that the whole performance had obviously been laid on for the Prime Minister's benefit. Unfortunately it was in that unexpectant frame of mind that I flew along, 'tail-end Charlie' in our formation of twelve, when, a few minutes later, we levelled out twelve thousand feet above Dover. I was still wondering whether there might yet be time to get into the fleshpots of London when the cannon shells from that unseen Messerschmitt ripped home and sent me spinning on my first face-to-face meeting with death.

. . . George Moberley came to see me [in Canterbury hospital]. He had been in action that morning when he had shot down a Messerschmitt 109. In the same action Sergeant Ridley had destroyed a Dornier 17, Jack Bell had claimed a Messerschmitt as probably destroyed and three more Messerschmitts and one Dornier had been claimed as damaged. George told me how Sergeants Westmoreland and Waring, both 'B' Flight pilots, had been shot down that day. Westmoreland was known to be dead; Waring was missing. Then he talked to me about personal affairs, about his family and his property. He told me that he wanted me to have his personal belongings if he were killed. I had a strong feeling that he had a premonition that he would be.

If indeed he had such a premonition, it was fulfilled next day, when, in a dogfight south of Dover, George was shot down and killed. He baled out at a very low altitude – so low that his parachute could not open properly. He hit the sea close to shore and his body was recovered.

In eight days, 616 Squadron lost five pilots killed or missing and five others wounded and in hospital. About fifty per cent of the pilots who had flown down from Leconfield had gone. But still the remnants fought on, greatly inspired by the courage and leadership of Denis Gillam, who now showed the fiery and utterly fearless character which was to make him one of the most distinguished RAF officers of the war. But . . . [then] he too was shot down and injured. It was the final, knock-out blow. Without him the squadron was incapable of continuing the fight. And so, exactly fourteen days after our carefree and confident departure from Leconfield, 616 Squadron – what was left of it – was taken out of the line to re-form at Coltishall, near Norwich. To set against its losses, the squadron claimed sixteen enemy aircraft definitely destroyed, six probably destroyed, fifteen damaged. Of these Gillam had personally destroyed seven and damaged three.

(Hugh Dundas, *Flying Start: A Fighter Pilot's War Years*,
Stanley Paul, 1988)

Well; your danger is as you have seen. And truly I am sorry it is so great. But I wish it to cause no despondency: – as truly, I think, it will not: for we are Englishmen.

(Oliver Cromwell)

92 SQUADRON – 'C'EST LA VIE'!

12 September

As my Anson transport plane made a quick circuit of Biggin, I had looked at the scene below. The whole environment was a mess of bomb-scarred earth and bombed-out buildings. The hangars were in ruins, the entire airfield pock-marked with bomb holes ringed with obstruction warning flags. There were newly laid patches on the runways where craters had been filled in and tarmacked. . . .

The ferry pilot wasn't going to switch off, and gestured me to get moving. He'd seen all he wanted to of Biggin Hill, for sure. No sooner had I humped my baggage out the back of the Anson than it swung around, and took off cross-wind.

The boys helped me stow my gear in the aircrew station wagon while I shot questions at them on the form.

'We shoot at Huns all day, dear boy, and get bestially drunk at night,' Brian* answered. 'Station stores has been blitzed, so you can help yourself to anything in the line of flying clothing. I got two of everything for a rainy day.'

As he spoke, the ack-ack guns started barking at a Ju 88 which had emerged momentarily from cloud cover over the airfield heading south, having, evidently, dropped his bombs, as he ignored us.

'What does one do on these occasions?' I asked, a little nervously.

'Just put on a tin hat, and strike a hostile attitude,' Brian said.

Suddenly the tannoy loud hailer crackled to life: '92 Squadron at 30 minutes available', and the fighter pilots made a concerted dash for the station wagon, which took off packed, with others hanging on the outside wherever there was a foothold.

'Where's my V8?' I shouted at Brian above the roar of the unsilenced exhaust.

'Sorry about that, chum. Norman drove it into a bus and wrote it off when you were on leave. Had up for drunk driving, but fortunately the local beak had a son in Fighter Command, and let him off with a pound fine.'

'I'll fix him for this,' I yelled.

'Been fixed already, poor chap, on the dawn patrol, yesterday,' Brian sighed. 'Tuck's taken over 257 Squadron at Martlesham. Hurricanes, poor sod. Al's got his flight.'

'Guess I'd better check in with the CO,' I said.

'He's out of action. Set himself on fire with his cigarette lighter. Seems someone had cleaned his uniform with a hundred octane,' Brian replied laconically.

Over a NAAFI lunch in the crew room, I asked John Bryson what the action was after dark, and he just winked 'plenty' . . .

. . . .

. . . Some days, we could only field five serviceable aircraft out of twelve. We fought all day, and played most of the night. We lived for the present and dismissed our future. The battle would be won, of course. We had no doubts about that. Meanwhile, the casualties mounted, but no one grieved as we knew it was inevitable. I found myself secretly watching the others, searching their faces for who would be next, and I thought I saw them looking at me the same way. But we never revealed our thoughts about fear. They were locked up as tight as the straps on our parachutes.

. . . .

. . . By now Fighter Command had got wind of the 92nd Night Club and . . . our habits . . . [and were] determined to give us a squadron

---

* Flight lieutenant Brian Kingcome, acting CO of 92 Squadron.

commander who would stick, . . . Johnnie Kent, a tough Canadian, had been selected.

When Kent was posted to command the squadron, 92 had made about the highest score in Fighter Command. He had been a flight commander in the famous Polish squadron 303 and already held a DFC, an AFC and the Virtuti Militari. We didn't take much more notice of John than we had of our two previous COs and he spent most of his time in the office when he wasn't flying, which suited us fine. No one had done any of the squadron paper work in two months, and unanswered correspondence and unfilled forms were piled high.

Then one morning Johnnie summoned his senior NCOs and pilots to his office. The interview went something like this: 'I have been watching the squadron's action for the past three weeks and all I can say is, it stinks,' he started. 'First, the station warrant officer tells me that the squadron airmen won't obey any orders except from their own officers and NCOs. You had better get this straightened out, but fast, or else someone's going to wind up in the glasshouse.' Then, turning to us: 'As for my officers, I can't find anything to like about you. You are the most conceited and insubordinate bunch of bastards it's ever been my misfortune to meet in my service career. You dress like bums, you steal air force petrol for your cars, you drink like fishes, you don't sleep and you've made a night club out of your billet, where your girl friends spend the night.

'One of my flight commanders comes out of hospital on crutches, and puts on an exhibition with an officer from another squadron. I won't have him in my squadron.'

'It was a damned good exhibition,' I said, my hackles rising.

'I'll come to you later,' said Kent, giving me the full blast of his ice-cold eyes.

. . . 'I have two complaints in front of me from the police. One concerns a gamekeeper who caught you poaching pheasants and the other a speeding violation. Your Lincoln Mercury, Bartley: I notice most of you all drive high-powered automobiles which are neither licensed nor insured, but I understand you have made an arrangement with a local constable whereby he tips you off before they run a check. As for your dress – I can hardly call it uniform – I will not tolerate check shirts, old school ties, suede shoes nor red trousers. Your record in the air is undisputed, but it could have been much better, and without your appalling casualties, so you are going to smarten up, and fast. You may dismiss.'

We filed silently from the office. 'How about that?' said Wimpy. 'Do you think he'll really sack Brian?'

'Over my dead body,' I said. 'I'll ask for a posting.'

. . . .

The WAAF officers were giving a party that night to which we were invited. I got hold of Bunty Hanbury, the senior WAAF, and told her in highly coloured terms what had happened, so that Kent could hear. I said I was going to ask for a posting to another squadron, in which case the others would follow. Bunty told me to cool it, and to go and find Paula, whom she'd invited especially for me.

Later, when we were all good and high, Johnnie got me in a corner. 'You know you're a sloppy bunch of bums,' he said. 'But pretty decent ones at that, so help me straighten things out. I know I can't win without you and Brian on my side, and I didn't mean what I said about sacking him. So give me a break, will you?' He held out his hand and I shook it . . .

. . . .

I found . . . [Paula] in another room, where a station band was playing. Bob had taken over the piano, and she was standing behind him. Golden hair, and blue eyes like the sky at thirty thousand feet. I took her in my arms and we started to dance. She was soft and delicate as Dresden china. We didn't talk. Our thoughts, we kept to ourselves. During our time together, she never asked me about my fear, or about our future. She understood, and accepted things as they had to be. She knew only two things really counted with me, the squadron and the war. She had become mine, and when all the drink and post mortems were done, I would take her, and she would make me forget my fear in the love we shared.

(Squadron Leader Anthony Bartley, DFC and bar, *Smoke Trails in the Sky: The Journals of a Fighter Pilot*, William Kimber, 1984)

Give me the wings, magician! So their tune
Mix with the silver trumpets of the moon,
And, beyond music mounting, clean outrun
The golden diapason of the sun.
There is a secret that the birds are learning
Where the long lanes in heaven have a turning
And no man yet has followed: therefore these
Laugh hauntingly across our usual seas.
I'll not be mocked by curlews in the sky;
Give me the wings, magician, or I die.

(Humbert Wolfe)

HIGH COMMAND MISJUDGEMENT

Galland's belief

The reproaches from higher quarters [with the Luftwaffe's Fighter Arm's 'failure'] became more unbearable. We had the impression that whatever we did we were bound to be in the wrong. Fighter protection created

many problems, which had to be solved in action. As in Spain, the bomber
pilots preferred close screening, in which their formation was surrounded
by pairs of fighters pursuing a zigzag course. Obviously, the proximity
and the visible presence of the protective fighters gave the bomber pilots a
greater sense of security. However, this was a faulty conclusion, because a
fighter can only carry out this purely defensive task by taking the initiative
in the offensive. He must never wait until he is attacked, because then he
loses the chance of acting. The fighter must seek battle in the air, must find
his opponent, attack him and shoot him down. The bomber must avoid
such fights, and he has to act defensively in order to fulfil his task: war
from the air. In co-operation between bomber and fighter, these two
fundamentally different mentalities obviously clash. The words of
Richthofen expressed during the First World War, summarizing the task
of the fighters, often came to our lips. Fundamentally, they are still valid
to-day: 'The fighter pilots have to rove in the area allotted to them in any
way they like, and when they spot an enemy they attack and shoot him
down; anything else is rubbish.'

We fighter pilots certainly preferred the 'free chase during the approach
and over the target area'. This in fact gives the greatest relief and the best
protection for the bomber force . . .

. . . .

. . . Göring refused to understand that his Luftwaffe, this shining and
so far successful sword, threatened to turn blunt in his hand. He believed
there was not enough fighting spirit and a lack of confidence in ultimate
victory. By personally taking a hand, he hoped to get the best out of us.

To my mind, he went about it the wrong way. He had nothing but
reproaches for the fighter force, and he expressed his dissatisfaction in the
harshest terms.. . . .

Failure to achieve any noticeable success, constantly changing orders
betraying lack of purpose and obvious misjudgement of the situation by
the Command, and unjustified accusations, had a most demoralizing
effect on us fighter pilots, who were already overtaxed by physical and
mental strain. . . .

. . . .

We fighter pilots, discouraged by a task which was beyond our
strength, were therefore looking forward impatiently and excitedly to the
start of the bomber attacks. We believed that only then would the British
fighters leave their dens and be forced to give us open battle.

(Adolf Galland [later *Generalleutnant*, General of the Fighters], *The First
and the Last: The German Fighter Force in World War II*, Methuen, 1955)

KEITH PARK'S HAND

As Commander [of 11 Group, Fighter Command] my main problem was not the plans and tactics of the German Air Force, as I knew from experience in 1917/1918, also from operations in 1940 over France, that the Germans worked to a regular plan and were slow to adopt new tactics.

My main problems were on the Home Front in England. My first aim was not to have my squadrons caught on the ground and destroyed as happened in Poland, Holland and France in 1940. At the same time I had to conserve my fighter strength by not being drawn into the air by false alarms or feint attacks by the German fighters.

My next concern was the exposed position of our vital radar stands on the coast, easy targets for tip-and-run raids which arrived without any warning but fortunately did not bomb accurately. My next concern was the endurance of my fighter squadrons which were sent into battle two or three times daily. Some squadrons lasted four weeks in the front line, but others were exhausted and had to be withdrawn after two weeks' fighting and sent to 12 or 13 Group for a rest and re-training. My instructions from Dowding were to call for replacement squadrons as infrequently as possible because we had practically no reserves. . . .

. . . .

. . . Number 11 Group was expected to protect from bombing many vital targets in south-east England:

London
Naval bases
Munition factories
Commercial ports
Fighting aerodromes

It was impossible to defend every target in such a wide area against a greatly superior enemy so I concentrated on covering the most vital and most obviously threatened . . .

Winston Churchill frequently visited my Operational Headquarters in August and September and never interfered with the conduct of operations.

(Air Vice-Marshal K. R. Park, *The Battle of Britain*, Icare, Paris, 1965)

THE CLIMAX – 15 SEPTEMBER

We must take 15 September as the culminating date. On this day the Luftwaffe, after two heavy attacks on the 14th, made its greatest concentrated effort in a resumed daylight attack on London.

It was one of the decisive battles of the war, and, like the Battle of Waterloo, it was a Sunday.

> (Winston S. Churchill, *Their Finest Hour*, Curtis Brown on behalf of the Estate of Sir Winston Churchill, C & T Publications, 1949)

'THE GREAT CHANCE . . .' HITLER

The Luftwaffe's assault on London on 15 September was designed to be decisive. On its eve, Hitler, Göring, Kesselring, and the RLM* chiefs were optimistic. They believed that RAF Fighter Command was broken. Its

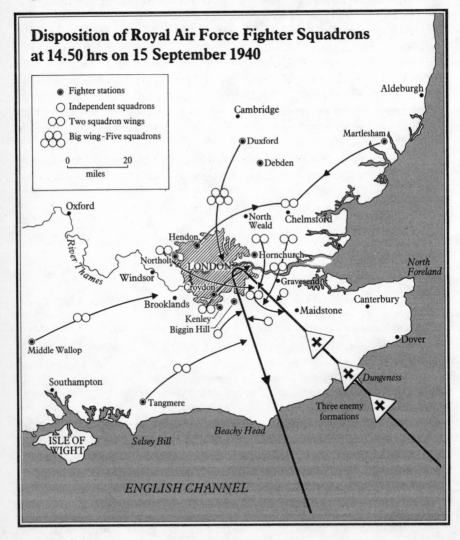

* Air Ministry.

resistance to the attacks on the 11th and 14th had been poor, in the main owing to mistakes by the RAF, and it was clear that significant numbers of its fighters were still being destroyed in aerial combat. Indeed, the Luftwaffe's air attacks were considered to be on the verge of success. It was believed that the British were being defeated by the Luftwaffe alone. . . . Hitler voiced the opinion that 'Britain's defeat will be achieved even without the landing.' On 10 [September] the Naval Staff, dubious about the new aims of the war, recorded in its diary: '. . . the Führer thinks the major attack on London may be decisive . . .'

. . . Reports coming in from the United States indicated that British morale was low and that physical damage was considerable. On the 14th, for example, OKH produced a memorandum which quoted a highly placed source in Washington to the effect that British aircraft production was in a critical state, while that same day the military attaché at the embassy reported that leading members of the US General Staff believed that 'England will not be able to hold out against the German attacks.'* On the 14th, the Führer told his military chiefs that '. . . the operations of the Luftwaffe are beyond all praise. Four to five days of good weather are required to achieve decisive results. . . . There is a great chance of totally defeating the British.'

. . . Whether or not Britain was in such a parlous state is not of such importance here; what is of interest is that the Germans believed it to be so.

(Matthew Cooper, *The German Air Force, 1933–1945: An Anatomy of Failure*, Jane's, 1981)

'WHAT OTHER RESERVES HAVE WE?'

During the morning of 15 September, Park received a visit from Churchill, accompanied by his wife and one of his private secretaries. He had no wish to disturb anyone, he said, but as he happened to be passing, he thought he would call in to see if anything was up. If not, 'I'll just sit in the car and do my homework.' Naturally, Park welcomed the Prime Minister and his companions and escorted them down to . . . [Group's] bomb-proof operations room fifty feet below ground level. Churchill sensed that something important might happen that day. (Park's wife had the same sense: when he apologized at breakfast for forgetting that 15 September was her birthday, she replied that a good bag of German aircraft would be an excellent present.) Once they were in the operations

---

* 'Joe Kennedy [father of John F. Kennedy, later President of the US], United States ambassador to the Court of St James, buddy of Ribbentrop and one of Wall Street's smarter slickers, [had written] Britain off and advised his President that John Bull was through' (Laddie Lucas, *Wings of War: Airmen of All Nations Tell Their Story*, Hutchinson, 1983).

room, Park tactfully explained to Churchill – not for the first time – that the air conditioning could not cope with cigar smoke. As the day's dramatic events unfolded, the Prime Minister was therefore obliged to observe them with no better consolation than a dead cigar between his teeth. He had met Park several times and regarded him highly, recognizing (as he wrote after the war) that his was the group 'on which our fate largely depended. From the beginning of Dunkirk all the daylight actions in the South of England had already been conducted by him, and all his arrangements and apparatus had been brought to the highest perfection.'

Soon after the visitors were seated in the 'dress circle' of the operations room, Park received a radar report of forty-plus aircraft over Dieppe, but no height was given. Then came another report of forty-plus in the same area and several squadrons were despatched to climb south-east of London. More squadrons were alerted to 'Stand By' (pilots in cockpits, ready for immediate take-off) and the remainder were ordered to 'Readiness' (take-off within five minutes). Having decided that a major attack was intended, Park had to guess its most likely targets, for his squadrons could not be everywhere. As always, he would concentrate on engaging bombers before they reached those targets, seeking to break their formations and cause them to jettison their loads into the sea or over open country.

Churchill remembered Park walking up and down behind the map table, 'watching with vigilant eye every move in the game . . . and only occasionally intervening with some decisive order, usually to reinforce a threatened area.' Churchill now broke silence. 'There appear to be many aircraft coming in.' As calmly, Park reassured him. 'There'll be someone there to meet them.' Soon all his squadrons were committed and Churchill heard him calling Dowding to ask for three squadrons from 12 Group to be placed at his disposal in case of another attack. He noticed Park's anxiety and asked: 'What other reserves have we?' 'There are none,' Park replied.

(Vincent Orange, *Sir Keith Park*, Methuen, 1984)

TO WIN OR LOSE IT ALL

The second and heavier attack on London [on the 15th] came about two hours later. The warning was shorter than in the forenoon, but gave time for six pairs of squadrons from 11 Group to take up positions over Chelmsford, Hornchurch, Sheerness, Northolt and Kenley while the leading German aircraft were still over the Channel. As the enemy approached the English coast 11 Group put up another seven and a half squadrons, four of them in pairs, while 12 Group again contributed five squadrons in a single tactical formation, and 10 Group one squadron.

Originally posted over Middle Wallop, the last was later transferred, with a second squadron, to the Kenley–Brooklands line.

Crossing the coast between Dungeness and Dover a little before twenty minutes past two, the attackers flew towards the capital in three formations. One was intercepted near Canterbury by a pair of squadrons ordered south from Hornchurch and later by a flight of Hurricanes posted over Maidstone; further west two squadrons moving north from Tangmere engaged another near Edenbridge and saw some of the bombers jettison their load and turn away while the majority continued towards London. Later Group Captain S. F. Vincent, commanding the Northolt sector, came in contact with the same force and had the satisfaction of seeing some of the bombers turn back in consequence of his single-handed attack delivered from head-on. The bulk of the fighting took place over London and its outskirts from Dartford westwards, where five pairs of squadrons from 11 Group and the wing from 12 Group were all in action between ten minutes to three and a quarter past, mainly with the third formation but probably also with survivors of the other two. In the course of the action the enemy distributed a big bomb-load over London and its outskirts, scoring several lucky hits on public utilities and railways. At East Ham a gas-holder and a telephone exchange were wrecked; and considerable damage was done to a variety of targets on both banks of the river at West Ham and Erith. Many other riverside boroughs reported hits; but the harm done was nothing like as great as that sustained eight days before in the first of the big daylight raids on London. Again retiring by two distinct routes, the attackers were engaged on the way out by another four squadrons, including two from 10 Group. Guns of the inner artillery zone and the Thames and Medway defences were also in action and claimed a number of successes.*

(Basil Collier, *The Defence of the United Kingdom*, HMSO, 1957)

CRISIS AVERTED

It was 4.30 p.m. before I got back to Chequers, and I immediately went to bed for my afternoon sleep. I must have been tired by the drama of 11 Group, for I did not wake till eight. When I rang, John Martin, my Principal Private Secretary, came in with the evening budget of news from all over the world. It was repellent. This had gone wrong here; that had been delayed there; an unsatisfactory answer had been received from so-and-so; there had been bad sinkings in the Atlantic. 'However,' said Martin, as he finished this account, 'all is redeemed by the air. We have shot down one hundred and eighty-three for a loss of under forty.'

---

* See map on page 144.

Although post-war information has shown that the enemy's losses on this day were only fifty-six, 15 September was the crux of the Battle of Britain.

(Winston S. Churchill, *Their Finest Hour*, Curtis Brown on behalf of the Estate of Sir Winston Churchill, C & T Publications, 1949)

'IT WOULD NEVER BE THE SAME AGAIN'

The last German night raiders flew eastward in the early morning of 16 September. As the dawn broke the columns of smoke arose over London and over the battered invasion ports. In the capital the sirens were silent and the streets echoed to the usual early morning sounds. Men came downstairs in their pyjamas to seize the newspapers and read the tremendous news: '185 SHOT DOWN AND MORE TO COME' said one headline. Across the Channel the German army turned out in the misty early morning for more invasion exercises. In the hangars and repair shops of the RAF and the Luftwaffe weary mechanics slipped outside for a smoke in early light. Another day. The war was still there. But from 15 September onward, it would never be the same again.

(Drew Middleton, *The Sky Suspended: The Battle of Britain, May 1940– April 1941*, Secker & Warburg, 1960)

THE OTHER SIDE OF THE COIN

On the German side, however, the battle was regarded as far from lost, even if the heavy casualties again made a change of tactics imperative. . . . Of the 56 aircraft that failed to return that day [15 September] 24 . . . [were] Dornier 17s and 10 Heinkel 111s. The damage to several dozen others was such as to require extensive overhaul. By the final count one quarter of the entire operating bomber force had been put out of action. Such a loss was far too high. If things went on like this, the Luftwaffe would bleed to death over England.

(Cajus Bekker, *The Luftwaffe War Diaries*, Macdonald, 1967)

The Londoners were very brave, and they went on being brave for a very long time.

(Peter Fleming)

THE SPIRIT OF LONDON

It was a battle now not only against the British air force but against the British people. But the people could 'take it', and none better than the long-suffering sons and daughters of the East End, upon whom the first cruel blow had fallen. For as on each succeeding night the German bombers returned to their task and the toll of broken bodies and buildings mounted, there was still no sign that nerve would crack or falter, no hint that London would prove unequal to its ordeal. Instead, a cheerful and unwavering fortitude, an immense patience, possessed the population; and in the flame and fury of 'The Blitz' were forged the links of a wider friendship and a deeper humanity.

Clearly the Londoners were not to be frightened easily, and the invasion plans must be pressed forward. Yet if to the virtually indiscriminate damage at night there could be added the destruction of key-targets by day, the task before the German armies might not prove so difficult after all. Besides, London was still farther inland than most of the 11 Group sector stations; it was certain to be defended in the greatest possible strength by the British fighters; and no other objective could offer the same chances of a vast and decisive air battle – a battle which would end, once and for all, the obdurate resistance of Fighter Command. So the German tactics were settled. The main weight of attack would fall on London by night, when losses would be agreeably small; the huge fighter formations, covering a small number of bombers, would force their way through to the capital by day, destroying in their path the final relics of Dowding's force.

(Denis Richards, *Royal Air Force History, 1939–1945*: vol. 1, *The Fight at Odds*, HMSO)

East Enders

Nearby was Christ Church. In the bone-deep chill of the crypt men, women and children lay on dirty quilts. Some slept in great stone coffins. The warden said they thought this protected them from blast.

A baby cried. A woman woke, comforted it, opened her dress and gave it her breast. The woman looked up, 'Awful ain't it, but we can't get in to them big shelters and those ones on the street are terrible dangerous.'

When I came out I saw Micky's small figure standing by the door of his shelter. There was the rumbling roar of a stick of bombs falling across the river and that never-to-be-forgotten, belly-turning rustling, crackling and cracking sound of a building crashing. 'Someone's copped it,' said Micky. As I left he said:

'Tell them we're not crying about it. It's like Churchill said, "It's up to us." But tell 'em it's no bloody picnic.'

Another night I visited a shelter beneath a warehouse close to the river. Over 200 people lay in groups on its cold stone floor. There had been some trouble on the first night. Lascars from the docks had raped a fourteen-year-old girl. Now the older men had formed a vigilante society. The Lascars were forbidden the place. The stink of sweat, dirty clothing, urine and excrement caught at your nose and throat.

These were the people who saved London's name. In their humility, their cheerfulness, their stolid, unspoken determination to continue there was a splendour. It was this quiet resolution that was far more impressive than the ribald jokes about Hitler and his court, the little paper Union Jacks stuck in the heaps of rubble, the slogans 'God Save the King' and 'Give it to them' chalked on blackened walls. All peoples are brave. When their time came, the Germans endured much heavier bombing with fortitude. What distinguished the British experience was that at a time when almost every broadcast, every newspaper headline told of reverses, defeats and defections, the people of London kept their heads and their hearts intact. They could not, they would not be driven or frightened out of what they dimly comprehended, they had to do. This was to fight on.

(Drew Middleton, The Sky Suspended: The Battle of Britain, May 1940–
April 1941, Secker & Warburg, 1960)

William Hickey reports

September 1940 . . . I wrote many descriptions of the heavy bombing of London and other cities. One of the first was of a night spent going the rounds of his parish with an East End parson, Father H. A. Wilson, Vicar of St Augustine's, Haggerston – a tall, nonchalant man in a black cassock, who 'permitted himself only one expletive, when a bomb fell too near: the appropriate "Blast!" ':

First he took me into his church hall, where a hundred or two people now regularly spend every night. Though of concrete, it is not technically a 'safe' building, he warns them; but they prefer its cosiness to the bleak, cold, unlit little brick surface shelters, some of which, in his parish, are still roofless. They smoke, play cards, play the piano.

In a corner of the floor a youth and girl were playing draughts. We picked our way among huddled groups; many were already asleep, wrapped in rugs. The vicar stopped to talk to a jocose old lady. 'This is the worst woman in east London,' he said, with an affectionate pat on her shoulder. 'She cheers me up a lot.'

'Bin 'ere forty years,' she said to me, 'and don't owe nobody a penny – through no fault of me own.'

At the side, on duty, sat one of the vicar's assistant curates, reading the letters of Mme de Sévigné, seventeenth-century French wit and beauty . . .

Meanwhile, we called at an almshouse; the aged inmates were sitting up in a downstairs room happily saying 'he's givin' us a quiet night, touch wood' . . . At a public shelter in the cellar of a disused brewery – the safest place in the parish – I thought I saw the vicar slip some sweets to an old woman . . . At a convent . . . also a recognized public shelter.

Along its narrow corridors the people slept sitting upright, crowded on narrow benches; one had to edge past them, now and then gently lifting and lowering a tousled cockney head, its owner too tired to wake.

The air was hot and acrid. In each room sat a white-coifed nun; when raids get bad they lead the people in singing hymns, to try to drown the bombs. Rollicking hymns go best. 'We Fought the Good Fight about fifty times last night between midnight and five o'clock,' said a nun.

Back at the clergy-house, I dozed. At four o'clock I was woken by a truly terrifying explosion; confused cries and wails followed it. I fumbled in the dark for my shoes, got them on somehow, went out. The vicar had been out and about all the time; blast from this bomb (or 'aerial torpedo') had rushed past him as he stood just inside his open front door. He thought it had hit the crowded hall; it hadn't; he hurried in there to comfort the people. An old woman ran past him wailing, 'Oh dear, I think it's our 'ouse, oh dear . . .'

In fact, the bomb had fallen some seventy-five yards away, wrecking a few small houses. When we got there they were carrying out a dead child. 'They're getting a young girl out; she's still alive,' said an ARP man. Over the shambles and misery an infernal glow in the sky shamed the first streaks of dawn.

(Tom Driberg, *Ruling Passions*, Jonathan Cape, 1977)

Mabel Knell, housewife

Her husband and eighteen-year-old son were both at work, her young daughter Mabel, aged fifteen, had just left school, and started to earn for herself; the little lad of eleven, and Freda, the baby girl of eight, had both to be seen off to school every day. The eldest son needed special interest, as he had just joined the Home Guard, and his meals had to be ready on time for his drills; the husband, too, was a voluntary Auxiliary Fireman, and, in addition to his practices, had to be on duty in all the frequent air attacks from which the town was constantly suffering. They had just reached the stage after years of hard work and struggle when, with the two older children earning, and the younger ones past the baby stage, they could spare a little time and money for themselves. They could go to the pictures in the evening, and a piano had been added to the sitting-room.

But to this whole-time job Mrs Knell managed to add just that extra quota of service which has resulted in her unassuming, simple, and completely normal life influencing many hundreds of her fellowtownswomen. She saw in the WVS Housewives' Service an opportunity for practical help which she could give her country . . . And so, on the night of 26 September 1940, the siren sounded as it had so often sounded before, and the husband changed into his uniform, and set off for his post of duty with his fellow-firemen at the docks, and this little, pretty, dark-haired woman saw him off on his dangerous mission, and then put her two small children into their bed under the stairs, for she would never have them in a public shelter lest they should lose their sleep, and by an abnormal way of living suffer next day in their school life; then, with an anxious thought to her son out on his Home Guard duties, she went into the kitchen, as she always did on 'raid nights', to make ready a hot drink to give her husband as soon as he came back.

But this particular night the fires were worse than usual; presently eight great pyramids of flame were shooting up, making a magnificent target for the rain of heavy bombs which followed, so Mrs Knell and Mabel joined the children under the stairs; but just before she sheltered there the mother placed beside her her little attaché case, which she had filled with all the necessary bandages and lotions which the doctor who gave the First Aid lectures had told her she would find helpful, if she could manage to get them, in case the Wardens brought anyone injured to her house for protection.

Later in the night they fetched the husband from the fire he had helped to get under control, and gave into his care his daughter Mabel and his little son. The baby girl lay beside her dead mother, where both had been instantly killed when the entire house was destroyed by a direct hit.

(Derek Tangye, *Went the Day Well*, Harrap, 1942)

Do not stand by my grave and weep
I am not there. I do not sleep
I am a thousand winds that blow
I am a diamond glint on snow
I am the sunlight on ripened grain
I am the gentle Autumn rain.
When you awake in the morning hush
I am the swift uplifting rush
Of quiet birds in circling flight
I am the soft starshine at night
Do not stand by my grave and cry
I am not there . . . I did not die.

(Author unknown)

BRITAIN UNDER THE US MICROSCOPE

16 October Last night for the first time I was continually wakened by bombing. As a rule I manage to sleep straight through, but the heavy cannonading plus the frequent whizz-boom of heavy bombs kept rousing me up. . . .

. . . For the first time [also] I could plainly hear a British fighter overhead and hope this betokens some consistent effort at bringing down at least a few of the German night flyers. At 4 a.m. nearby explosions got me out on the balcony. The heavens were full of flares dropped by the Germans and down in the street below a string of little fire engines went gonging along toward a huge rosy glow beyond Regent Street from which flames were roaring up above the housetops. This was the most disturbed night I have experienced so far.

The British are working very hard on a scientific detector which will enable their fighters to shoot these Boche raiders down at night [air-to-air radar]. If they evolve this soon they will have gone a great way toward winning the war. . . .

. . . In the meantime, a small number of fighters prowling around in the darkness last night managed to shoot down three of the raiders, which is a small step in the right direction.

Gerald Maxwell came in, to my surprise, as I had no idea he could get away from his job at the Coastal Command where he runs the photographic intelligence section – a most fascinating, scientific and precise business. Apparently he has been given a kind of roving commission to size up the situation in the Fighter Command. He was not only one of the best British aces in the . . . [First World War] but he has one or two young brothers in a fighter squadron and is intensely interested in their success. As a preliminary to [his] investigations, he had the admirable nerve to get into a Hurricane and fly at night to familiarize himself with this new machine, which goes three times as fast as the old SEs which he fought in during the [first] war.

He showed me a copy of a memorandum he had prepared at the Prime Minister's request and which has been presented to Churchill. It pointed out an extremely dangerous situation in the Fighter Command, in which it would seem that dour, dogmatic, stuffy old Dowding has managed to lose the confidence of . . . the fighter pilots. The complaint seems to be that he never has any contact with them and fails to appreciate how important it is for him to see and talk with them, especially with some squadron that has suffered severe losses. The whole trend of affairs indicates that there is a strong movement to replace Dowding by someone who is more of a leader. At the same time one must admit that he has done a magnificent job and is largely responsible for the successful defense of this country so far. It can easily be said about him, as was said about Jellicoe in the last war, that he is one man who can lose the war in a single afternoon by a bad error of judgement.

Of course, Maxwell feels very strongly about the matter. One of his young brothers has already had eight of the most terrific experiences, in all of which he was either shot down or wrecked, and once or twice under conditions which made his rescue a miracle.

While I was waiting for the party in the lounge of the Carlton, Sir John

Reith* came over and said fiercely that he did not think much of the American Ambassador's leaving London and that if he had his way about it the British Government would not grant him an exit visa. Of course I don't know what [Joe] Kennedy has in his mind, but from a soldier's point of view he is deserting his post at a critical time.

> (General Raymond E. Lee [US Military Attaché in London], *The London Observer: The Journal of General Raymond E. Lee*, edited by James Leutze, Hutchinson, 1972)

He should have stuck to Wall Street

Secretary of State, Washington DC
From United States Ambassador, Joseph Kennedy
Dateline: London, 27 September

For the President and the Secretary
The night raids are continuing to do, I think, substantial damage, and the day raids of the last three days have dealt most serious blows to Bristol, Southampton, and Liverpool. Production is definitely falling, regardless of what reports you may be getting, and with transportation smashed up the way it is, the present production output will continue to fall. . . .

My own feeling is that . . . [the British] are in a bad way. Bombers have got through in the daytime on the last three days, and on four occasions today substantial numbers of German planes have flown over London and have done some daylight bombing. . . .

I cannot impress upon you strongly enough my complete lack of confidence in the entire [British] conduct of this war. I was delighted to see that the president said he was not going to enter the war because to enter this war, imagining for a minute that the English have anything to offer in the line of leadership or productive capacity in industry that could be of the slightest value to us, would be a complete misapprehension.
[Editor's italics]

From Murrow, a different slant

This is London . . .
During the last week you have heard much of the bombing of Buckingham Palace. You have probably seen pictures of the damage. You have been told by certain editors and commentators who sit in New York that the bombing of the Palace, which has one of the best air-raid shelters in England, caused a great surge of determination, a feeling of unity, to sweep this island. The bombing was called a great psychological blunder. I do not find much support for that point of view amongst Londoners I've talked with. They don't like the idea of their King and Queen being

---

* Director General of the British Broadcasting Corporation.

bombed. But remember that this is not the last war. People's reactions are different, minds have become hardened, calloused. It doesn't require the bombing of Buckingham Palace to convince these people that they are all in this thing together.

There is nothing exclusive about being bombed when there are houses down in your street, when friends and relatives have been killed, when you have seen that red glow in the sky night after night, when you are tired and sleepy. There isn't enough energy left to be outraged about the bombing of a Palace. The King and Queen have earned the respect and admiration of the nation, but so have many tens of thousands of humble folk who are much less well protected. If the Palace had been the only place bombed the reaction might have been different. Maybe some of these German bomb aimers are working for Göbbels instead of Göring. But if the purpose of bombing the royal residence was to strike terror into the hearts of Britishers, then the bombs have been wasted.

That fire bomb on the House of Lords passed almost unnoticed. I heard a bus full of people laughing about it, when one man said 'That particular bomb wouldn't seriously damage the nation's war effort.' I'm talking about these things because the bombing of the Palace appeared to have affected America more than Britain. But in order that you may understand that this war has no relation with the last war, so far as symbols and civilians are concerned, you must understand that a world is dying. The old values, the old prejudices, the old bases of power and prestige are going. One of Britain's armies today is made up of that tide of faces that is London . . .

. . . In the West End of London life follows some kind of pattern. The shops are still full of food. The milk arrives on the doorstep each morning. The papers too, but sometimes they are a little late. A couple of people have left a change of clothing in our apartment, just in case a delayed action bomb should land near their residence and prevent them going home for a night or two. How long the people of the city can stand this sort of thing I don't know. I know only that they are not near their limit. Most of them expect the worst to come. If the city is stripped for action, if the Government trusts the people and tells then what is happening, and proves by swift action that the welfare of the relatively few who have lost all is the concern of the whole community, then I think the battle of London will be such a thing as men will try in vain to describe. There is still humour in this town.

(Edward Murrow, CBS broadcast to the US from London,
00.05 BST, 16 September 1940)

Methinks I see in my mind a noble and puissant nation rousing herself like a strong man after sleep, and shaking her invincible locks. Methinks I see her as an eagle mewing her mighty youth, and kindling her undazzled eyes at the full midday beam; purging and unscaling her long abused sight at the fountain itself of heavenly radiance, while the whole noise of timorous and flocking birds, with those also that love the twilight, flutter about, amazed at what she means.

(John Milton)

. . . *And Schickelgruber it became*

My greatest buddy was Quentin Reynolds, the husky New York Irishman, whose gravel-voice is remembered still by millions for his Sunday night postscripts to the nine o'clock news.

To one of these broadcasts I made a contribution. It was a Saturday morning and Quent's manuscript had to be with the BBC for censorship by 6 p.m. The night before had been heavy in every sense of the word. Quent's suite at the Savoy had been crowded with newspapermen and RAF fighter pilots on leave, and as he kept open house till the last guest had gone, both the bombs and the bottles had given all present a bit of a 'shellacking'.

'Come round and help me, old bean,' growled the host, who liked to imitate the London slang of thirty years back. 'I am short of ideas, old bean.'

When I arrived at the Savoy, Quent was propped up in bed with a portable typewriter that rocked from side to side on his knees.

'Order me a gin and lime, with lots of lime,' he groaned. 'Let's see if that will help.' But the gin and lime took so long to arrive that we batted out a couple of thousand words and reached the peroration without it.

Quent was orating from his bed and I was typing on a dressing-table as he reached the climax.

'Come on, Hitler!' he croaked derisively.

'Alter that to his real name, "Schickelgruber",' I suggested. 'Nobody in England could take a man with a name like Schickelgruber seriously.'

'You're darn right, old bean,' said Quent. And Schickelgruber it became on Sunday night. The name was hurled like the blast of a Sahara sandstorm into the microphone, and it bounced out of five million radio sets. People laughed that night as the bombs fell. Britain's contempt for Hitler became as valuable as several squadrons of bombers in prosecuting the war.

(Arthur Christiansen [Editor, *The Daily Express*],
Headlines All My Life, Heinemann 1961)

Quentin Reynolds contributed, in addition to his famous BBC postscripts, a compelling commentary for the Ministry of Information's spectacularly successful propaganda film London Can Take It, *made during the Battle by a young documentary director named Harry Watt. It played for weeks to packed houses in the UK and North America.*

Reynolds, who was covering the Battle for Collier's, *the US magazine, refused payment for his written and spoken text, a copy of which now follows.*

I am speaking from London. It is late afternoon and the people are preparing for the night. Everyone is anxious to get home before darkness falls – before our nightly visitors arrive. This is the London rush hour.

Many of the people at whom you are looking now are members of the greatest civilian army ever to be assembled. These men and women who have worked all day in offices or in markets are now hurrying home to change into the uniform of their particular service.

The dusk is deepening. Listening crews are posted all the way round the coast to pick up the drone of the German planes. Soon the nightly battle of Britain will be on. This has been a quiet day for us; but it won't be a quiet night. We haven't had a quiet night for five weeks. They'll be over tonight and they'll destroy a few buildings and kill a few people. Probably some of the people you are watching now.

Now they're going into the public shelters. This is not a pleasant way to spend the night, but the people accept it as their part of the defence of Britain. These civilians are good soldiers.

Now it's eight o'clock. Jerry's a bit late tonight. The searchlights are in position. The guns are ready. The People's Army of volunteers is ready. They are the ones who are really fighting this war. The firemen, the air-raid wardens, the ambulance drivers.

The very young and the very old, with that deep wisdom given only to the very young and the very old, sleep in the shelters. Do you see any signs of fear on these faces?

And there's the wail of the banshee . . . and that was a bomb.

Now the army of people swings into action. The bombs have started fires. When a bomber starts a fire he immediately returns, uses it as a target and drops more bombs, hoping to spread the fire.

Yet the People's Army ignores the bombs and the spent shrapnel, which rains down constantly. Brokers, clerks, pedlars, merchants by day – they are heroes by night.

The night is long. But sooner or later the dawn will come. The German bombers are creatures of the night. They melt away before the dawn and scurry back to the safety of their aerodromes.

And there's the wail of the banshee again – this time a friendly wail . . . The 'All Clear' signal tells us that the bombers have gone. It's just 6 a.m. In this last hour of precious sleep, this strange new world finds sleep: peace.

Britain raises her head, shakes the debris of the night from her hair and takes stock of the damage done. Britain has been hurt during the night. The sign of a great fighter in the ring is: 'Can he get up from the floor after being knocked down?' Britain does this every morning.

Britain doesn't look down upon the ruins of its houses, upon those made homeless during the night, upon the remains of churches, hospitals, workers' flats. Britain looks upwards towards the dawn and faces the new day with calmness and confidence.

The People's Army goes to work as it did in that other comfortable world, which came to an end when the invader began to attack the last stronghold of freedom.

Dr Paul Joseph Göbbels said recently that the nightly air raids have had a terrific effect upon the morale of the people of Britain. The good doctor is absolutely right. Today, the morale of the people is higher than ever before. They are fused together, not by fear, but by a surging spirit of courage the like of which the world has never known. They know that thousands of them will die. But they would rather stand up and face death than kneel down and face the kind of existence the conqueror would impose on them.

Not all the services run as they did yesterday, but they manage to get to work on time – one way or another. In the centre of the city the shops are open as usual – in fact, many of them are more open than usual.

And they know, too, and are comforted by the thought that England is not taking its beating lying down. They are guarding the frontiers of freedom. It is hard to see five centuries of labour destroyed in five seconds. But England is fighting back.

I am a neutral reporter. I have watched the people of Britain live and die ever since death in its most ghastly garb began to come here as a nightly visitor many weeks ago. I have watched them stand by their homes. I have seen them made homeless. I have seen them move to new homes.

And they know that every night the RAF bombers fly deep into the heart of Germany, bombing munition works, aeroplane factories, canals; cutting the arteries which keep the heart of Germany alive.

It is true that the Nazis will be over again tomorrow night and the night after that and every night. They will drop thousands of bombs and they'll kill thousands of people. But a bomb has its limitations. It can only destroy buildings and kill people. It cannot kill the unconquerable spirit and courage of the people of Britain.

London can take it!

SMART COLONEL

Now in the darkness the first of over 250 bombers began to thread their way towards the capital. What some called the Battle of London and what the Londoners themselves called 'the Blitz' had begun.

I dined that night, very tired and shaken, with a colonel of the United States Army Air Force I had met recently. His name was Carl A. Spaatz and he had been in London for some weeks watching the battle. We dined at Rules and midway through the meal we heard the high, keening scream of a bomber in a shallow dive. Paddy, the waiter, volunteered that the Germans were 'at it again'.

'By God,' Spaatz said, 'that's good, that's fine. The British are winning.' I remarked that it hadn't looked like it that afternoon. 'Of course they're winning,' he said vehemently. 'The Germans can't bomb at night – hell, I don't think they're very good in daylight – but they haven't been trained for night bombing. Nope, the British have got them now. They've forced them to bomb at night. The Krauts must be losing more than we know.'

I suggested that night bombing in the end might succeed in beating the British to their knees.

'Not in a million years,' Spaatz said. 'I tell you the Germans don't know how to go about it. And look at this bunch here. Do they look worried or scared. We're both a damned sight scareder than they are. The Germans won't beat them that way. Nope, the Germans have been licked in daylight.'

Four years later when he was General Spaatz, commanding the United States Eighth Air Force and a mighty figure, I reminded him of the conversation. 'Goes to show you that colonels are mighty smart fellows – sometimes,' he said.

(Drew Middleton, *The Sky Suspended: The Battle of Britain, May 1940– April 1941*, Secker & Warburg, 1960)

BLUNT WORDS OF A JUNKERS 88 PILOT

The task of destroying the Royal Air Force called for . . . above all . . . large fighter forces with ranges covering southern England, including London. A wholesale offensive with bombers was doomed to failure unless these fighter forces could remain in the air over enemy territory long enough to bring the enemy up to fight and beat him there or destroy him on the ground. Without fighter cover, bombers, even when flying in dense formation, were easy meat for the British fighters. And the fighters of the Royal Air Force were good.

The vital question whether the German fighters could perform the double task of protecting our own bombers and shooting down the enemy fighters had to be answered in the negative. That was how our fighter aces on the Western Front saw it . . .

The flying time, and therefore the range of the Me 109 was so short that only under the most favourable circumstances was an air battle in the vicinity of London possible for more than a few minutes. If our fighters and bombers missed their rendezvous at the exact moment or got separated on the approach, the whole sortie was wrecked and cost the bombers heavy losses. For one thing was plain – the Royal Air Force fully realized how critical the position was, and the English fighters had no hesitation in going bald headed for our bomber squadrons . . .

The German fighters, which could not be detected [by radar] from the ground, literally had their hands tied, tied to the Continent by an invisible but none the less potent thread – the question of fuel. Over and over again they had to return to base before the enemy could be caught and held. When action was actually joined the German fighters usually showed themselves to be superior. But the Royal Air Force had the advantage of fighting on interior lines and made wonderful use of it . . .

. . . .

. . . After extremely heavy losses, the Luftwaffe's daylight attacks on airfields in southern England and the Midlands, the southern harbours and London had to be abandoned in October. Radar and the few fighter squadrons had gained the day. On the German side, the effectiveness of British radar was not fully realized and no serious measures were taken to interfere with the wireless organization or destroy it from the air.

The German reports of victories, designed for propaganda purposes to conceal the failure of the Luftwaffe against England, were a very sore subject with our formations employed in the operations. When Field-Marshal Milch, as Inspector-General of the Luftwaffe, visited certain bomber groups which were based in Holland, 30 Group made no secret of its indignation. The squadron leaders who had actually flown in these operations bluntly told the Field-Marshal that it was impossible to produce the results required of them with the aircraft, bomb-sights and armament at their disposal, that the English fighters were just as superior to German bombers as German fighters were to British bombers and that night bombing could have no decisive effect, as we had neither bomb-sights for night operations nor enough bombers. Milch seemed grateful for our frank statement and said he would immediately seek a remedy.

He did produce a remedy. One Wing of the Group which had borne the heat and burden of the attacks . . . was broken up 'as punishment for mutiny and defeatism'. The officers were transferred and reduced in rank. A new staff officer arrived who had promised Göring that he would restore the efficiency of the Group in a fortnight if he were given command. His request was complied with.

Werner Baumbach, Broken Swastika: The Defeat of the Luftwaffe, Robert Hale, 1960)

Waiting Upon 'Mein Führer'

With forty victories in the Battle, Adolf Galland was called to Berlin to receive, by Herr Hitler's hand, the Oak Leaves to the Knights Cross.

Hitler received me in the new Reich's Chancellery. It was the second time I sat opposite him. On the first occasion, after my return from Spain with the Cóndor Legion, our meeting had been in the form of a collective reception, but now I was alone with him. Our conversation was a lengthy one. I expressed my great admiration for our enemy across the water. I was embittered by several insidious and false representations and commentaries by the Press and on the radio which had referred to the RAF in a condescending and presumptuous tone. Although I was expecting contradiction or anger from Hitler when I gave him a different picture, he did not interrupt me, nor did he try to change the subject, but nodded repeatedly and said that my description confirmed his beliefs. He too had the greatest respect for the Anglo-Saxon race. It had made it all the more difficult for him, he said, to decide on waging this life-and-death struggle which could only end with the total destruction of one or the other. He called it a world historical tragedy and said that it had been impossible to avoid this war, despite all his sincere and desperate attempts. If we won the war, a vacuum would be created by the destruction of Great Britain which it would be impossible to fill.

In most convincing terms, Hitler expressed not only his sympathy for the English race, but also his admiration for the class of political and industrial leaders which down the ages had developed on a much broader basis than anything that had so far existed in Germany. In their political development, favoured by different circumstances, the English were a hundred years ahead of us. All the virtues an eminent race had developed over long periods became manifest during critical phases in its history, as that which England was going through then. He regretted that he had not managed to bring the English and the German people together, in spite of a promising start.

(Adolf Galland, The First and the Last: The German Fighter Force in World War II, Methuen, 1955)

And Göring's stag party

From Berlin I flew to see Göring in East Prussia and at the gate of the Reichsjägerhof in the Rominterheide met Mölders. As Commander of the 51st Fighter Group, also based on the Channel, he had received the Oak Leaves three days before myself for his fortieth kill. He was in a hurry to get back to his station, but to his annoyance had been detained until now by Hitler and Göring. The obligation to defend your title as the most successful fighter pilot in the world was still taken very seriously. After a hurried farewell, he called to me: 'Fatty promised me he would detain you at least as long as he did me. And by the way, good luck with the stag I missed.'

The Reichsjägerhof was a log cabin made of huge tree trunks, with a thatched roof jutting far over the eaves. Göring came out of the house to meet me, wearing a green suède hunting jacket over a silk blouse with long, puffed sleeves, high hunting boots, and in his belt a hunting knife in the shape of an old Germanic sword. He was in the best of humour. Both the disagreeable memory of our last meeting and his worries about the Luftwaffe in the Battle of Britain seemed to have been spirited away. We could hear the stags out on the heath: it was rutting time.

After congratulating me, he said that he had a special treat in store for me: permission to hunt one of the royal stags which were usually reserved for him, a so-called 'Reichsjägermeister stag'. He knew them all and each one had a name; he watched over them, and was loth to part with one of them. 'I promised Mölders,' Göring said, 'to keep you here at least three days, so you've got plenty of time.' That night no mention was made either of the war in general or the Battle of Britain in particular.

Next morning at ten o'clock I had bagged my stag: it was really a royal beast, the stag of a lifetime. There was no further reason to prolong my stay at the Reichsjägerhof.

(Adolf Galland, *The First and the Last: The German Fighter Force in World War II*, Methuen, 1955)

ALL ALONE?

A story . . . [Johannes Steinhoff*] likes to tell concerns his Battle of Britain days. A formation of battered German fighters was returning to France after a daylight escort mission over England. The badly clanked pilots flying with Steinhoff were maintaining radio silence, since they were not anxious for any further encounters with the RAF. In their headphones came a pitiful wail from some helpless, wandering German fighter pilot:

'I'm all alone . . . I'm all alone,' moaned the lost German.

After several minutes of this dolorous caterwauling, Steinhoff heard one of his formation's R/T transmitters switch on.

'Shut up, you stupid bastard,' barked Steinhoff's squadron mate. 'You are not alone. There's a Spitfire on your tail.'

The moaning stopped abruptly.

(Trevor J. Constable and Raymond F. Toliver, *Horrido*, Macmillan, 1968)

---

* Postwar: General Johannes Steinhoff.

THE TALE OF THE GREMLINS

Gremlins* only make their appearance when pilots are in a tight position. They have many tricks up their sleeves. They can, for example, lay hands on the gauge which indicates to a pilot that his engine is being fed with oil at the requisite pressure, and cause the indicated pressure to drop dangerously, which is one of the factors all-important to his survival. A more mischievous Gremlin might decide to meddle with the instrument showing the glycol temperature of the Merlin engine, causing it to flicker, thus putting up the pilot's pulse-rate.

The Merlin had two banks of six cylinders with separate magnetoes, and any Gremlin worthy of his salt could easily make one bank misfire, thus causing the whole airframe to shudder in an alarming manner. They could make gauges misread, fuel warning and other indicators flash; they could even manipulate the pneumatic pressure indicator sufficiently to make one wonder whether the undercarriage would come down on selection, or if the guns would fire when the button was pressed – both systems relied on air pressure.

A senior Gremlin could, with the greatest ease, make one believe the oxygen was tainted – but he would usually delegate to a subordinate Gremlin the duty of disrupting the oxygen needle and swinging it into the red danger area, only to return it five minutes later, to indicate that the oxygen cylinder was half full.

The most remarkable thing about the Gremlins was that they departed from one's aircraft when the dangerous period was over. No Gremlin, for example, laid so much as a finger on my aircraft when I was in the airfield circuit preparatory to landing. I think, on the whole, they preferred to do their work at a great height, or while one was over the sea in a single-engine aircraft.

... There must have been hundreds of thousands of Gremlins, both British and German, operating over the skies of England in 1940.

(Wing Commander H. R. [Dizzy] Allen, DFC, *Who Won The Battle of Britain?*, Arthur Barker, 1974)

DEFENCE OF FREEDOM

Why did I go to England? Because I felt it was my duty. It was seeing where one's duty lay, not doing it, that had become so difficult.

(Capitaine François de Labouchere, 249 and 615 Squadrons, on his decision to quit France and join his Free French comrades in England)

---

* Gremlin, n (RAF sl.). Mischievous sprite alleged to cause mishaps (*The Concise Oxford Dictionary of Current English*, edited by H. W. and F. G. Fowler, Clarendon Press, 1960).

FREE FRENCH . . .

I don't really know what happened. I was 'weaver' when I heard a loud noise . . . At the same time my cockpit was filled with glycol vapour. There was a big hole above the engine from which a not-too-thick stream of white smoke was coming. Detling airfield was just below. Life was fine – but I stopped appreciating the joke when I saw flames instead of smoke . . . I was, however, low enough to land wheels up.

My beautiful brand-new uniform, covered with oil, was irrecoverable . . . I immediately put in . . . for another. The quartermaster general did not agree. 'If you had a fire,' he said, 'you must in some way be to blame.' . . .

That was 'my' battle of Britain. A succession of never-ending alerts, of take-offs in three minutes to try to intercept an elusive enemy; and the superior performance of the adversary who always had the advantage [of height and sun] . . .

Our score at the end [of the battle] was a blank . . . I remember that period as one of exultation mixed with a little . . . regret that, despite my efforts, I arrived a little late in this Battle of Britain.

(Henri Lafont, *247 and 615 Squadrons*, Icare, Paris, 1965)

THE ENDURANCE OF MAN

It was inevitable that the Battle produced its legendary characters. One such was Geoffrey Page of 56 Squadron. After being shot down and cruelly burnt, and undergoing months of plastic surgery, he returned marvellously to operations, played out a long innings and finished the war as a highly decorated wing commander with a tally of fifteen enemy aircraft standing to his credit.

Barely conscious from his terrible burns, he had baled out of his blazing Hurricane into the sea, some eight miles north of Margate. Then his Maker intervened.

Only one problem remained. It was one of keeping afloat for just another minute or two before all energy failed.

. . . Then I heard it – the unmistakable chug-chug of a small motor boat growing steadily louder. . . . In it sat two men in the strange garb peculiar to sailors of the British Merchant Service. . . . Slowly the boat circled without attempting to pick me up. A rough voice carried over the intervening water 'What are you? A Jerry or one of ours?'

My weak reply was gagged by a mouthful of water. The other man tried as the boat came full circle for the second time. 'Are you a Jerry, mate?'

Anger flooded through me. Anger, not at these sailors who had every

164

reason to let a German pilot drown, but anger at the steady chain of events since the explosion that had reduced my tortured mind and body to its present state of near-collapse. And anger brought with it temporary energy. 'You stupid pair of fucking bastards, pull me out!!'

The boat altered course and drew alongside. Strong arms leaned down and dragged my limp body over the side and into the bottom of the boat. 'The minute you swore, mate,' one of them explained, 'we knew you was an RAF Officer.'

. . . The first sailor produced a large clasp knife. 'Better get this wet stuff off you, mate. You don't want to catch your death of cold.'

The absurdity of death from a chill struck me as funny and I chuckled for the first time in a long time. To prove the sailor's point the teeth chattering recommenced. Without further ado the man with the knife set to work and deftly removed pieces of life jacket and tunic with the skill of a surgeon. Then my naked body was wrapped up in a blanket produced from the seat locker.

One of them went forward to the engine and seconds later the little boat was churning her way back to the mother ship. The other sailor sat down beside me in silence, anxious to help but not knowing what to do next. I sensed the kindness of his attitude and felt that it was up to me to somehow offer him a lead. The feeling of sickness was still there from the revolting smell of burnt flesh, but I managed to gulp out 'Been a lovely . . . summer, hasn't it?'

. . . By now the tall sides of the old tramp steamer were looming above the little boat as they lined the rail looking down at me. A voice hailed us. 'What you got there, Bill? a Jerry?'

The man with the knife cupped his hands and called back, 'No, one of our boys.'

Swiftly a gangway was lowered and two pairs of strong arms formed a hand chair and carried me to the deck aloft. The grizzled captain came forward to greet me with outstretched hand. Clasp knife spoke quietly. 'He can't, Skipper. Both hands badly burned.'

'Bad luck, lad,' the captain said. 'But never mind, we'll soon have you fixed up.' To the sailors he said, 'Bring him into the galley.' . . .

Roughly the crew attempted to console me as whimpers of suffering escaped through my lips. It was obvious that their inability to ease the suffering was causing them acute mental discomfort.

Nature offered her own relief-valve, and for a few minutes I escaped into unconsciousness . . .

. . . .

Dim recollections of an ambulance ride, the outside of the general hospital, followed by a long journey down endless corridors on a trolley, a heave, and I was lying on top of a comfortable bed in a small private room. Soon blessed relief from pain was injected into my arm . . .

. . . .

. . . It was pointed out to me that burns ran a grave danger of septicemia and that the blood must be kept cleansed . . .

. . . I was [then] trundled away to the operating room on a trolley. The surgeon, anaesthetist and a gowned nurse comprised the skeleton staff for surgical cases. All three helped to lift me on to the table beneath the huge over-hanging light.

The nurse and surgeon disappeared to scrub-up and the anaesthetist prepared his hypodermic syringe.

A sudden desire to know the extent of my facial injuries absorbed me and I pleaded for a glance in a mirror. Sensibly the second doctor refused the request and changed the subject to safer topics.

The masked and gloved surgeon returned with his assistant. Neatly the anaesthetist tied a rubber cord round my bicep and searched the hollow of the elbow joint for a suitable vein. Not wishing to see the needle enter the skin, I looked away and upwards, catching sight of myself in the reflector mirrors of the overhanging light. My last conscious memory was of seeing the hideous mass of swollen, burnt flesh that had once been a face.

The Battle of Britain had ended for me, but another long battle was beginning.

(Geoffrey Page, *The Tale of a Guinea Pig: The Exploits of a World War II Fighter Pilot*, Bantam Books, New York, 1981: Pelham Books, London, 1981)

Tom Gleave was another heroic figure from the Battle who survived his terrible burns to give the Royal Air Force noble service.

I finally managed to get the hood [of the cockpit] open. Then . . . there was a God Almighty explosion. I went straight up in a huge sheet of flame. The aircraft just disappeared. I came down head over heels, pulled my ripcoard, and my parachute opened. My hands were swelled up, and my face and legs. Most of my clothes had gone. I was pretty badly burnt – about 30 per cent burns. I lost all the skin off my right foot. I still get holes occasionally, things sometimes come out, bits of bone. I lost all the skin off my hand and most of my face. My eyelids and nose went. We carried loaded guns. We could have shot ourselves, and I would have . . . [done so had I got] to the state where I hadn't a hope in hell. No doubt some pilots did . . .

. . . .

. . . Sister came in [at the hospital] and said my wife had arrived. I was well enough to worry about her seeing me as I was: my hands, forearms, and legs were encased in dried tannic acid. My face, which felt the size of the proverbial melon, was treated in the same way, and I peered through slits in the mask. I heard footsteps approaching the bed and then saw my wife standing gazing at me. She flushed a little and said, 'What on earth have you been doing with yourself, darling?'

I found it hard to answer. 'Had a row with a German,' I replied.

(Squadron Leader [later Group Captain] Tom Gleave)

> I have been half in love with easeful Death,
> Call'd him soft names in many a mused rhyme,
> To take into the air my quiet breath;
> Now more than ever seems it rich to die,
> To cease upon the midnight with no pain.

(John Keats)

BRILLIANT SURGEON

Archie McIndoe, the plastic surgeon of finely developed skills, brought succour to the crews who had sustained grievous injury from burns in the Battle. The New Zealander, whose work at East Grinstead, in Sussex, was recognized with a knighthood, became the saviour of many who had made their sacrifice and were reconciled to live with their wounds. Cyril Jones, then a leading aircraftman, was an operating-room assistant at the hospital and witnessed McIndoe's work at first hand.

We were a specialized unit for treatment of burns and reconstructive surgery. We received pilots and ground crew who were burnt as a result of German bombings and accidents on the airfields. The pilots came mostly because of flash burns caused by the high-octane spirits of their fuel tanks. The burns were up to 60 or 70 per cent of their bodies. The difference between being burnt to a cinder and coming to us might have been just three seconds exposure to the flames in a burning plane.

Most of our patients were young men, in the prime of their lives. Most had been good-looking. The pilots who came to us were also well educated. To suddenly look the way they looked after being badly burnt was very shaking. It hit them hard. The advantage of our unit was there was always someone worse off. You may have lost a leg, but right next to you might be a chap who'd lost his hands. A man might have no ears, but there was another chap who was blind.

McIndoe insisted on putting these men together. He'd never allow rank to get special privilege. He was always asked by other services to take special cases. We once had a captain in the Royal Navy who needed treatment. The navy in those days was all posh. There was a lot of tradition and this, that, and the other and, of course, the under ranks weren't even spoken of. This captain came to us one day. He'd lost an eye and McIndoe was asked to rebuild his eye socket. McIndoe admitted him into a ward with ordinary airmen who had suffered bad burns. This captain, who expected VIP treatment, was put into a ward with forty men. On one side was a leading aircraftman. On the other side was a sergeant. Well, this navy captain was in high dudgeon about it. He went straight to McIndoe and said, 'It is ridiculous for me to be nursed in a ward where I've got ordinary ranks around me. I must have a private room of my own.' McIndoe told him, 'You asked to be treated by me. If you wish to be treated by me, you will take the treatment I am offering. If you don't like the ward, then go and find someone else to treat you.'

. . . .

There was terrific camaraderie among the patients. You'd often see fifteen wheelchairs being pushed to town, all going to the pub. McIndoe wanted the men to be accepted by the general public as normal human beings. He wanted to give them back their normal functions and their dignity. In the early stages, we had to go through the stage of men not wanting to live. They were terrible to look at. But to see then now, after so many years – they are accepted and have been for years, though some had to go through as many as sixty operations. Some decided, 'Right – my wife accepts me and that's good enough.' This is where many of the women played an important role. Some of our nurses – good-looking young girls – married those men when they were at their worst.

In his treatment, McIndoe paid most attention to eyelids and hands. He would take a single layer of epidermis from the arm of the man to replace his eyelids. He wasn't looking to give a man back his looks. It couldn't be done. He was aiming at restoring their normal functions – opening and closing the eyes, opening and closing their mouths, restoring their noses, and restoring the use of their hands. They went through phases. From healing the burns to starting reconstructive surgery could be anything from three days to three years.

(Norman Gelb, *Scramble*, Michael Joseph, 1986)

THE NIGHT BATTLE: ABORTIVE START

I had only been there [No. 6 (Operational Training) Group, Bomber Command] just over three weeks when, much to my delight, I received a personal signal from the newly appointed Chief of Air Staff* offering me command of a night-fighter wing in 11 Group [Fighter Command], if I were prepared to revert to the rank of Wing Commander [from Group Captain]. I gratefully accepted the appointment and next day reported to Park, the AOC of 11 Group, who told me that two new night-fighter wings were forming, one at Southend and the other at Gravesend, and that he proposed I should command the former. . . .

---

* Air Chief Marshal Sir Charles Portal.

The wing was to be made up of 264 Squadron equipped with Defiants and 151 equipped with Hurricanes, but at that time only 264 Squadron was actually at Rochford and I asked for the arrival of 151 to be postponed for a few days until I had organized the accommodation. . . .

Many of the airmen were youngsters who had joined the Service shortly before the outbreak of war, and owing to the necessity of getting mechanics into newly formed squadrons as quickly as possible, disciplinary and general service training had been substantially reduced. We now paid the penalty for this as some of these men were not as steady under fire or in the face of bombings as they should have been, but the strong measures I had to adopt were soon effective, and when I moved my bed into the detonator store they decided I was crazy and more to be feared than enemy action. . . .

The wing was . . . not a satisfactory organization. Firstly, the airfield was unsuitable for the operation of Defiants at night because when taking off towards the Thames, two miles distant, the aircraft had to make a quick turn almost as soon as they became airbourne to avoid the balloon barrage flown from barges moored in the river. This was the cause of two fatal accidents in ten days. . . . Secondly, the Defiant was a thoroughly bad night fighter. It was slow and unmanoeuvrable, it had no AI* and it carried no fixed front armament but relied on a four-gun turret for its fire power, and when the guns were swung to the full-beam position, the aeroplane became very unstable. . . .

All these [and other] difficulties were fully appreciated, and early in December [two months after the start], the wing was disbanded and I was sent to take over the Wittering sector [covering the Midlands].

(Air Chief Marshal Sir Basil Embry, GCB, KBE, DSO (3 bars), DFC, AFC, *Mission Completed*, Methuen, 1957)

EVENING FLIGHT

The blue bound fires of evening
 sink quietly in the West;
the soft twilight is deepening
 and teal return to rest.

But we sit by the salting
 to meet their flight with lead,
and here they do no halting
 but the halting of the dead.

(A. N. C. Weir†, DFC, *Verses of a Fighter Pilot Flying Officer*, Faber & Faber, 1941)

* Airborne radar.

† Nigel Weir, a Wykehamist, survived the fighting in the Battle only to be killed a month or so later, in November 1940. Ed

AIR–SEA RESCUE: LUFTWAFFE'S LEAD

Germany, in contrast to her sea power enemy, had entered the air battle with a well-planned service for fishing air crews out of the sea, drying them off, and returning them to action. The Luftwaffe's sea rescue service began training before the war in He 59 float planes and fast launches. As the battle wore on it introduced a luxury sea rescue float. Equipped as a wave-bobbing 'oasis', each float was fitted with four bunks, blankets, clothing, food and water, and stationed at intervals in mid-Channel.

The Luftwaffe gave the lead in most aspects of air–sea rescue. It introduced the yellow colouring for rubber dinghies, skull caps and jackets. The RAF followed suit and also adopted the Luftwaffe's practice of issuing crews with bags of fluorescine which stained the water a bright green colour . . .

While Me 109 pilots carried inflatable dinghies, their single-seated opponents flying Hurricanes and Spitfires had to rely on their 'Mae Wests'. Only when an Me 109 pilot's dinghy had been captured and examined did successful development of a dinghy for RAF fighter pilots take place. It was a great improvement on the German prototype, but by that time the Battle of Britain was over and many airmen had drowned.

. . . .

. . . The life of every operationally trained fighter pilot was at a high premium but, despite courageous rescues by the volunteers in the lifeboats of the Royal National Lifeboat Institution, the sea was taking its toll of pilots who ought to have been rescued.

Upon occasion the lifeboatmen were themselves inspired by the pluck of 'amateurs' making private rescue bids. At five minutes past six on the morning of 14 August the *Charles Cooper Henderson* was launched to seek a British bomber down in the sea between Hythe and Dymchurch. Taking in tow a fishing boat which had picked up two survivors before they arrived, the lifeboatmen discovered that a Miss Peggy Prince had also put out in a small canoe and paddled back with another survivor. She was awarded the OBE . . .

. . . .

. . . Obviously a 'crash' emergency scheme was required, and like so many British 'lash-ups' to meet a crisis situation, air–sea rescue was helped into being under the 'old pals act'. A quick arrangement between Air Vice-Marshal Park and Vice-Admiral Sir Bertram H. Ramsey, Vice-Admiral, Dover, launched a local Channel rescue service which combined Park's RAF launches, Ramsey's light naval craft and twelve Lysander aircraft borrowed from the Army Co-operation Command to drop dinghies. Truly a 'combined op' in the very best British make-shift tradition, [but] air–sea rescue was not regularized until the end of August.*

(Edward Bishop, *The Battle of Britain*, Unwin Hyman Ltd, 1960)

* Once established in strength, the Royal Air Force's ASR service (air and waterborne) performed prodigious feats – in home waters and overseas – often in the face of the enemy's fire. Ed.

'They Kept the Ferry Moving'

The men and women of Air Transport Auxiliary were civilians in uniform who played a soldier's part in the Battle of Britain and who performed, throughout the war, a task of supreme importance to the RAF.

They brought the airplanes to the squadrons. In foul weather and fair, by night and day, they kept the ferry moving.

I came upon the ATA almost at the start of its activities. I watched it grow from a mere handful of pilots into a vast organization. And I saw how the fine courage and cheerfulness of the early days endured as numbers swelled and responsibilities multiplied.

(Lord Beaverbrook, Minister of Aircraft Production)

One arm and one eye

When delivering aircraft to the front line, [ATA] pilots had to chase squadrons from place to place and their taxi planes followed even when the squadrons were being bombed at the time.

One pilot who led a flight of six Hurricanes to a coastal aerodrome, was greeted with 'Thank God you've brought us something. Now we can fight again!'

Keith-Jopp himself volunteered one day in early September for his fifth job of the day.

It meant flying from South Wales to Kent, tracking the Squadron through two intermediate airfields, and finally running it to earth at Croydon. It was almost dark when he reached them and delivered a Mark 1 Spitfire (with a broken reflector sight) which had that morning been in use at a Training Unit.

The squadron was at half strength and the crews almost 'all in'. The ATA pilot went to the Mess before leaving the Station and one can imagine the surprise and possible pleasure of the young pilots, tired as they were, to find in their midst the one-armed, one-eyed veteran of another war who had brought them a desperately needed replacement aircraft with which to fight the next day.

(E. C. Cheesman, *Brief Glory*, Petty & Sons, 1946)

Masters of their fate

Air Transport Auxiliary was founded . . . by Gerard ['Pops'] D'Erlanger, banker and peacetime private flyer. It offered a specialist service because its pilots were trained to fly any aircraft on sight whether or not they had ever flown the type before. The key to this – apart, of course, from flying ability – lay in the pages of a small blue book.

This was a brilliantly compiled edition containing every item of necessary flight information for every aircraft, British or American, flown by the Royal Air Force or the Fleet Air Arm. . . .

We were masters of our own fate. In collecting and delivering aeroplanes we could overrule station commanders and chief flying instructors.

(Commander Francis Francis, [CO of No. 1 Ferry Pool, ATA, White Waltham, Berkshire], *Personal collection*)

THE EAGLES' WAR

By the autumn of 1940, with the Royal Air Force still sorely pressed by the German Luftwaffe, the beginning of a stream of American pilots was moving to swell the ranks of the RAF – while the organizational procedures were being implemented to create the fighting unit.

Charles Sweeny – a staunch friend of Britain and founder of the Eagle Squadrons – re-captures the mood of the times:

In 1940 and 1941 – 'Our darkest hour' as Winston Churchill termed it – a number of young Americans came to England determined to defend with their lives the principles of freedom and democracy. They were banded together within the Eagle Fighter Squadrons of the Royal Air Force and set up a very distinguished record. When the United States came into the war in December 1941, they were absorbed into the United States Army Air Force as the 4th Fighter Group and again were extremely successful. Among the names that spring to mind are Tobin, Mamedoff and Keough, the first three volunteers, followed shortly afterwards by Peterson, Goodson and Blakesley. These boys, as well as others, will live . . . wherever brave men and their deeds are recounted . . .

The Eagle Squadrons were formed by me in May 1940 after conversations with Churchill, Beaverbrook, and a meeting with the Air Staff. They listened to my suggestions and in due course, I received a letter saying that 71 Squadron had been activated by the Royal Air Force to house the Eagle [volunteers] but in the first instance they wanted 25 pilots and 25 pilots in reserve before they became operational. The same formula was followed up when the other two squadrons were formed, but of course, they were acting [then] through the Empire Training Scheme which provided a steady flow of pilots.

Oddly enough, the name 'Eagle Squadron' was suggested to me by my father and I took the shoulder patch from my American passport and added the initials 'E.S.'.

. . . Eventually, we had over 240 volunteers and some 80 were lost in action, which as you realize, was a very high percentage.

(P. D. Mason, *Fighting Church Fenton*: A Detailed History, 1937–1989, Pegasus Studio, 1989)

COMBAT REPORT

Pilot Officer David Scott-Malden, RAFVR, 603 Squadron
The aerial combat which remains most vividly in my mind was over Kent on 12 October 1940 soon after joining 603 Squadron. The Squadron was depleted by losses and eight aircraft were directed into a large 'gaggle' of Me 109s. The Squadron split up individually and passed head-on through the enemy formation. There was a sense of shock, as a distant series of silhouettes suddenly became rough metal with grey-green paint and yellow noses, passing head-on on each side. At the far end I had a few minutes' dog-fight with the last 109, scoring hits which produced a tail of black smoke. Then we were alone at 20,000 ft, the German gliding down with an engine which coughed and barely turned over, I with no ammunition and very little petrol. He glided hopefully towards the Channel: I looked for an airfield before the last of my petrol ran out. Strangely I felt inclined to wave to him as I left. But then, I was only twenty years old.

(Fighter Pilot Profiles, Military Gallery, Bath, 1985)

By a remarkable historical coincidence, the remains of the Me 109 which Pilot Officer [later Air Vice-Marshal] David Scott-Malden, of 603 Squadron, stationed at Hornchurch, shot down on 12 October 1940 have recently been found by Trevor Williams and a colleague from the Rebel Air Museum at Andrews Field, in Essex.

Williams recorded the details of the find in a letter to the Air Vice-Marshal dated 30 March 1989, after the checks had been completed.

The Me 109E – S, Werks Nummer 1966, with a black 'eleven' in front of the fuselage, crashed high up on the Kent Downs at Deans Hill, Hollingbourne. . . . scattering its wings and DB 601 engine down the steep slope. We gathered as much of the aircraft as we could – at least enough to make a nice display for the Museum. . . .

The pilot, Staffel Führer, Oblt Buesgen, of 1/JG52, [based at] Coquelles or Peuplingues, was engaged on a free-lance fighter sweep. Slightly injured, he baled out and probably ended his war as a prisoner in Canada.)

REGIA AERONAUTICA'S BATTLE INTERVENTION

When we were about 12,000 feet up, I saw nine planes of a type I had never seen before, coming along. They were in a tight 'V' formation. I did not like to rush in bald-headed, until I knew what they were, so the squadron went above to have a good look at them. Then I realized that any rate they were not British, and that was good enough for me so we went into attack starting with the rear starboard bomber . . .

I must say that the Italians, as they turned out to be, stood up to it very well.

(*Winged Words: BBC Broadcasts*, Heinemann, 1941)

Whoever has the Italians on his side will lose.
(Adolf Galland, from J.E. [Johnnie] Johnson's
personal collection)

Czech at war with Mussolini

It was just my luck that, on this day [of the Regia Aeronautica's attack], the engine of my Hurricane wasn't developing its usual power. I pushed all the levers forward, but there was not the proper response. Try as I might, I couldn't keep up with the formation. Dropping 100, 200, 500 yards behind, I became highly vulnerable to attack.

As Rabagliati manoeuvred the squadron [No. 46] up-sun for the attack, two other squadrons from the North Weald sector, 249 and 257, were also hurrying to get their chance at this rare quarry. Engagement took place over Maidstone. All I could do with my lazy engine was to stay where I was hoping to pick off any stragglers. . . .

At that moment I saw, just above, thirty or forty unknown biplanes. They looked like Avia B 534s, the standard fighter aircraft in my country. Then I realized that here was a gaggle of Italian CR 42s, supposedly protecting their bombers [BR 20s]. A fat lot of good they were doing!

I struggled to get my lazy beast of a Hurricane up to their level. As I did so two of the fighters were falling in flames and then two more broke away from the main formation, looking as if they might have had enough of the fighting. As they crossed my path without seeing me I gave the second aircraft a short burst with my machine guns, allowing full deflection. It exploded and went down like a fireball. . . .

By now I was over the sea and then, holy mackerel, six CR 42s started diving at me out of the sun to come to the aid of their comrade. I was now the prey. It was time for me to quit so I turned away putting my nose down at about 6000 feet. I quickly left the Italians behind, recrossed the coast and eventually landed at Rochester, in Kent, . . . with my fuel tanks almost empty. I had ten bullet holes in the wings, and fuselage of my aircraft.

After refuelling I returned to Stapleford, claiming one CR 42 destroyed and another probably destroyed from my personal war with Mussolini. . . .

My claims were never credited. In the excitement, I had forgotten to switch on my ciné camera and, because I had been on my own, separated from the squadron, there was no other confirmation!

(Karel Mrazek* [later Group Captain], personal collection)

FAMILY TIE

(Letters written during the Battle are still cherished. In the family of the 3rd Earl of Leicester there is a letter written to a beloved childhood nanny – 'Susie Q' – by the younger son, David Coke,† a member of 257 Squadron, as he lay wounded in the Royal Naval Hospital at Gosport, near Portsmouth, which is specially treasured.)

Darling Susie,   Tuesday
   I had half the stitches taken out today, and the rest out tomorrow. Afraid it will be a little time before [the wound] heals completely . . . I hope to get out of here at the end of this week and go and spend a couple of weeks with Mummy and Daddy at Eastern Grey [in Wiltshire], but it seems they're very reluctant to let visitors out of here!
   Several Merchant Navy lads are in here whose convoys have been bombed. Poor devils, they have a devil of a life, and don't get nearly enough credit for what they are doing. I've seen them myself bombed and machine-gunned in the Channel – little cargo ships with no armour and perhaps only one machine gun. Tho' they lose a ship now and then nothing stops them . . .
   I was amazed at the number of ships and convoys coming up the Channel and Thames Estuary. I wish old Hitler could have seen the effect of his boasted 'command of the North Sea and Channel!' The latter looks awfully narrow from the air . . . and France looks so lovely in the evening sun. It's difficult to realize there is so much nastiness over there.
   . . . Our boys have been doing pretty well, tho' I can't help thinking they are getting more than their fair share of the limelight. Half the praise is due to the designers and manufacturers of the Hurricane and Spitfire.
   The bomber boys, too, are not getting half enough praise . . . Where our fighting is just slapdash enjoyment, their work is relentless . . . They undergo ten times more strain and danger . . .
   I was so sorry Mummy came rushing down from Scotland just when she was looking after Anne and Carey. I hear the fools at the Air Ministry said at first I was seriously wounded. How damn silly of them! Had a

---

* Karel Mrazek was the first Czech to be posted to 46 Squadron. Ed.
   † Flight Lieutenant the Hon. David Coke fell in action with 80 Squadron at Acroma, south-west of Tobruk, on 9 December 1941 in the rough desert fighting. The DFC for which this gallant officer had earlier been recommended was gazetted after his death. Ed.

grand letter from Grandpa who says 'you have made a capital start in life' referring to my being wounded!!

I hope perhaps to see you all. I'll certainly try. Love to Sissie and the Bobbins . . .

Your loving David

BODIE HAD DONE HIS BEST

Bodie was our local ace, and a true one at that. He didn't claim anything he didn't see explode in front of his very eyes. He was, was 'Bogle', a bloody good hombre. . . . He recounted his experiences of one of his last days with 66. . . . These are his own words; take a lot of trouble reading them:

The second [enemy aircraft] was spinning. There was a piece off one wing. He spiralled crazily down into the water. It reminded me of chestnut leaves in the autumn, fluttering down onto the school playing fields. He hit, exploded, and petrol and oil burned fiercely on the surface of the sea . . .

I then remembered having seen another Dornier explode and burn – let me think, when was it? Why, only that very morning! It was still Sunday, 15 September. The day had been a year.

I flew to the coast and set course for home. Passing low over fields and villages, rivers and towns, I looked down on labourers working, children at play beside a big red-brick schoolhouse, a bomb crater two streets away; little black heads turning to white blobs as they heard my engine and looked up. I thought of workers in shops and factories, or stretcher-parties and ARP [Air Raid Protection] wardens. I hoped the All Clear had gone. I was tired, I'd done my best for them. . . .

Cor, stone the crows! Could John Milton have written better prose than that? '. . . Thrones, Dominations, Princedoms, Virtues, Powers. . . . No fear lest dinner cool. . . . All night the dreadless angel unpursu'd. . . . Arms on armour clashing bray'd horrible discord. . . .' Don't ask me whether Bodie did any better than Milton. That is my secret . . .

(Wing Commander H. R. [Dizzy] Allen, personal collection)

Their shoulders held the sky suspended;
They stood, and earth's foundations stay.

(A. E. Housman)

HOST TURNED GUEST:
FROM AUGSBURG TO A KENTISH HOP FIELD

In a contest which produced many bizarre stories, Michael Lister Robinson, an attractive and charismatic Royal Air Force leader, could tell one of the strangest of all. From his schooldays at Downside until his entry into the Service in the mid-1930s, Robinson lived to fly. He flew aeroplanes with the angels, and this ability, allied with an engaging personality, brought him two rather special commands in the Battle – a flight in 601, the County of London Auxiliary Air Force Squadron, and, a little later, leadership of 609, its West Riding counterpart. Two years later still, as Sailor Malan's successor at the head of the Biggin Hill Wing, Robinson, by now impressively decorated, was lost in action. Nearly a score of enemy aircraft stood to his credit when he fell.

On 31 August 1940, as 601 engaged the opposition, Michael had damaged two Me 109s and then, out of ammunition, had chased after a third. His combat report, given afterwards, withheld one fact:

He [the German pilot] never rose above 100 feet until well south of Maidstone and then throttled back. I overtook him and formated on him, pointing downwards for him to land. He turned away so I carried out a dummy quarter attack, breaking very close to him. After this he landed his Me in a field . . . I threw him a packet of twenty Players and returned to base.*

But Robinson hadn't at once returned to base – as the extraordinary sequel to the incident was later to confirm.

Some while after Robinson had taken over command of 609 on 4 October 1940, he and Squadron Leader J. S. Ward, the 11 Group PRO, prepared a script to be broadcast by the BBC. Michael was to deliver it. It told how, six months or so before the outbreak of war, he and two young Army friends, one from the Welsh Guards and the other from the Argylls, were on leave, skiing at Garmisch. One evening in the 'local' they had encountered a group of Luftwaffe officers, also on leave, from the Richthofen Geschwader, based at Augsburg in southern Germany, some 60 or 70 miles away.

After 'rather a long Kümmel session', the senior German officer had invited the British contingent to a Guest Night in the Mess at Augsburg three or four days hence. The invitation was accepted. Robinson's script picks up the tale.

We set off from Garmisch in a taxi about six o'clock on a cold and starry night to drive to Augsburg . . . Eventually we reached a gloomy and windswept expanse reminiscent of Lincolnshire and were escorted to the Richthofen *Geschwader's* Mess. It's difficult to describe one's first

* (Frank Zeigler, *The Story of 609 Squadron: Under the White Rose*, Macdonald, 1971)

impressions, but generally I was very impressed. We were shown into the anteroom, which was sparsely furnished, but clean and attractive and decorated with pictures of aerial battles of the First World War – only, of course, the Fokkers were always on top and the odd SE 5As and Camels were spinning down in flames. I pointed out to a young *leutnant* that we, too, had the same sort of pictures in our Messes except that the role of the principal characters was usually reversed. This seemed to amuse him, and the remark was passed round the room in German.

The officers were most polite, clicking their heels and generally being anxious to bring us as many drinks as they could. Personally, I was very impressed by the appearance of all of them . . .

We were led into the dining room and were placed by ourselves at the two ends and the middle of a long refectory table. I sat at one end beside the CO, a First World War pilot. My friend from the Welsh Guards was at the far end beside the adjutant, another last-war pilot. The third member of our party was down the middle of the table next to the second-in-command . . .

The room was lit only by candlelight. The walls were panelled, and the only decorations were squadron banners hung along the sides. The general effect was very good. Like most Guest Nights the dinner started rather pompously, and I was surprised when the CO turned to me and said: 'You must not be surprised if you find my boys getting rather out of hand after dinner.'

'Well, sir,' I said, 'I shouldn't worry too much about that. I think we know the form all right.'

He hesitated. 'I'm afraid you don't understand me. You see, your Air Force and mine, as things used to be, were brought up to certain definite traditions. You may have to excuse my pilots, but remember they are very young and perhaps lack some of the training.'

The dinner was good and very well and impressively served. We reached the coffee stage and it was apparent that they were determined to put us under the table as quickly as possible . . . More and more *Kirsch* arrived until I felt that so long as I remained upright at the table I could cope. I did notice, however, that gradually, one by one, the pilots were disappearing . . . Seeing a doorway leading into the open air we went outside, rubbed our faces in the snow . . . and ran a couple of times round the Mess . . .

We came back into the Mess expecting to find the boys turning somersaults over chairs and that sort of thing . . . Instead, they were gathered about in odd groups having drunken arguments in German.

A young *leutnant* came up to me. 'You've got Hurricanes?' he asked.
'Yes,' I replied.

'Well,' he said, 'we've got Messerschmitt 109s and God help you if you ever have to fight us in your old tubs.'

It was their Mess so I didn't want to provoke an argument. 'You know,' I said mildly, 'even so, we still think our Hurricanes are pretty good, too.'

'Then,' he countered, 'you don't believe me? . . . When the war starts (and I hope it does soon) I will take on any three Englishmen with Hurricanes in my Messerschmitt.'

A few days later, we returned home.

I was destined to meet that young *leutnant* once again – not in southern Germany, but in southern Kent, in a hop field near Maidstone . . . It was a most perfect day and the dust he had created by landing his 109, wheels up, hung over the field. I followed him down, landed nearby and walked across two fields to where he was lying in the sunshine.*

I recognized him before he recognized me. 'Hello,' I said, 'are you all right?' He nodded. 'Then,' I asked, 'may I have your pistol?' As he handed it over I said to him: 'Your face seems familiar, haven't we met somewhere before?'

'Yes,' he said, 'wherever was it?' His English was immaculate, I think he had been at Oxford.

'Augsburg, February 1939,' I said. 'It was a good dinner.'

'Ah, yes,' he murmured. 'But tell me – why didn't you shoot me down when I was in the air? I couldn't have escaped.'

'As a matter of fact, I couldn't shoot you down,' I said. 'I had to force you down the way I did. I had used up all my ammunition on some other 109s!'

Then the Home Guard came and took him away.†

(Michael Robinson's personal papers)

'Noblesse Oblige'

As the Battle wore on and the autumn leaves began to fall, field and covert offered respite for some from the rigours of the aerial conflict.

The permanent staff at Kirton Lindsey welcomed us back with lavish hospitality . . . for they regarded 616 [South Yorkshire Auxiliary Squadron] as their own.

Each of the Auxiliary squadrons had its own honorary air commodore, and ours, the Marquis of Tichfield,‡ drove over from his country seat in Nottinghamshire to welcome us back at a guest night in the mess. After

---

* A most hazardous and frowned-upon action! Ed.

† In the event, the broadcast was never made. It was too strong meat for the anti-fraternizing, vetting authority. Ed.

‡ Later the Duke of Portland.

dinner the conversation turned to shooting. Were we interested, Tichfield inquired?

. . . Two days later there was a phone call from Welbeck. Lord Tichfield would like the squadron to provide four guns next Thursday, [operations allowing]. Bring plenty of cartridges and some lunch. Yes, it would be all driven game, no walking. . . .

Our new CO was a natural shot and would lead the expedition to Welbeck. Nip* could hit a pheasant and was quite safe with a loaded gun. As the fourth member I selected Jeff West,† newly commissioned and keen to see some of our country life. He had never shot game before, but he could bring down Messerschmitts, where the same principles of deflection shooting held good. . . .

. . . Personally, I found my own game and wild-fowling experience to be of the greatest value. The fighter pilot who could hit a curling, down-wind pheasant, or a jinking head-on partridge, or who could kill a widgeon cleanly in a darkening sky had little trouble in bringing his guns to bear against the 109s. The outstanding fighter pilots were invariably excellent game shots. . . .

We were confident that Jeff would be all right once we had given him some elementary training . . .

We reported at Welbeck. It was a crisp, firm, . . . [autumnal] day which promised well for the sport. The customary draw for positions took place and for the first drive Jeff found himself between our host and a famous amateur golfer, and I was next along the line of guns. The horn sounded and the partridges swung across the sugar beet, fast, jinking and very low. The first few coveys came straight at Jeff, and he went into action. The guns on either side fell silent and with good reason, for Jeff had his sights on the enemy and swung his gun from front to rear at shoulder height! His lordship and his retinue – loader, under keeper and dog handler – took suitable avoiding action, as did the amateur golfer.

After the first drive I had strong words with the New Zealander and suggested to our host that since West was very inexperienced at this sort of thing it might be wise to put him well behind the guns as a stopper. Lord Tichfield never batted an eyelid and said he was sure Mr West would soon pick up the drill and that we had better get along to the next drive. For me the day was not improved when one of our more enterprising airmen, acting in the temporary capacity of loader, decided to take a hand in the proceedings and brought down a wild duck!

We continued to shoot at Welbeck until the end of the season, and for us those days were some of the happiest of the war years. We always shot until it was nearly dark. Some very old men acted as beaters, for the

---

* Flight Lieutenant Philip Heppell.
† From New Zealand.

youngsters were away at the war . . . [later one] afternoon when the light began to fade, we finished a drive and our host addressed the beaters, who were bunched together: 'Would you fellows mind if I asked you for another drive?'

The simple reply came straight back from an aged countryman: 'We'll beat till midnight for 616, m'lord.'

(J. E. [Johnnie] Johnson, Wing Leader, Chatto & Windus, 1956)

SMALL IS BEAUTIFUL?
THE ENDURING CONTROVERSY

The most practical size for Fighter Command's formations to oppose the large enemy gaggles was the subject of acrimonious argument between Air Vice-Marshal Keith Park, the 11 Group commander, who fought the day-to-day battle, and Air Vice-Marshal Trafford Leigh-Mallory, commanding 12 Group, whose contribution was largely confined to reinforcing the southern area. Park contended that time did not usually allow squadrons to be assembled into wings. Leigh-Mallory, on the other hand, echoing Douglas Bader's belief, was a strong protagonist of the Big Wing used in the appropriate way. The controversy raged and reached high places; it continues to this day.

Opinion

From [my] personal experience, there were very few occasions in the 11 Group area when it would have been possible to scramble and assemble two squadrons as a wing – let alone five as finally used from Duxford – in time to make an effective interception before the enemy bombers reached their target. Almost one hundred per cent of the interceptions by the Duxford wing were over or just short of the target, and sometimes after the bombs had fallen, which supports the contention that much vital time was lost in forming up, and proceeding to the target, in mass formation. On this basis, I wonder how many of the 11 Group Sector airfields would have been in commission on 7 September, when the Germans finally ceased bombing airfields, and how many aircraft would have been destroyed on the ground or caught in the act of getting airborne, had Park relied on wing formations to fight his battle. . . .

From a fighter pilot's point of view, I hold that Bader's wing concept was wrong, and I consider that the German fighter tactics against the American daylight bombers prove my point. The Germans faced the same problem in 1943 as did Fighter Command in 1940, but with vastly more experience behind them, a more sophisticated radar control system, and a longer period of defensive operations in which to experiment and learn.

181

Most important of all, they had adequate early warning of attacks on their Homeland and time in which to concentrate their mass formations where and when they wanted them. In the end, having tried the mass formation technique, they resorted to small mobile formations of fighters concentrated in time and space, but operating independently. They found that too many fighters tied to a single leader sterilized flexibility of action and thought on the part of individual pilots, and usually resulted in only the leader getting a decent shot at the raiding bombers before the rest of the formation was set upon by the escorting fighters.

(Air Commodore Alan C. Deere, DSO, OBE, DFC, *Nine Lives*,
Hodder & Stoughton, 1959)

What Bader actually wanted

[Douglas Bader's] . . . plan for the 12 Group wing was positive, practical and pretty pugnacious. He saw it as being complementary to Keith Park's use of the 11 Group squadrons and as a means of buying them the precious time they lacked to gain height and position in the face of the incoming raids. It rested, like all his air tactics, on a few plain and clear tenets.

It required, first, that the wing should be called off the ground as soon as the radar had begun to show that the Germans were building up in strength over the Pas de Calais and that a major raid was imminent. With this kind of warning, the Duxford squadrons could have been at 20,000 feet over the estuary (with the Spitfires 4,000 or 5,000 feet above) by the time the attacking force was setting course across the Channel.

Another 15 minutes on a south-easterly course and the wing would be in position, well forward over East Kent, covering a broad area bounded by Canterbury, Ashford, Dungeness and Dover, with all the height and freedom to manoeuvre into a good, tactical, attacking position as the first enemy formations crossed the coast. The wing leader and the 12 Group squadron commanders would then have had *control of a battle of their own seeking* – the overriding requirement for a successful defensive action. . . .

. . . .

Two years later, in the autumn of 1942, Keith Park, then the AOC, Malta, used this forward interception plan with devastating effect in the last phase of the desperate defence of the Island. The circumstances were virtually identical. Sending his squadrons and wings, across the Straits, and sometimes as far as the Sicilian mainland, he met the enemy's attacks head-on. It was the lethal left hook which finally shattered Kesselring's jaw.

(Laddie Lucas, *Flying Colours: The Epic Story of Douglas Bader*,
Hutchinson, 1981)

C-in-C's view

I have the honour to forward a copy of a report rendered by AOC 12 Group on certain operations recently carried out by Wings of Fighters dispatched from 12 Group to reinforce 11 Group in their engagements with enemy mass raids . . .

It will be seen from these figures that the losses inflicted on the enemy were not increased in relation to the number of our fighters engaged on the later patrols when a larger number of Squadrons took part. Nevertheless, the losses incurred by the Wing were reduced and *I am, in any case, of the opinion that the AOC 12 Group is working on the right lines in organizing his operations in strength*. [italics added]

> (Air Vice-Marshal D. C. S. Evill, Senior Air Staff Officer, on behalf of the Air Officer Commanding-in-Chief, Fighter Command, to the Under Secretary of State at the Air Ministry, 24 September 1940. [Reference FC/S. 18507/Air.])

BROADHURST'S STANCE – AN AUTHORITATIVE VIEW

On 30 June 1940, Harry Broadhurst led the Wittering Wing – 229 and 266 Squadrons – on what his log book records as a 'wing patrol'. This was the first time in the Battle that fighter squadrons were operated as a so-called Big Wing. Sometimes, he would borrow another squadron from nearby Digby, and later he led four squadrons. Few could approach, let alone match, Broadhurst's combined experience and authority. With this background, I therefore put the point straightly to him.

'Over the years,' I said, 'there has been a lot of argument about the Big Wing theory. What now, with hindsight, are your views about it?'

The response was positive and clear. 'I never discussed the subject with L-M,* but I did discuss it with Douglas Evill [Dowding's brilliant Senior Air Staff Officer] at his instigation. He contended that the Big Wings had their place in the overall scheme of things, but he did not think they could be related to 11 Group's day-to-day operations, which was where the argument started. The main disadvantage was the time it took to scramble three, four or five squadrons from an airfield. There is no doubt, also, that the top brass in Fighter Command were worried about being over-confident about the defence of the industrial areas of the Midlands and the North, and did not want to denude 12 and 13 Groups more than was absolutely necessary in case the Germans switched the targets *from* the south. The great attraction in having a wing airborne in 12 Group, after the first alarms had sounded in 11 Group, was that . . . [it] could

---

* Air Vice-Marshal Trafford Leigh-Mallory.

reinforce 11 Group from a reserve already airborne but not committed to specific targets.

'The argument created a lot of misunderstanding and bitterness. If reasoned discussions could have been held at a suitable level, great benefits could have ensued to the overall defence system. As it was, jealousy and self-opinion prevailed; we were all the losers, but it did expose the big failure in Dowding's method of command. As far as I know, he tried to avoid getting involved in the argument, whereas he should have held high-level meetings so that proponents and opponents alike could all have had their say, and a firm policy agreed . . .

'. . . It was, of course, true that when we heard all the chatter and vectoring on the RT [Radio Telephone] there was a tremendous temptation to get in on the act like, by his own admission, Douglas [Bader] did, who often took the Duxford Wing into 11 Group territory seeking his own battle. But the trouble with that began when the 11 Group controller suddenly saw thirty or forty aeroplanes plotted on his table not knowing if they were friendly or hostile.

'It certainly upset the plotting and I had a certain amount of sympathy for the 11 Group controllers because I knew their problems from my own stint at 11 Group Headquarters. I had been there for a short time as Wing Commander Training, and my deputy was Squadron Leader Lord Willoughby de Broke. We wing commanders at 11 Group were on a roster of Duty Operations Officers and Willoughby and I spent much time together in the operations room. He was a good and astute man, and, because I kept in touch with him, I knew the problem.'

'What, then, was the problem?' I asked. Again, the answer was quite direct.

'Sometimes in 1940,' said Broady, 'our control and reporting system was unreliable so that the plotting of enemy raids on the ops [operations] room tables at Fighter Command and 11 Group was not always accurate. I remember at least one occasion when there were no hostile plots on the table and yet some of our chaps were shot down. It was, therefore very important for a fighter leader to obey the controller's instructions so that, down in the hole, he would know exactly where the leader was. If, like Douglas, you went darting about all over the place, it upset the whole plotting table. So, when I led the Wittering Wing, I obeyed instructions and did what I was told to do.'

'Of course,' I said, 'Douglas was a great protagonist of the leading air fighters of the First War – Ball, McCudden, Bölcke and Richthofen; the very essence of their tactics was free-lancing over enemy territory – like you and I were doing over France in 1941. Is that not so?'

'You are quite correct,' replied the Air Chief Marshal, 'but there was one big difference. In 1940, we were on the defensive, when we had to obey orders. In 1941, we were on the offensive. Then our free-lancing fighter sweeps were in order.'

I then switched my questioning to the personalities in the Battle. 'In his book, Wright* relates how, one day in 1940, an angry Leigh-Mallory came striding into Park's office after an interview with the Commander-in-Chief and said that he would "move heaven and earth" to get Dowding sacked from his job! When you were at Wittering did you have any inkling of ill-feeling between Dowding and L-M, or between L-M and Park?'

Broadhurst paused. 'Only towards the end of the Battle when there was a conference of station commanders at Fighter Command which Stuffy chaired. He told us that our speeches should be limited to five minutes. L-M always prepared his speeches, and when it was his turn, he began to read from his paper. After six minutes, Stuffy interrupted him. "The trouble with you, Leigh-Mallory," he said, "is that you cannot see beyond the end of your nose!" '

'Do you mean to say the Commander-in-Chief actually said that about his Group Commander in front of a bunch of wing commanders?'

'He certainly did,' replied Broady.

'Now, regarding Park and L-M,' he went on, 'I remember in early October I was leading my wing – four squadrons I had that day – over the Thames Estuary at 18,000 feet when, through broken cloud, I saw a large formation of Italian bombers unescorted, as far as I could see, by fighters. They were not then being attacked so I asked the Hornchurch controller if I could send a squadron down. My request was refused on the grounds that the "situation was being dealt with". However, on returning to Wittering I found that the Italians had not, in fact, been attacked at that particular stage.

'Wanting to get to the bottom of it, I called Willoughby who happened to be the duty controller at 11 Group. I explained the facts and said I wanted to know why we had not been allowed to attack. He said. "Hold on, I'm handing you over to the AOC." '

'I was then in a quandary. The last thing I wanted to do was start an argument with Park as I knew L-M would be furious at one of his station commanders talking direct to the AOC, 11 Group. However, there was no going back and I described the fruitless interception to Keith Park who said curtly: "I will investigate it at once," and that was the last I ever heard of the affair.'

The Air Chief Marshal let his mind run on.

'Later, as you know, the whole thing got out of hand after a visit by the Secretary of State, Sinclair, to Duxford. Douglas [Bader] aired his views to Sinclair complaining that his Big Wing was being held back by 11 Group. On his return to Whitehall, Sinclair asked his Under-Secretary, Balfour, to go down to Duxford and make a thorough investigation.

* Robert Wright, *Dowding and the Battle of Britain*, Macdonald, 1969.

Balfour's "Duxford Memorandum" was the result. The findings were passed on to the CAS.* It caused great umbrage and eventually culminated in that unsavoury conference at the Air Ministry on 17 October, chaired by Sholto Douglas.'

'Was not a lot of the fuss started by Bader's adjutant, Peter Macdonald?' I asked. He was then a Member of Parliament and therefore had access to ministers like Balfour and Sinclair. I did not realize until I read Laddie Lucas's book about Douglas† that Macdonald had actually exercised his right, as an MP, to ask to see the Prime Minister and was closeted with the Great Man for an hour and a half. But from what you have now said it appears that the idea of Big Wings did not originate with Douglas and L-M as is generally supposed, but at Fighter Command with the Air Staff's idea of airborne reserves.'

Broadhurst was in no doubt. 'That is quite correct,' he replied. 'There were many occasions during the Battle when concentration of force was the ideal to aim for if you had the time to assemble your squadrons into a wing. But the size of the fighting unit – squadron or wing – was determined by the time taken to intercept before the bombing; and the fact was that Park simply did not have the time to build his squadrons into wings. It was no use intercepting after the bombing when the damage had been done. So he was right to stick to small, flexible formations. But he did not take advantage of the Duxford and Wittering Wings until he was forced to.'

(J. E. [Johnnie] Johnson, personal collection)

Ministerial postscript

These two very different characters [Park and Leigh-Mallory] had individual views on air fighting strategy and tactics. They disliked each other to the point of strong personal antipathy and took no trouble to hide this fact from their staffs. Dowding knew of this personal relationship. He should have ... taken steps to rectify the position. He should have called in the two AOCs and told them in no uncertain terms that this quarrelling had just got to stop; if not, he would sack them both.

(Harold Balfour [Lord Balfour of Inchrye, PC, MC], Wings over Westminster, Hutchinson, 1973)

---

* Chief of the Air Staff, Air Chief Marshal Sir Cyril Newall.
† Laddie Lucas, *Flying Colours: The Epic Story of Douglas Bader*, Hutchinson, 1981.

FAMOUS AIR MINISTRY MEETING, 17 OCTOBER 1940

Present:

Air Vice-Marshal W. S. Douglas	DCAS
Air Chief Marshal Sir Hugh C. T. Dowding	AOC-in-C, Fighter Command
Air Marshal Sir Charles F. A. Portal	
Air Marshal Sir Philip P. B. Joubert de la Ferté	ACAS (R)
Air Vice-Marshal K. R. Park	AOC 11 Group
Air Vice-Marshal Sir C. J. Q. Brand	AOC 10 Group
Air Vice-Marshal T. L. Leigh-Mallory	AOC 12 Group
Air Commodore J. C. Slessor	D of Plans
Air Commodore D. F. Stevenson	DHO
Air Commodore O. G. W. G. Lywood	PDD of Signals
Group Captain H. G. Crowe	ADAT
Squadron Leader D. R. S. Bader	OC 242 Squadron
Wing Commander T. N. McEvoy	
Mr J. S. Orme	

The purpose of the meeting, which has sometimes wrongly been described as a post-mortem on the Battle of Britain and, as such, a sinister device, designed by the Air Ministry and its supporters to pave the way for Dowding's removal as the AOC-in-C, Fighter Command, was contained in its title. This disclosed it to be a discussion to consider 'Major Day Tactics in the Fighter Force'. . . .

The Air Staff paper of 14 October, covering the agenda, and the minutes confirming the outcome, leave no possible doubt about its intent. Far from it being a critique of the Battle of Britain and those who were primarily concerned with its conduct, its aim was to project thought forward to the challenging months to come and the tactics to be employed in the daylight air. Night was not excluded.

> Vigorous and heavy as the enemy attacks have been against this country, we must have regard to the possibility that more determined, better organized and heavier attacks may be made in the spring of 1941, if not before. . . . It is necessary that the lessons we have learned should be applied generally to enable the fighter defence to operate at maximum efficiency. . . .

The note was quite explicit.

. . . .

Sholto Douglas [the chairman] asked Bader, at one point, for his views on leading and operating big formations. 'You are the one,' he said, 'who

187

has actually done it operationally.' It was a testing moment. The room seemed to go extra quiet.

'I did not speak for long. In spite of my embarrassment, I remember thinking that this would be the only time that a fighter pilot might ever be asked for his views by the Air Staff.'

In fact, Douglas stuck to a single, broad theme. 'You, gentlemen,' he recalls saying, 'learnt the lessons in the First World War. They are still the same today. Height, sun, position and strength in numbers – this is still what counts. It follows that to gain the tactical advantage we must be got off the ground in time to win it. Time and good warning is what we need more than anything.' He wasn't too sure, but he hoped he had managed to get his point across. . . .

. . . .

Was Leigh-Mallory right to have taken Bader to the meeting? Some have criticized him and, indeed, imputed to him certain base motives for having done so.

(Laddie Lucas, Flying Colours: The Epic Story of Douglas Bader,
Hutchinson, 1981)

Two views

I knew nothing of the Park–L-M controversy until – for some unaccountable reason which I still cannot imagine – I attended the famous conference on 17 October shortly before my departure for America; I can only think that Cyril Newall, being sick, had told me to attend and give him an independent account of what went on; but I honestly do not remember. The only impression I can now recall is that it was amazing, and entirely wrong, that young Bader was allowed not only to attend such a high-level conference but also to air his views on the tactics of 11 Group. If I had been in Stuffy's place I would not have put up with that for a moment. The curious thing is that I have no recollection of Stuffy ever saying a word – though I suppose he must have.

(Marshal of the Royal Air Force Sir John Slessor, Chief of the Air Staff,
1950–1952: correspondence with Lord Balfour of Inchrye, Under-Secretary
of State for Air, 1938–1944, 28 October 1969)

When Dowding came to the meeting he was shocked to see a young Squadron Leader sitting behind Leigh-Mallory. It was Douglas Bader, brought along by his AOC. Maybe it was against service discipline and custom for such a junior to be present at this high-level conference but even today I can see no real objection. Here were a lot of middle-aged experts met to resolve differing views on fighting strategy and tactics. Here amongst them was one of the men actually doing the daily job and I

188

think it must have brought a real and refreshing breath of reality that Bader was there to give his views if asked.

> (Harold Balfour [Lord Balfour of Inchrye, PC, MC] *Wings over Westminster*, Hutchinson, 1973)

Salient findings (extract from minutes)

(20) DCAS* said he thought the views of the meeting could be summarized as follows: The employment of a large mass of fighters had great advantages, though it was not necessarily the complete solution to the problem of interception. In 11 Group, where the enemy was very close at hand, both the methods described by AOC 11 Group and those of AOC 12 Group could, on occasions, be used with forces from the two Groups co-operating.

(21) The AOC-in-C said that it would be arranged for 12 Group 'wings' to participate freely in suitable operations over the 11 Group area. *He would be able to resolve any complications of control* [editor's italics]. In reply to DHO, the C-in-C said that co-operation of this kind could, in the present circumstances, hardly be employed generally throughout the Command as similar conditions seldom arose elsewhere.

VICTORY FOR FIGHTER COMMAND

For Operation Sea-lion, for the Battle of Britain, for Newall, for Dowding and for Park the sands were running out. For Fighter Command, though its losses substantially decreased, October provided 'one of the most severe tests of the whole Battle'.[†] The 'hit-and-run' raids by the German fighter-bombers called for exceptional vigilance; they also

> shattered one of the basic principles of Fighter Command organization, namely economy of effort by keeping planes grounded until they were needed.[‡]

Instead, with great reluctance, Fighter Command had to revert to the concept of standing patrols. . . . What it meant was that 12-aircraft squadrons were averaging 45 flying hours a day – sometimes 60. Added to the extra strain of high-level fighting, this meant that the weariness factor was now critical:

---

* Deputy Chief of the Air Staff, Air Vice-Marshal W. Sholto Douglas, in the chair.

† Derek Wood with Derek Dempster, *The Narrow Margin: The Battle of Britain and the Rise of Air Power*, Hutchinson, 1961.

‡ Ditto.

It was estimated in the summer of the Battle that every pilot kept in action for more than six months would be shot down because he was exhausted or stale, or even because he had lost the will to fight. In terms of flying hours the fighter pilot's life expectancy could be measured at eighty-seven.*

With squadrons flying their October average, this meant that a pilot could only expect some four or five weeks of life. It cannot be disputed that

although it is true that there were more squadrons in the Command at the end of October than at the beginning of July its fighting strength had fallen considerably.†

It was fortunate indeed for Fighter Command (and for Britain) that the German *Schwerpunkt* had shifted to the attack on cities. Fighter Command was stretched like the strings of a violin – but with characteristic opportunism the German High Command switched to the 'soft target':

The attraction of London was the German Air Force's undoing. Like an indestructible sponge it absorbed punishment and diverted what might have been the death blow from the sorely tried organism of defence.‡

The outcome of the battle . . . is quite clear:

The objective of the *Luftwaffe* in the Battle of Britain was not achieved. The Battle of Britain was lost by Germany.§

Thus, Dr Klee; *Luftwaffe* General Werner Kreipe adds:

. . . though the air battles over England were perhaps a triumph of skill and bravery so far as the German air crews were concerned, from the strategic point of view it was a failure and contributed to our ultimate defeat. The decision to fight it marks a turning point in the history of the Second World War. The German Air Force . . . was bled almost to death, and suffered losses which could never again be made good throughout the course of the war.**

* Derek Wood with Derek Dempster, *The Narrow Margin: The Battle of Britain and the Risk of Air Power,* Hutchinson, 1961.
† Air Historical Branch (RAF) II/117/2(B).
‡ Wood with Dempster. See * above.
§ Dr Karl Klee, *Decisive Battles of World War II: The German View,* André Deutsch, 1965.
** W. Richardson & S. Frieden, *The Fatal Decisions,* Michael Joseph, 1956.

Both German authorities agree that from all angles the Battle of Britain has to be viewed as a decisive battle of the war; in Klee's words:

> . . . the invasion and subjugation of Britain was made to depend on victory in that battle, and its outcome therefore materially influenced both the further course and the fate of the war as a whole.
>
> (John Terraine, *The Right of the Line: The Royal Air Force in the European War 1939–45*, Hodder & Stoughton, 1985)

STOOD DOWN

RETROSPECT

This victory made possible all that followed after, as pilots from the allied nations came with courage and devotion to join us. Free men everywhere will always cherish the memory of those who made victory possible. The pilots themselves and the ground crews, the men in the factories, Lord Beaverbrook who inspired them, Mr Churchill who led the nation, all have their place in a proud memory

(The Rt Hon. Anthony Eden, Secretary of State for Foreign Affairs)

I have often wondered . . .

What would have happened if we had not had radar, the Hurricane and Spitfire and a crowd of dedicated youngsters, many of them, like myself, from the Dominions, Colonies and foreign lands. I wonder too how the Germans would have reacted had they known how untried so many of our pilots were and that often the boy who was shooting at them was firing a gun for the very first time in his life!

In any case it is all over now and from my observance there was no lack of guts or skill on either side but I would like especially to say that amongst the bravest, most skilful and most dedicated I place the Poles as equal to any and superior to most. In this Battle they truly evoked the spirit of John Sobieski and his Winged Hussars.

(Squadron Leader [later Group Captain] J. A. Kent, 303 [Polish] and 92 Squadrons)

I have often wondered . . .

What would have happened if two hundred thousand German storm troops had actually established themselves ashore. The massacre would have been on both sides grim and great. There would have been neither mercy nor quarter. They would have used terror, and we were prepared to go all lengths. I intended to use the slogan, 'You can always take one with you.' I even calculated that the horrors of such a scene would in the last resort turn the scale in the United States. But none of these emotions was put to the proof. Far out on the grey waters of the North Sea and the Channel coursed and patrolled the faithful, eager flotillas peering through the night. High in the air soared the fighter pilots, or waited serene at a moment's notice around their excellent machines. This was a time when it was equally good to live or die.

(Winston S. Churchill Their Finest Hour, Curtis Brown on behalf of the
Estate of Sir Winston Churchill, C & T Publications, 1949)

My sister and I

My sister Tig and I joined the WAAF before war was declared and we did not take it too seriously. Even when war was declared and we marched off to Tangmere, it was still a glorious game, and this illusion continued into the early summer of 1940.

Then one day the Stukas came howling down at us out of the sun and, after the first stunned disbelief, we tumbled into the shelters whilst they beat and hammered us into the ground. We ascended to chaos.

The squadrons thundered off the ground tirelessly. Off they pelted, day after day, those glorious, radiant boys. We were with them in sound and spirit. We heard their shouts of 'Tally Ho!' There was one boy who always burst into song as soon as he caught sight of the enemy and swung into the attack. We only heard these private war cries when they forgot to switch off their transmitters in the heat of battle, an awful yet uplifting experience. But that feeling of lead in the stomach when they failed to return was all too familiar. . . . There were so many. I remember when Caesar Hull was killed – we *all* admired him. The gay and gallant American Billy Fiske; the two Wood-Scawens, inseparable brothers, devout Catholics, charmers both – and all of them so young and so well endowed, and such a wicked, wicked waste. I mourned them then, now and for ever.

(Aircraftwoman Anne Turley-George, in Richard Hough and Denis
Richards, The Battle of Britain: The Jubilee History,
Hodder & Stoughton, 1989)

Generous opponent

I can only express the highest admiration for the British fighter pilots, who, although technically at a disadvantage, fought bravely and indefatigably. They undoubtedly saved their country in this crucial hour.

(Adolf Galland, The First and the Last: The German Fighter Force in World
War II, Methuen, 1955)

Dowding's letter

Transcending my relationship with Dowding, I like to remember him by his letter to me on 2 October 1940 thanking me for my congratulations on his award of the GCB:

Bentley Priory
2. 10. 40

Dear Balfour,
Very many thanks for your letter of congratulation which I very much appreciate.

If I could I should like to cut the Decoration up into a thousand pieces and distribute it to the Fighter Boys who are the ones who have really earned it.

Yours sincerely
(Signed) H. C. T. Dowding

(Harold Balfour [Lord Balfour of Inchrye, PC, MC], *Wings over Westminster*, Hutchinson, 1973)

'We had the glory'

It was always fine, that summer and autumn [of 1940]. Sound, smell and touch were vivid, as well as sight. They linger still: the freshness of a September morning outside the dispersel hut, with mist clinging to the grass undulations of the airfield; the crossing white trails in the blue sky, showing the first squadrons already in action; the puffs of blue-black smoke as the Merlin engine started; the exhilaration of climbing in tight formation; London, spread out like a map, hazy against the sun and partly obscured by the burning oil tanks of Thameshaven; the feel of the bevelled ring on the stick, carefully turned from 'safe' to 'fire'. The enemy is a thing, not a man. First a string of tiny silhouettes against a distant cloud. Then suddenly, all round you, so close that you note with a sense of shock the rough metal and grey-green paint, with sometimes a vivid yellow nose. You are turning savagely, trying to stay with your leader, trying to keep track of the crossing enemy, pressing the gun-button with a fierce exultation as the sight comes to bear. Then – just as suddenly – the utter solitude of the sky. How can you be so alone, where only seconds before was the heart of a battle? As that autumn wore on, fatigue dulled the impressions of the senses. Sleep was hastily snatched between sorties, in a chair or on the grass at dispersal, on a sofa in the Mess. At last, as darkness fell, there was relaxation. Ancient cars were packed with pilots bound for their favourite pub. Often we were not allowed to pay for our drinks; though meat was scarce, steaks would appear in a back room. Sturdy, cloth-capped figures in the bar would come up, shake hands, and return in silence to their seats.

How does the Londoner express his feelings at such a time? In the language of another age, we were their champions, sallying forth from the walls of the beleaguered city. They would not have recognized such language; but they showed, by a proffered drink or a silent handshake, that they understood and wished us God-speed.

We had the glory. They went back to work in office or factory, railway yard or dock, and gathered round their radios for the news. Strength came from the man who offered them nothing but blood, toil, tears and sweat. I saw something which I have never forgotten. If the heart of a nation is sound, danger brings out unexpected kindliness. As on the battlefield, men facing the unknown become considerate to each other. Friendly greetings were exchanged between strangers, as each morning brought the threat of new attack. Small services were done for neighbours, without thought of thanks or reward. For one moment in history, the nation felt like a family. Un-British, often comic in its embarrassed emotion, this was the true meaning of 'Their finest hour'. It is only in the aftermath of victory or defeat that greed, meanness and self-interest flourish, like weeds in a forgotten garden.

(David Scott-Malden [later Air Vice-Marshal], *603 Squadron*, Icare, Paris, 1965)

The incomparable sailor

After our disastrous start to the Second World War, Sailor [Malan] and Douglas [Bader] did more than anyone else to get our tactics right, and we owe much to them. Douglas, twenty-two victories, was brought down after two years of flying, and Sailor, thirty-two victories, was taken off operations at about the same time when he was completely exhausted. During the Battle no one fought harder or led his men better than the lion-hearted South African, and his combat claims were always very modest. For the remainder of the war Sailor continued flying and teaching. He embarked on what amounted to a private crusade to spread the word about his ten basic rules of air fighting – soon called 'the ten commandments'. He did much to improve our gunnery training, returning home when it was all over. The RAF's greatest fighter pilot and leader died in 1963, after a long and painful illness.

(J. E. [Johnnie] Johnson, *Full Circle*, Chatto & Windus, 1964)

Russian shock

Field Marshal Gerd von Rundstedt had no illusions. He told some Russian officers in 1945 that had the Luftwaffe won the Battle of Britain in 1940, Germany would have defeated the Soviet Union the next year. They had come to ask his view on the decisive battle of the war, thinking, of course, that he would name Stalingrad. When, his old eyes cold, his face stiff and proud, von Rundstedt told them 'the Battle of Britain', they closed their notebooks and went away.

(Drew Middleton, *The Sky Suspended: The Battle of Britain, May 1940– April 1941*, Secker & Warburg, 1960)

VERDICT

The composition of the RAF though largely and basically British, was broadly international. And this was right: for the Battle of Britain, as we now see it was not a national or an insular affair. It was international. Like the battle for Magna Carta and the Petition of right, it affected not only Great Britain but the world; and like them it was not the end of a struggle for something, but only the beginning . . .

(Squadron Leader H. E. Bates, in Squadron Leaders R. Raymond and David Langdon (eds.), *Slipstream: A Royal Air Force Anthology*, Eyre & Spottiswoode, 1946)

Reichmarschall Hermann Göring was the exact opposite of the aloof, yet knowledgeable, Air Chief Marshal Sir Hugh Dowding, and 'Dolfo' Galland had told me how, during the Battle, he and Werner Mölders visited their obese commander at his opulent hunting lodge in East Prussia. There, strutting about in his absurd uniforms, surrounded by paintings and *objets d'art* looted from the vanquished and feeding his bison and lions, he had the utter conceit to dictate fighter tactics to his able young fighter leaders.

Göring, unlike Dowding, had not done his homework. Perhaps the key to his strange behaviour was that in addition to directing the Luftwaffe he was a powerful political figure. There was no one except Hitler to hold him back. But Hitler disliked and did not understand air warfare. In 1940 he was content to leave the Luftwaffe to his 'loyal Hermann', to Göring, the extrovert, who lived in the past and still fancied himself as an expert on fighter matters; and so, as Galland said after the war, instead of delegating some authority, especially about tactical matters, to better qualified subordinates, he had to be in the swim all the time and to make all the decisions himself. Apart from his high-level conferences at Karinhall, he often flew down to the Channel coast to see how things were going, and to issue orders which contravened his previous instructions. His fighter pilots were dismayed and baffled by these ever changing orders, and when some of the brighter spirits complained he displayed the gangster methods which he and his cronies had used on their way to power and threatened to have them shot – a habit not conducive to the maintenance of good order and discipline in any military organization, including that of a totalitarian state.

Germany had the aeroplanes, the aircrews and the opportunity to win the Battle, but Göring went about it the wrong way. He should have put out the eyes of Fighter Command by destroying the nineteen radar stations between the Wash and the Isle of Wight, destroyed RAF fighters by strafing, and their communications by bombing. Simultaneously with the radar attacks the six fighter airfields near the coast between Tangmere and the Thames, the five sector stations near London, and the head-quarters of Fighter Command and 11 Group, at Bentley Priory and Uxbridge respectively, should have been struck. Small, compact formations should have attacked each of these thirty-two targets two or three times a day until reconnaissance showed that further blows were unnecessary. The enemy's night bombers should have been dovetailed into the same plan and directed against the sector stations and aeroplane factories.

Since the object of the daylight raids should have been to knock out Fighter Command in the south, and not merely indulge in a series of exciting yet inconclusive dog-fights, surprise was absolutely necessary, and the bombers and their escorts should have crossed the Channel below 500 feet to avoid radar detection. Having crossed the coast, these forces, proceeding well inland, should have remained at treetop height, navigating by visual reference and changing direction every thirty miles or so, to confuse the Observer Corps, until their goal was reached. The low-level raid on Biggin Hill, by nine Junkers 88s and twelve Messerschmitt 109s, was the most successful attack against a sector airfield, and this sort of surprise attack ought to have been carried out against the coastal airfields, the sector stations and the two headquarters, all of which lay within the radius of action of the 109.

Two years after the Battle of Britain the Luftwaffe exploited the low-level approach when enemy fighter-bombers often crossed the Channel at about 200 feet to bomb and strafe towns on Britain's south coast. Sometimes they penetrated well inland, achieved surprise, and were gone before any of the numerous defending squadrons could intercept. In 1943 I often led a few Spitfires at treetop height over France in search of parked aeroplanes on enemy airfields. You wanted good visibility to navigate properly, and when the airfield lay a few miles ahead you got the sun at your back, eased up to a hundred feet, and took the pilots in. Usually the flak was appalling, and we did not linger after the first pass, but we wrecked many aeroplanes, and I once saw a dozen enemy fighters, assembled for take-off on a runway, completely ruined by two strafing Spitfires; and when the Americans began operating their fighters deep into Germany they often came home 'on the deck' and destroyed many hundreds of combat aeroplanes by low, front-gun attacks. As for low-level bombing, Mosquito light bombers later specialized in this role and carried out many successful daylight raids, sometimes without fighter escort, against such targets as the jail at Amiens (to release some hundreds of Resistance fighters), a five-storey building used by the Gestapo in the centre of The Hague, and another Gestapo headquarters in the middle of Copenhagen. Just after Hitler's War we carried out many trials to try to find the answer to the fast, low-level intruder, but there is no adequate defence, and it is significant that today both America and Britain are producing strike aeroplanes which can operate at low altitudes. Indeed the young German, Matthias Rust, recently exploited Russia's low-level radar 'gap' when, undetected in broad daylight, he flew his Cessena trainer from West Germany's northern border to Moscow's Red Square.

Dowding's airfields were not well protected by light or heavy guns. Anti-aircraft resourses were so stretched that captured Stuka machine guns were used to defend Tangmere; and one obsolete brass-bound cannon was the only heavy weapon available to another sector station.

In early August a small force of Junkers 88s destroyed the buildings of the Ventnor radar station, which, two months later, was not back to full efficiency. Four years later a Canadian Spitfire squadron, each fighter carrying a 500-pound bomb, destroyed a *Würzburg* radar station on the French coast, and Typhoon squadrons enjoyed similar successes. But the Stuka was a more accurate dive bomber than either the Spitfire or the Typhoon, could plant a bigger bomb within a few yards of the aiming point, and was the ideal aeroplane, providing it was operated properly, to take out the conspicuous radar stations. Flying in squadron strength of seven or eight Stukas and escorted by a similar number of 109s, the Stuka force was capable of mounting at least two daily strikes against the fourteen nearest radar sites. Like the twin-engined bombers, they should have flown as low as possible in order to avoid combat, and should have then climbed steeply to their bombing height of a few thousand feet while the 109s covered the attack. Follow-up attacks should have used the skip-bombing technique, with delayed-action bombs, so that the Stukas remained at a very low height throughout the mission. Because of the longer sea crossing the fast twin-engined Junkers 88s and Messerschmitt 110s should have been used against the eight more distant radar sites.

It would not have been possible, or desirable, to provide a fighter escort for every bombing formation, because surprise was essential, and big, clumsy formations were more easily detected than small, mobile raiding parties. Owing to their extreme vulnerability, the Stukas required a fighter escort; so did bombers flying into the London area. But the remainder of the daylight bomber force, attacking radars and coastal airfields, should have relied on fighter sweeps to provide general support and reception escorts to cover their withdrawal. Had the bomber and fighter forces been employed in this fashion, it should have been possible for the Luftwaffe to hit the radars, the sector stations and the head-quarters twice daily, and the coastal airfields three times daily and still have had night bombers to carry on against the sector stations and the aeroplane factories.

These attacks should have been well coordinated, because a bad planning error might have flushed RAF fighters too soon. A good planner would have concentrated his initial strikes against the radars and coastal airfields, so easing the task of the aircrews who, say two days later, had to penetrate to the London area. Surprise would certainly have been achieved against the radar and forward airfields, and had the attacks been well delivered, the eyes of Fighter Command would have been put out after, at the very most, three or four strikes. Once the radars and forward airfields were out of the way, it only remained to concentrate against the sector airfields and the headquarters until the dispersed aeroplanes were written off and landline communications destroyed.

Working to such a plan, how long would the Luftwaffe have taken to achieve air domination over southern England? When I put this question to Park he replied, 'This was the one thing I dreaded, because had they come in very low we could not have intercepted from ground readiness, and I should have had to resort to standing patrols, which were no substitute. There were more airfields in the south not belonging to Fighter Command yet available to us, but they did not have good signals [communications] and without signals the only thing I commanded was my desk at Uxbridge!'

In my view the Luftwaffe could have won air domination over southern England within two weeks and would then have been ready for the next phase of their campaign – the isolation of the battlefield – by blasting cities, towns, railway centres and harbours [editor's italics]. Then, opposed only by a British Army still handicapped by the loss of much equipment at Dunkirk and by a Royal Navy fighting at a great disadvantage in the narrow confines of a Channel dominated by the Luftwaffe, the German airborne troops might easily have seized a suitable piece of Kent in which to establish and build up an invading force.

Despite Dowding's withdrawn character, and the fact that he was rarely seen at squadron level, his pilots knew he stood four square behind them and, at this time, he was becoming something of a father figure. Apart from his ability to manage people, he had the qualities of leadership which were inherent rather than acquired. He was a leader of the highest integrity. He possessed abundant moral courage as we have seen when he made his unprecedented appearance before the War Cabinet. He was a professional who fully understood the tools at his disposal. He had the will to lead.

'I often wondered', said Harry Broadhurst, 'why "Stuffy" took all the trouble to fly to Wittering and cross-examine me that day late in May 1940 when he could so easily have telephoned. But now, nearly 50 years later, I realize that he was looking for moral support. You see, he had the Establishment, Churchill, the Chiefs of Staff and the French Government all pressing for more Hurricanes and no one to turn to for support. The more I think about him resisting all those chaps at the top the more I realize what he did for Fighter Command and his country.'

Much play has been made with the size of the fighting formations; but if one ponders the defensive arrangements made on the afternoon of

15 September, when more than twenty-six squadrons – including Bader's Big Wing, nine small wings and three (plus) independent squadrons – were in action (see map on page 144), Park's tactical genius shines through the fog of battle.

We must, however, always remember that Park was Dowding's lieutenant, and it was the Commander-in-Chief himself who made certain that his remaining thirty or so squadrons, deployed throughout the United Kingdom, were held in reserve to meet the possibility of other attacks developing against the Midlands and the North.

Few men in our long history have shouldered such a burden and Dowding was one of the great commanders of all time. During the contest the strands of leadership in Fighter Command flowed down from the Commander-in-Chief through our simple chain of command – groups, stations and squadrons – to a thousand fighter pilots and their ground crews, and produced that priceless pearl, high morale, which made men bigger than their normal selves . . .

High morale – the greatest single factor in the waging and the winning of the Battle of Britain.

(J. E. [Johnnie] Johnson, personal collection)

AFTER BATTLE

Many things we had forgotten, we who knew
 The boundless unpossessive joy of living –
 One to another giving –
When Death had brushed our wingtips as we flew:

Who proudly soared to battle, when the span
 From dawn to sunset was eternity,
 And Death's simplicity
Laid bare the naked living soul of man.

First, we forgot that war had not removed
 From those at home the toil, the sweat, the tears
 The hopes of earlier years;
War is the absence of the one beloved.

Their hearts were numb with sorrow, in the sense
 Of others dying, which is death in life
 More pitiless than strife;
War is the sense of age's impotence.

And lastly, we forgot the constancy
  Of those who burned the lantern at the gate
  And sat, content to wait;
Peace is the finding of fidelity.

                   (David Scott-Malden)

APPENDIX A
FIGHTER COMMAND ATTACK NO. 6
(FROM DEAD ASTERN)

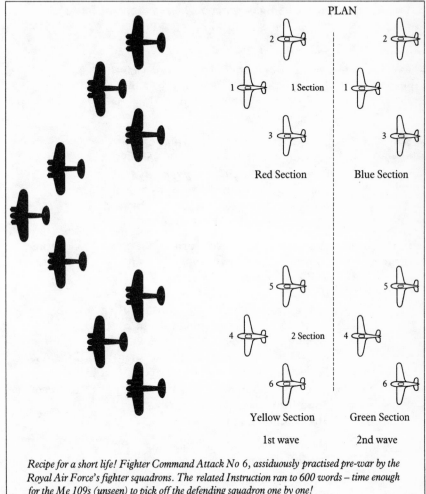

PLAN

2   2

1   1 Section   1

3   3

Red Section   Blue Section

5   5

4   2 Section   4

6   6

Yellow Section   Green Section

1st wave   2nd wave

Recipe for a short life! Fighter Command Attack No 6, assiduously practised pre-war by the Royal Air Force's fighter squadrons. The related Instruction ran to 600 words – time enough for the Me 109s (unseen) to pick off the defending squadron one by one!

While the Luftwaffe was being bloodied in combat in the Spanish Civil War, the Royal Air Force's Fighter Command had its head buried in the text book – but not for long after the Battle of Britain started!

Contrast the (summarized) Instruction which follows with the three simple statements which Sailor Malan, Douglas Bader, Bob Stanford-

Tuck and other leading exponents made the basis of their dog-fighting skills:

> *He who has the height controls the battle.*
> *He who has the sun achieves surprise.*
> *He who gets in close shoots them down.*

(A Squadron of Single-Seater Fighters Attacks 9 Bombers
in Squadron Formation)

Phase	Description	R/T Order
Two types of approach	In this attack the form of approach to be adopted will depend on the course and position of the enemy at the time of sighting.	
Approach (Pursuit)	A Squadron in search formation on sighting the enemy ahead or 45° on either bow and *proceeding away from the fighters* will form 'Sections astern' and close to a position about 800 yards astern and slightly below the enemy.	'Sections Astern GO'
Approach (Turning)	A Squadron in search formation, on sighting the enemy ahead or to a flank and *proceeding in the opposite direction* will form 'Sections astern' as in the Approach (Pursuit), but in order to make a rapid sweeping turn in closing to the position for deployment, i.e. about 800 yards astern and slightly below the enemy, it is necessary to form individual aircraft 'Line Astern'. Squadron re-forms 'Sections Astern' after completing the turn.	'Sections Astern GO' 'Line Astern GO' 'Re-form Section Astern GO'
Deployment	Having arrived in position astern of the enemy, the Squadron Leader gives the order to deploy in preparation for the attack. On receipt of this order Nos. 2 and 4 Section Leaders will lead their Sections to positions in Sections abreast to *Port* of their Flight Leaders.	 'No. 6 Attack Deploy GO'

Phase	Description	R/T Order
	When a Squadron of single seater fighters is deployed for No. 6 Attack both flights should be, therefore, in Sections abreast to Port with B Flight directly astern of A.	
Attack	On the order to attack A Flight (Nos. 1 and 2 Sections) will go forward *simultaneously* and carry out the first wave of the attack on the starboard and port Sections of the bomber formation respectively. They will open fire at optimum range and will break away on the order of the Squadron Leader. The second wave (B Flight), whilst awaiting to attack, will maintain a position 800 yards astern, slightly to a flank and below the enemy. The second wave will go forward when A Flight break away and carry out a similar attack.	'No. 6 Attack GO'
Break Away	On completing their attack, Sections will break away downwards and outwards to either flank.	'Break away GO'
Reform	Squadron will re-form Sections Astern, below and in rear of the enemy, and await further orders from the Squadron Leader.	

Operational note

It is considered that, in war, a number of the bombers will be shot down during the first wave attack. It is most important, therefore, that the Leader of the second wave should form his six fighters into a formation suitable for an attack on the remaining aircraft in the bomber formation.

This deployment is to be carried out by the Flight Leader selecting the extreme right flank of the remaining bombers; the other five fighters will take their target numbered from right to left, in the bomber formation, according to their own number in the Flight, e.g. the Flight Leader (No. 1) attacks the right flank bomber and No. 2 fighter will attack the second bomber counted from the right flank of the formation . . .

In the 1930s, the Royal Air Force actually took it all seriously! Tried once in the battle conditions of 1940, what then remained of the squadron (if anything) would have been sent packing north the next day to re-equip, re-group and re-think!

APPENDIX B
THE BROTHERHOOD OF
FIGHTER COMMAND

2,944 pilots and aircrew flew in the Battle of Britain and these were later to become known collectively as 'The Few'. They were not only of British nationality. Pilots and aircrew of fifteen nationalities flew in the Battle. They were:

Americans	Czechoslovakians	Poles
Australians	Free French	Newfoundlanders
Belgians	Irish	New Zealanders
British	Jamaican	South Africans
Canadians	Palestinian	Southern Rhodesians

They flew with 71 Squadrons, Flights and Units, including two complete naval squadrons, 804 and 808; one complete Canadian squadron, (Can) (401); two complete Polish squadrons, 302 and 303; two complete Czechoslovakian squadrons, 310 and 312; and also 22 Fleet Air Arm pilots who were seconded to Royal Air Force squadrons.

Not only Spitfire and Hurricane aircraft were used in the Battle. [Altogether] six types of aircraft were in use. They were:

Beaufighters
Blenheims
Defiants
Gladiators
Hurricanes
Spitfires

and two naval aircraft, the Martlet and Fulmar. Also, the Royal Navy flew the Sea Gladiator.

The conditions for any pilot or aircrew to qualify as one of 'The Few' and to be entitled to wear their distinguishing characteristics, were laid down in an Air Ministry instruction and I quote: 'Any pilot or aircrew must have flown at least one operational sortie with any of the 71 accredited Battle of Britain Squadrons, Flights and units between 0001 hrs on 10th July, 1940 and 2359 hrs on 31st October, 1940'.

Appendix B

In post-war years, it became an obsession with me to find out who, as individuals, 'The Few' were and to see that their names and accurate statistics, in the fullest detail, [were] recorded for posterity in the form of a Roll of Honour . . . This Roll . . . [would] be placed in the Imperial War Museum in London for all to see.

Little did I know that the project I started in 1957 would not be completed until 1976, except for the collection of a few more signatures; the search for these continues. All of these years were needed, firstly, to search through past official records to obtain the names of those pilots and air-crew who qualified to be known as 'The Few', and secondly to contact those of them who survived and the next-of-kin of those who were killed, all of whom were resident in many parts of the world. The task was made more difficult since it was not commenced until seventeen years after the Battle of Britain took place.

(Flight Lieutenant J. H. Holloway, MBE,
The Battle of Britain: 'The Few', 1980)

Index

Index